Michael Erickson

And Other Ericksons

Dedicated to Harold and Eileen Erickson,
for all they did, for all of us.

With sincere appreciation to John Erickson,
whose support made the original writing possible.

And a special thanks to another long-suffering
"Mrs. Erickson" — my adorable wife, Lori, for
patiently tolerating the countless hours required
to do this "Pandemic-era" revision. She's a
gracious sweetheart of the highest order.

Editor's Note:

This book was revised to be printed as a paperback. But it will be read, for the most part, as an eBook. Because the technology has not yet caught up, eBooks do not carry the same page composition as printed books. Many photographs were intentionally centered to fill the width of the printed page. The eBook pretty much keeps them there. But many other photographs and illustrations move from the sides of pages, where they might be just minor references to the accompanying paperback text, to the middle of the eBook's page where they often take on more prominence than intended. Also, eBook layouts differ for those reading with tablets, on Kindles, and with phones. If you're reading this on a phone, you'll see that the photographs and, especially, their captions, are often very small. You might want to enlarge them. And Kindles, surprisingly, don't have color. Also, I have moved the Table of Contents to the back of the book so it doesn't dominate Amazon's "Look inside" pages. Unorthodox, but more serviceable.

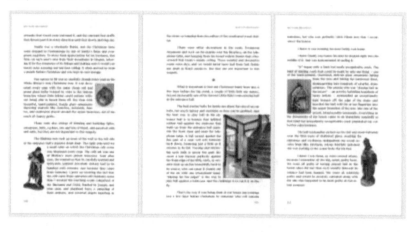

CHAPTER 1

Big Things
Come In Small Packages

There is a large box in one of the two upstairs bathrooms at the Erickson house in Chattanooga.

This box is a cube. Thirty inches high by thirty inches deep by thirty inches the other way. This two-and-a-half-foot cube came from Green Bay, Wisconsin, home of the Packers. It was shipped from the Northern Tissue Company.

It is filled with toilet paper.

Five hundred and twelve rolls of single ply Northern toilet paper. Enough to keep the Erickson household going for a year at a time back when the Erickson household was in its prime. The box is still there. The prime has settled elsewhere.

It was one of Mr. Erickson's roles in life to make sure all three bathrooms were always adequately supplied with paper. Whenever he reached through the carefully cut opening at the top center of the box and had to lean well in to reach rolls from the back, he knew it was time to order another cube.

In 20 years the Erickson household never once ran out of toilet paper.

As all the little Ericksons grew up and became big Ericksons, one of their most difficult adjustments to life in the real world has been keeping up with toilet paper. Never running out. That's an item the flood of little Ericksons thought the Lord provided.

Mr. Erickson was not the Lord. He was a wholesale florist. His skills at buying in large quantities and maintaining inventory were critical to the operation of his household.

Besides toilet paper, he made case purchases of toothpaste, potato chips, applesauce, peanut butter, jelly, lunch sacks, Cokes, and beer. Mr. Erickson bought beer four cases at a time. For 10 years it was Champagne Velvet. Then, for the next ten years, Carling's Black Label. Now he inventories Busch — a brand tolerable to family and friends alike. For better or worse, communal beer drinking became a family ritual. Much like pregnancy became a family routine.

From 1940 to 1958, Mrs. Erickson was more than just a little pregnant. She was mostly pregnant.

She spent 126 months, or ten-and-a-half years of that 18-year period, gestating. She reduced pregnancy from an event to a pastime.

When her oldest son, Harold, Jr., was in the fifth grade at Notre Dame Elementary School, her second oldest, Frank, was in the fourth grade; Allen was in the third; John was in the second; David was in the first. Philip, Michael, and Eileen were at home. Douglas might have reached rug rat status, but was probably still in the womb wondering why life was so noisy.

Ten thousand eight hundred and fourteen wash loads later Mrs. Erickson's ninth-born, Douglas, had evolved to sixth grade status at Notre Dame Elementary School, Louis was in the fourth, Cecilia was in the third, Paul was in the second, Charles was in the first, and Carol, the last of the youngest, was at home trying to figure out why life was suddenly so quiet.

The Ericksons were a large family.

Fourteen children.

Eleven boys.

Three girls.

Two parents.

No twins.

The Ericksons were the largest family in Chattanooga. Maybe even the largest in Tennessee. It wasn't a very Catholic state.

Mr. Erickson used to say, "Only a fool would have a larger family than this."

CHAPTER 2

Success
Is Relative

Once our individual diaper dirtying days were over, each of the Ericksons took on the airs of an over-achiever.

Harold, the oldest, set the pace by earning a Ph.D. and quickly distinguishing himself in scientific circles.

In his wake came four attorneys, two CPAs, a combination attorney-CPA, a physician, an engineer, a self-made millionaire, two girls who married into millions, and an unemployed writer.

Success is relative. But from where the unemployed writer sits, it often looks absolute.

CHAPTER 3

Prologue, Meet Epilogue

Dear Nieces and Nephews,

When I first wrote this book in 1979, there were 15 of you. The oldest was ten, but is now, with this very slight 2022 revision, much older than I was at the time of its writing. Six of you, though not inconceivable, had yet to be generated by that parental process you'd rather not dwell on.

Much has changed. Because everything changes.

Except the past. And this is the past.

This was intended to be, ostensibly, allegorically beneficial to the direction of your lives. But you are all so deep into those lives I expect its only benefit will be, at best, supportive, or remonstrative. Either way, it's part of who you are.

7

∞—∞

Your grandfather had a lot of wisdom.

Questionable, at times, but wisdom was all Mr. Erickson had to counter Mrs. Erickson's prodigious knowledge. Her propensity for facts.

In a different life, she could have been an almanac.

In this life, she was a baby-making machine.

Your father, possibly your mother, was a by-product of this long-term mingling of apocryphal wisdom with absolute fact.

I don't mention that background to justify the eccentricities the Erickson side of your parentage foisted upon you. Those peculiarities stem from neither brains nor imagination. He or she is simply suffering from dilution.

One of your parents grew up in a place where there were more people than there were available personalities. Everyone had to share, and no one, as you will see, came out whole.

Relatively yours,
Uncle Rags

P.S. The main driver in my revising this book was to fix the embarrassing number of typos I wasn't able to correct before the person who hurriedly typeset the original version many years ago Xeroxed copies for the parents' 50th wedding anniversary (Oct. 16, 1985). Some typos have, no doubt, survived. And others have, no doubt, been created. But not nearly so many, I hope. I have followed most basic grammar and style rules, but, for ease of reading, not all.

Photos have been added, and a few are intentionally used more than once. Photographs used to cost money. Because our mother's father ran a store in Missouri that developed photographs, she respected the art. And took far more than someone pinching pennies normally would have. At least, until children became more a routine than a wonder. Many siblings were not photographed as often as others.

CHAPTER 4

You Can't Mind Manners
You Never Learned

The Ericksons seldom gather in whole these days.

But, when we do, our behavior immediately reflects the table manners we never learned.

The steady influx of outsiders — aka wives — wisely cemented a tradition of not getting together for chaotic Christmases.

Occasionally, though, word might leak that a couple of the older ones are planning to visit the parents in Chattanooga over some minor holiday and pressure will mount for others to make the trip. Alarmed by the threat of a loud, degenerative reunion, the more experienced wives quickly fill those weekends with school recitals, swim meets, dental appointments, imaginary funerals, or any remotely plausible reason why neither they nor their husband can travel.

But women are sentimentalists and forever fall for the allure of weddings. All of our recent reunions have coincided with the marriage of yet another brother, or even a sister. Since only two or three are still single, we won't be reunioning much in the years ahead.

Tying reunions to weddings is as unpardonable as it is unavoidable. The wedding becomes secondary as we take advantage of the pre- and post-nuptial parties to become re-acquainted with ourselves. At the expense of becoming acquainted with the family and friends of the bride.

We huddle in the corners. The large corners. Ideally, the large corners nearest the bar.

Fortunately, there are three socialites in the family: Frank, John, and Eileen. They make us all look better than we are. Practiced at winning friends and influencing people, they drift through the rooms talking with the strangers and answering the inevitable, "Now which one are you?"

The rest of us have a prodigious propensity for drinking wherever we happen to be out of whatever quantity of beer it has to offer. When all the beer is gone, the reclusive Ericksons are equally hard to find.

Our old tradition of shouting at one another until one or two in the morning from around our crowded kitchen table in Chattanooga has been replaced by the new tradition of abandoning the pre-wedding party or reception in the hometown of one new bride after another and relocating to a suitable hotel room where, armed with bottomless coolers of beer, we stay up until one or two in the morning loudly rekindling one another's awareness of personal and professional defects that certain brothers or sisters might have forgotten they harbor. One of many reasons why the sisters-in-law, those who married these defective deadbeats, prefer root canals to reunions.

Mother is rightfully ashamed of the manners we never learned. And never hesitates to let on.

Daddy gets far more pleasure out of sitting around a motel room listening to our ceaseless banter than he does from standing in some nice family's living room being the father of the groom.

CHAPTER 5

Shall We Gather
At The Tables

They ask. They always ask.

They ask, "Which one are you?"

And then the second question is always, "How did you eat?"

I'm one of the skinny ones. Beanpole statures run in the family. But that doesn't answer the question. What they want to hear is that we fought and scrapped like caged beasts when food was on the table. That we stabbed at each other's hands and wrists with bloodstained forks. Those would be exciting answers. But the pertinent answer is: "We ate at two tables."

The two tables lived in separate rooms — what was called the breakfast room, and dining room. They were joined by a doorway. That doorway was sealed on more than one rude occasion when we in the older persons' room determined those at the babies' table, which included the parents, were creating too much clamor.

The older persons' table was in the dining room, and was called the dining room table. The babies' table was in the breakfast room, I'm guessing a realtor gave it that name. It was just off the kitchen, and had what was called the kitchen table.

We in the dining room would demand at times, "Could you all keep it down at the kitchen table!" The inevitable retort from a future lawyer seated at that table would be, "There isn't a table in the kitchen!" And all the babies would cheer for their side. Arguments were always based on the letter of the law since we were not allowed to dispute its spirit.

The dining room table was reserved for high schoolers, a few privileged grade schoolers, such as Little Eileen, and anyone returning from college.

We never really achieved maximum residency at the house. Carol, the youngest, was born a few weeks after Harold, the oldest, left for college. Harold, like the others, returned during the summers. But once someone left for college he never regained full status. He was lucky to even get his old bed back.

During those summers, Harold, Frank, Allen, John, David, Philip, myself, and Eileen squeezed into the six spaces the dining room comfortably offered.

Mr. and Mrs. Erickson held down the head and foot of the kitchen table, with Douglas, Louis, Cecilia, and Paul fitting into the four side positions. Charles and Carol flanked Mrs. Erickson from their highchairs.

It was somewhat acceptable to spill milk but absolutely forbidden to spill highchairs.

As each new older brother left for college, the oldest one at the kitchen table, usually a seventh-grader, could move to the dining room, opening a seat at the kitchen table for whoever was still eating from a highchair. Making this move away from the other babies became a rite. A recognition of grown-up status. A cut-rate bar mitzvah.

Douglas and Louis, numbers nine and ten, were the last to leave the kitchen table. After them, there was finally ample room there for the parents and leftovers. The four youngest — Cecilia, Paul, Charles, and Carol — were never allowed to eat without parental supervision. The Little Kids. They never officially matured.

The eternal Little Kids: Cecilia, Paul, Charles, and Carol.

CHAPTER 6

"Make That A Guinness"
One For The Books

Doctor Doug, Number 11, was thumbing through a copy of the Guinness Book of Records.

Douglas, a pathologist, was in the family room of his suburban home in Macon, Georgia, one Saturday afternoon, idly working his way through the book of records one of his three young daughters had bought for a dime at a garage sale.

Longest fingernails . . . tallest twins . . . fastest turtle . . . biggest taco . . . most college degrees in one family . . .

"Thirteen."

"Just thirteen?!?"

Douglas's initial surprise that there was such a thing as an official world record for the number of college degrees quickly gave way to his realization that our 14 degrees bested that piddling family's paltry achievement.

A few long distance calls later, back in the days when long distance cost dollars and when all non-emergency family calls were made in the discounted hours from 5 p.m. Friday to 5 p.m. Sunday, it was determined by Michael, a competent researcher from his days of working for newspapers, that the first step toward staking a claim to one of their records was for someone to

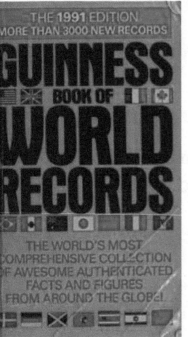

actually call the publisher's London office. An overseas long distance call. The cost was high . . . but so were the stakes.

An editor in London welcomed a challenge to their existing record but required proof all 14 siblings graduated from accredited colleges or universities.

In their original excitement over snaring such an easy and completely unexpected share of the world's pie merely from the serendipity of Douglas's daughter having brought home a used book that her father happened to randomly open and thumb to a surprisingly relevant page, Michael agreed to do the groundwork necessary to securing the record so it would be a surprise for the parents who orchestrated this achievement. Quickly daunted by the prospect of securing letters of affirmation from ten or more different universities, aware of his crippling propensity for procrastination, and already a renowned and well-documented quitter, Michael wisely threw in the towel and recruited the family member far better suited for this demanding task: Mrs. Erickson, herself. Thus assuring the job would be done, and done well.

Within two months, she mailed a hefty package to London with detailed documentation of the Erickson family's claim to a record it had, in fact, held for at least the previous decade.

We became official record holders in the 1991 edition. And when the publishers asked if they could get a photograph for the 1993 edition, we had a loud, raucous gathering in Naples, Florida. The first reunion not tied to a wedding.

OO

Of course, this record is more a reflection of numbers than actual achievement. Many parents see all of their children graduate from college. But, for 14 to get through that process without a single blip is, in fact, commendable. I came the closest to blipping. Having already indistinguished myself by quitting the band, the Boy Scouts, and the altar boys, it proved fortunate, for those counting, that I didn't follow through on plans to skip my senior year of college in 1969 and dodge the draft by, instead of just driving up to Canada, jumping all the way to London.

The thought of six older brothers, several with advanced degrees, scornfully shaking their heads at every future mention of my name led me to spend my last $1,000 in savings on another year of tuition, books, and apartments rather than on a flight to the core of the "British Invasion" music scene. But I'm pretty sure that life unflown would have been an interesting adventure for a writer.

I might have ended up working with a famous London brewer — helping it publish its annual book of world records.

Oldest in Britain The title of existing school in Britain is claimed that King's School bury, Kent was a foundation of some time between his arrival in AD 597 and his death c. 604. (College of Theodosius) at Major, South Glamorgan, burnt down in AD 446, was after a lapse of 62 years, by 508, and flourished into the Winchester College was 1382. Lanark Grammar School have been referred to in a papal up in 1183 by Lucius III.

In 1988/89 Rizal High School, Philippines had an enrolment 658 regular students, although year 1991/92 the number had 16 419.

with the most pupils in Great was Banbury Comprehensive, 2767 in the 1975 summer term. Exmouth Community College, the most pupils, with 2129. The enrolment in Scotland has been at Roman Catholic High School, Lanarkshire, with a peak of 1977. The highest enrolment was at Holyrood School, Glasgow, with 1831 pupils. The Holy Child School, Belfast, Ireland reached 2752 in 1973 school was split up. The highest in 1990/91 was 2474 at St comprehensive College, Belfast.

Most expensive The most expensive schools in the world tend to be prestigious international finishing schools, such as those in Switzerland. One of these is the Gstaad International School, which had annual fees in 1991/92 rising to $55 000. It claims to be the most exclusive school in the world.

Excluding schools catering for specialist needs, the most expensive school in Great Britain which is a member of the Headmasters' Conference is Harrow School, Middx (headmaster N.R. Bomford). The maximum annual fee for boarders in 1992/93 is £11 925.

The most expensive school which is a member of the Girls' School Association is Roedean School, Brighton, East Sussex (headmistress Mrs A.R. Longley), with annual fees in 1991/92 of £10 740 for boarders.

In the academic year 1991/92 St Andrew's Private Tutorial Centre, Cambridge (co-founders W.A. Duncombe and C.T. Easterbrook) charges £13 230 for full-time science students (predominantly individual tuition plus accommodation).

Earliest comprehensive school Windermere Grammar School (then in Westmorland), adopted the non-selective comprehensive principle as early as 1945. It closed in 1965, and together with two other schools in the area, formed a new comprehensive school The Lakes School, in Troutbeck Bridge, Cumbria. The

Calder High School, near Hebden Bridge, W Yorks, opened as a comprehensive school in 1950, and was established through the amalgamation of Hebden Bridge Grammar School and various 'through schools' which served the vicinity. The earliest purpose-built was Kidbrooke Comprehensive for Girls, in south-east London, opened in 1954.

Oldest PTA The parent-teacher association with the earliest known foundation date in Britain is that for Lawrence Sheriff School, Rugby, Warks, formed in 1908.

Most schools The greatest documented number of schools attended by a pupil is 265, by Wilma Williams, now Mrs R.J. Horton, from 1933–43 when her parents were in show business in the USA.

Most O and A levels Since 1965 Dr Francis L. Thomason of Hammersmith, London has accumulated 70 O and O/A levels, 16 A levels and 1 S level, making a total of 87, of which 36 have been in the top grade. A.F. Prime, a prisoner in HM Open Prison, Sudbury, Suffolk accumulated a total of 1 S level, 14 A levels and 34 O levels between 1968 and 1982. Environmental difficulties tend to make study harder in prison than elsewhere.

The highest number of top-grade A levels attained at one sitting is seven, by Stephen Murrell of Crown Woods School, Eltham, London in June 1978, out of eight passes. Robert Pidgeon (b. 7 Feb 1959) of St Peter's

■ **Most graduates in a family**
Mr and Mrs Harold Erickson of Naples, Florida, USA saw all of their 14 children — 11 sons and three daughters — obtain university or college degrees between 1962 and 1978. Bringing them together for a family photograph more than ten years later also required a great deal of work and organization, involving flights home from nine different cities.
(Photo: Moment-In-Time Photography)

CHAPTER 7

An Embarrassment Of Riches

Dear Little Nieces and Nephews,

Let enough time pass and you can admit to almost anything.

Enough time had passed for your grandfather to admit one night, "There was a time when I was embarrassed to be seen with the whole family."

He explained that one of his greatest thrills used to be walking down the aisle of the church as Sunday Mass was about to begin, proudly leading his parade of little progeny. That was back

21

in the 1950s. We were still a growing nation. California was only half full.

Times changed. Large families, like outhouses, plummeted out of style. Busybodies convinced the children of the Sixties that we were running out of air. As with the original Original Sin, everyone was judged guilty of the crime of living. Excess was deemed sinful. Large families were the epitome of excess.

Suffering from this new social stigma, Daddy started going to an earlier Mass than the rest of the family. He admits to having felt a sense of shame and guilt if he had to appear in public with more than six or seven of us at a time.

But that sense of shame has also faded. Helped as we all — with the possible exception of myself — grew into such model citizens, became so distinguished and successful, that if you lined us up we might look almost as intimidating as we once looked cute.

A little money goes a long way when it comes to social acceptance.

A lot of money goes a lot farther.

Relatively yours,
Uncle Rags

CHAPTER 8

Why?

Mrs. Erickson did not have 14 babies. Not all at once, anyway.

She did not just spew them, guppy-style, into the rambling two-story house that contained their bedlam.

Still, there is no real question that she had the babies. And there is no real answer as to "Why?"

Being Catholic must have had a lot to do with it. It always did, back in the days when the Pope's, or even just a priest's, word weighed more than a woman's life.

But fervent and fertile as she was, it is doubtful the pulpit is the only culprit.

One very plausible theory is that Mr. and Mrs. Erickson simply settled into a routine of having babies. They were never ones to alter their routines.

They changed their brand of beer about once a decade. They have never changed their brand of toilet paper: Northern. Or shampoo: Prell. And once they started, they only occasionally changed their brand of babies: Boys.

The pregnant Mrs. Erickson with No. 1 (Harold) center,
No. 7 (Michael) left, No. 6 (Philip) right,
and No. 8 of 14 (Eileen) in the bonnet.

A viable explanation might be found buried in a very fine novel Mr. Erickson wrote in his late-50s. In this unpublished work of fiction, the romantic, dashing husband comes home from the office many evenings and tears his loving, adoring wife away from the toddlers at her feet. They grab a quiet 30 minutes together before settling down to supper and evening chores. No one recollects Mr. Erickson tearing our cook away from the stove, but those novel insights at least offer a hint.

Mrs. Erickson has threatened for years to make a full disclosure. Always promising it for some time in the never-arriving future.

It has long been suspected in certain circles that sex might have played at least a trifling role in the size of the family. If so, it is doubtful that Mrs. Erickson's exposé will ever flower.

CHAPTER 9

Spilt Milk

Take an ordinary glass of milk. Tip it over. It spills.

Science recognizes only two ways of spilling milk. Intentionally or accidentally.

But since the day milk was first extracted from a moo cow's gland and served at a growing family's dinner table, children have been spilling it a third way: Inevitably.

Sit a child at a table and he or she will spill milk.

Not every time, of course. If more than just a few children spilled milk every time they came near it, adults would long since have abandoned procreating. No. Children spill milk only often enough to prove to their parents they are incapable of mastering life — that they will take their own good time learning how mean ol' Mr. Gravity works.

A child's fearful look as the milk forms a river on the table and then begins a waterfall to its lap says instantly that he or she did not do it on purpose. Of course, it's usually apparent to everyone else at the table that it couldn't have been just an accident. You can't accidentally turn a glass of milk slowly to its side — even if you didn't mean to do it. To the child, though, Mr. Gravity, like God, works in mysterious ways.

⦿

I grew out of the milk spilling stage at about the same age any reasonably awkward child would. But I had the misfortune of spending the next several years experiencing Eileen, and then Douglas, then Louis, then Cecilia, then Paul, etc., discovering to their individual little capacities to be endlessly surprised by the phenomenon that when you knock a glass of milk over the contents spill across the table.

Our eating arrangements around the kitchen table were tight, to say the least, so the bungler spilling the milk seldom suffered the wet, sticky aftermath alone. Usually two or three of our laps would be targeted by the panoramic waterfalls. Mrs. Erickson, who was pregnant nearly all the time, sat at the end of the table nearest the kitchen and closest to the nasty old dishrag she used for cleaning up spills. Daddy sat at the other end where he was helpless to do more than growl and hiss through his teeth at the culprit — often as not hissing at the wrong toddler.

Eileen, Douglas, and I would sit along one side of the table, with Philip, Louis, and Cecilia facing us from the other; Louis always being at an appropriate end position to accommodate his chronic left-handedness. Paul, Charles, and/or Carol would be in the highchair at Mother's right, depending on which of them was currently dirtying diapers. Whoever was presently

Front row milk spillers: Eileen, Douglas, Michael, Philip,
baby Cecilia, and Louis.

occupying the highchair, and thus frequently distracted by bowel movements, was expected to spill milk. The rest of us were supposed to know better. I hardly understand why. It seems that if Harold, Frank, and Allen didn't know better at a particular age, then Louis, Cecilia, and Paul should hardly be the wiser.

Regardless, spilling milk was an intolerable offense punished by a series of loud grunts and sighs from Mother as she swabbed it up and by Daddy's excitement at the commotion and his fear of a change in his pregnant wife's disposition. As his hissing and mean looks began to wear down, Daddy would usually grit his teeth to convey the tone of a shout and demand from the visibly shaken offender, "Now why did you do that!?" The teary-eyed ne'er-do-well would always stammer, "I-I-I was j-j-just trying to d-d-drink it."

Often there were two or three of us in various stages of milk spilling. Getting milk dumped onto your lap was almost worth it if the bungling dumper happened to be an older brother. Made you feel like it must not be so stupid to spill milk after all. And when the spiller was younger, you were allowed to sit there and gasp loudly like Mother, hiss between your teeth like Daddy, and even stand up or shift frantically in your seat to add to the commotion and the seriousness of the crime.

It was fair for the older ones to ridicule the crying perpetrator. "Good gosh, Douglas! You're such a ba-by!" "Yeah, Douglas!! When are you going to grow up!?" "Douglas isn't ever going to grow up. When he goes to school he'll be carrying a rattler instead of a lunch box." "He'll be the only kid in his class who has to wear a bib." "Yeah, Douglas is always going to be just a little b-a-b-y!"

There was nothing we string of babies hated more than to be called a baby. Worst of all was for a big baby to be called a "little ba-by." "I am *not* a little baby!" we would cry whenever accused of such depravity. "Then why did you spill your milk?" the prosecution would retort, always laughing loud enough at its own wit to drown out the whimper of, "I was just trying to drink it."

Milk was spilled at least every third night. Sometimes every night for a week, by which time every baby at the kitchen table was too traumatized and superstitious to drink. The high points came on those occasional instances when two glasses of milk would be spilled during the same meal. Sometimes this could be accomplished by the same little ba-by. A few times a year one glass of spilled milk would cause someone else to jerk out of the way and spill his simultaneously. Daddy, trapped against the wall at his end of the table, was visibly devastated, his life flashing quickly before him in an attempt to discern how it came to this, by those two-milk spills.

As though cramming from six to nine fledglings around a table wouldn't cause enough spilling on its own, the parents greased our miscreant conduct by having the older ones, the Big Boys who ate at the table in the dining room, serve themselves buffet style from dishes placed every night in the middle of our crowded little table. This meant that if you were one of the babies the older ones were always balancing plates of hot gooey food over your head. No matter where you sat, an arm or two would be reaching in between you and your neighbor scooping something out of the middle of the table.

You might notice a stringy clump of hot macaroni and cheese or a glob of cold applesauce ready to drop off David's serving spoon, angled directly at your little bare forearm. The Little Kids spilled gallons of milk trying to protect themselves from the carelessness of the Big Boys. The Big Boys were known to personally upset a glass of milk on occasion with their own carelessness and immediately cast a blaming look at the little one below who would be so shell-shocked by the white-washing that he could not muster a convincing defense. The guilty Big Boy always denied any involvement, loudly testifying as an expert witness to the innocent baby's long history of similar "accidents." They were usually specific as to just how the "ba-by" spilled his milk in this instance and were quick to support their evidence by recounting said baby's frightening inability to grow up.

(O)

There is a classic piece of film in which a drop of milk is magnified about one hundred thousand times and captured by slow motion as it falls into a puddle of milk. The drop creates an art form that can inadequately be described as a cross between a volcanic eruption and a blossoming tulip. A solid wall rises around where the drop landed and then breaks at its crest showering a circle of new little drops onto the milk's surface. My theory is that if you magnified just one of those little drops falling from the first drop's crest, it would create the exact same volcanic tulip as it in turn splashes down. And each of the drops created by its shower would create the same effect. *Ad infinitum.*

31

Yes, to infinity. Each little drop is still creating ever smaller drops which are still creating even smaller drops. "The Spilt Milk Theory of the Universe."

Somehow, hard as it would be on Daddy if he should get his head around this theory, all those tumblers of milk we spilled over all those years are still out there infinitely cascading away.

(Editor's Note: This and two other chapters in the opening section will be repeated later in the book in order to maintain context from when the book was first printed.)

CHAPTER 10

When The Roll
Is Called Down Yonder

After the dreaded evening family Rosary, it was time for lunches. Not lunch. Lunches.

Mrs. Erickson, who might or might not be pregnant at the time, plants herself in the kitchen — cleaned up from supper before the Rosary — and methodically arranges all the necessary items for making the lunches we would be eating the next day at school.

Tucked into a shelf below her long linoleum-surfaced work counter is a bin of 500 small brown paper lunch bags. The bin might be full and stacked to the top of its space in the cabinet portion of the counter's superstructure, or it might be nearly empty. It doesn't matter because there is always a box in the garage with thousands more brown paper lunch bags.

Also shelved below the counter is a cardboard case of giant-sized jars of peanut butter. If full, that case has 12 half-gallon jars of Peter Pan smooth. Another cardboard container tucked into her cabinet has up to a dozen 16-ounce jars of Bama grape jelly. We were big peanut butter and jelly eaters. Daddy was a wholesaler who bought family staples in bulk.

To her left, Mrs. Erickson places two fresh loaves of white bread. To her right is a jumbo roll of waxed paper or Saran Wrap, depending on the era and the evolving state of sandwich-making arts. Between the bread and wrappings are the condiments — jumbo jars of mustard and mayonnaise.

She begins by pulling out the right number of lunch sacks and, working in numerical order, scribbles a name across each bag with one of the stubby little pencils that live among the ownerless change in a back corner of that same work counter. Always our full Christian names — except for Frank, the only one who was never called by his Christian name, and the only one who later

took religious vows. But I'll position both Harold and Frank in college at the time of this night's lunch making. So, being in Pittsburgh and at a seminary in the middle of Alabama, they are too far away to hear their names called — even with Mrs. Erickson resorting to her higher registers. They will just have to buy their lunches tomorrow. Also, in this time frame, Mrs. Erickson is not pregnant. Miracles happen.

⓪

The action begins with Mother's scream from the kitchen. She screams, "ALLEN!?!"

"WHAT!?!" resounds from upstairs in the Big Boys Room where he is racing through *All the King's Men* instead of laboring over his chemistry.

"What do you want for lunch!?!" Mother bellows from her post at the kitchen counter, her voice piercing through the breakfast room, around a corner and on through the dining room, rounding another corner and clipping along a wall of the entrance hall before climbing the 16 carpeted stairs, crossing the hardwood landing, and finally blasting into the far corner of the Big Boys Room where Allen is propped on his bed reading.

"What do you want for lunch!?!" was the demand.

Allen, like everyone, has to think and answer quickly lest our tender little ears be pilloried by the beam-rattling second call. In order to answer quickly, we usually order what we ordered the day before. Allen shouts back his concept of daily bread and there is a pause while his peanut butter and jelly sandwiches are constructed by the world's best peanut butter and jelly sandwich maker and stuffed into his brown bag.

"JOHN!?!"

"I want two peanut butter sandwiches and a banana!" John calls back from his room upstairs where he is installing a homemade, illegal phone in a desk drawer. John knew he was next and was ready. John had his own, private bedroom in a house where everyone else was bunked three to four deep? Yes. John ruled. There is another pause for spreading and sack stuffing.

"DAVID!?!"

"What!?!"

David, also upstairs in the Big Boys Room but lost in the wiring of his science club project, has not noticed all the prior shouting — an evening noise as routine as the roar of traffic from our busy street and the crying of babies.

"What do you want for lunch!?!" booms up from the distant kitchen.

"I want one spam and one liverwurst and all the other stuff!" David calls back down. He was a big lunchmeat eater. He and Frank were the biggest lunchmeat eaters in the family. By "all the other stuff" he means coat the bread with mustard and mayonnaise and throw in anything like bananas or cookies or raisins that she might have at hand. David was an all-around big eater. Frank, too. They both looked like real people, rather than skeletal victims of an African famine.

"PHILIP!?!"

He answers thoughtfully from one of the upstairs bathrooms, "I'll have one salami with spicy mustard and an apple butter!" We had different kinds of mustard, so if you wanted something out of a smaller jar you had to be specific about it. Mother tried very hard to please. She was good at it. Good at trying. And good at pleasing.

"MICHAEL!?!"

I would probably be in the living room watching *Yancy Derringer* and looking at geography. "Two peanut butter and grape jellies!" I call back. During the course of my early education I ate no fewer than 3,687 peanut butter and grape jelly sandwiches. I also ate at least five-hundred-thirty-three peanut butter and apple jelly sandwiches, just for variety.

Much of our "fine china" consisted of virtually unbreakable jelly jars bought by the case.

"EILEEN!?!"

On the phone. The upstairs phone.

"EI-LEEN!?!!!"

"Tell her I'm buying my lunch tomorrow," she says to anyone in the adjacent Big Boys Room, who shouts, "She's buying her lunch tomorrow!" just loud enough for someone downstairs, maybe me in front of the television, to pick up on this drifting bit of information and pass it onto someone doing homework on the dining room table, who holds on to it because it's too late because he had already heard Mother inhale for blasting a third and deafening "EIII!!-LLLEEEEN!!!," while Daddy, who is hard of hearing for reasons easily understood, sits peacefully reading the evening newspaper at the table in the breakfast room, just a few feet from the turbine at the work counter.

"She says she's buying her lunch tomorrow," the relay in the dining room conveys in the calm before the next building storm. Mother, in her despair over the effort it took to learn the status of "Eileen" sighs loud enough to cause static in transmissions to pilots from the control tower at the Chattanooga airport 12 miles away. And she sighs again at the brown paper bag with that name already scribbled across it as she tucks it under the counter for use the next night.

⑩

Cosmopolitan Eileen. Everyone else was too shy to buy his lunch — hot food from the school cafeteria. There is much less anxiety in ordering the night before from Mrs. Erickson and carrying it in your own bag with your own name on it. But Eileen learned early that buying lunch with a lunch card was one of the tricks that made students acceptable. Waiting in lines and all. The best way to become one of the crowd is to join its lines.

I was jealous of how well Eileen handled buying her lunch. My anxiety soared whenever I forgot my lunch on the dining room table in the morning and Jim Jones, who worked for Daddy, for some reason couldn't get out to the house and retrieve it. Those rare days, I had to "buy my lunch," choosing between exotic entrees like country fried steak or beef tips with noodles and feeling pressure from the server behind the glass to buy one of those ugly, steaming vegetables . . . having to choose foods with that looked completely foreign . . . pointing while saying, "Let me have some of 'that,'" knowing I would not like "that" because I had never tasted "that" before. Never tasted country fried steak with brown gravy because I was raised on round steak with black gravy. But Eileen handled it all beautifully. Born to eat out.

⦾

"DOUGLAS!?!"

Nothing.

"DOUG!-LASS!!"

"He's asleep," someone finally figures out and relays down the line. "He has a headache," is the necessary explanation. Douglas had terrible headaches. Mother would guess at what he will want for lunch the next day. Douglas seldom complained about anything, not even his headaches, so that made her guessing easier.

"LOUIS!?!"

"I'll have one-and-a-half baloneys and a half a peanut and butter and jelly!" Louis shouts from the next room where he has been doing his homework on the dining room table.

"You don't have to shout!" Mother shouts back.

Daddy does not look up from his newspaper.

"CE!-CIEL!-LIA!?!" . . . "PAUL!?!" . . . "CHARLES!?!" . . . "CHAR!-ELES!?!!!". . . "CAROL!?!"

Actually, if the roll call began with Allen during his senior year of high school, it would have stopped with Cecilia, in the first grade. I just drew it out to show that Charles was one who could never recognize his name on a mere first shout basis not even if he was sitting in the adjacent breakfast room pestering Daddy and his newspaper.

⚭

All of the more than 30,000 lunch bags Mrs. Erickson filled over the years would be crammed in turn into the open space reserved on the top shelf of the rounded refrigerator with its small frosty top freezer and ice trays behind its heavy door, to be kept cold overnight and then laid out the next morning on the dining room table where we could forget them if we were stupid.

CHAPTER 11

Either I Forgot My Shoes,
Or I'm Wearing Someone Else's Feet

As we were rushing out of the house in the morning and piling into the station wagon in our frantic, but always successful, effort to get to school on time, Mrs. Erickson kept up a constant barrage of shrill shouts and shrieks about how slow we all were and how she could not understand why it was always so hard for us to leave on schedule. In her daily barrage she often insisted that "other families" did not find it so difficult to leave for school.

How dare she, of all people, taunt us with what life was like in normal families!

⦿

School started with eight o'clock Mass at the circa 1890s church downtown that was a block from the large brick, barely younger building that housed 12 grades of Notre Dame elementary school and high school.

I won't trouble you with details of when eight o'clock Mass started, but we had to leave the house by no later than 7:45 or we might all tramp into the quiet church late — something we never minded, but something Mrs. Erickson found more offensive than cockroaches. She liked us to be out of the driveway no later than 7:30. I doubt we ever made that. We had thousands of chances over the years, but I doubt we ever left by 7:30. Except on those many occasions when a team of the many boys was "serving" eight o'clock Mass — meaning they were the altar boys — and had to be there at 7:50. In those instances, she liked to see us leave at 7:15 and maybe we would pull out of the carport by 7:35.

No matter when we left the house, Mother would be screaming at us. She screamed at all of us in general, but at Allen or Douglas or Charles in particular because they were the three who were notoriously slow in the morning. In exasperation as the last of the station wagon doors was finally slamming, she often shouted the cliché about how they would be late for "their own funerals." We don't know about that, yet. But, to his credit, Charles wasn't late for his own wedding. The ones late for that one were Allen, David, and Philip; and me and Louis and Carol. Douglas wasn't able to make it to Boston and be late with us.

⦿

When she could hear the station wagon's motor running and see we were almost in, Mrs. Erickson would take her screaming demeanor away from the carport door for a moment and stalk it quickly back into the house to see if anyone's lunch was still on the dining room table. There was usually something — if not a lunch, at least a school book — and she raced back to the carport door with it, letting the forgetful owner know what she thought of *his* inability (our pure sisters never did anything wrong) to deal with life's simplest requirements.

Sometimes a lunch or a book escaped her searching eye and Jim Jones, who made deliveries for Daddy's wholesale flower shop for the thirty years of our growing up, had to drive the delivery truck out from town, pick up the forgotten book or lunch, drive it back to town, take it to the school, and give it to a nun who would pass it on to the forgetter.

We forgot our homework a lot and this was a hard thing for Mother to spot during her last minute searches. The dumb kids at school who didn't really do their homework were always telling the nuns they had forgotten it. Mrs. Erickson, who was pregnant at the time, routinely made Jim go through all the pick-up-and-delivery motions for one page of long-division arithmetic because she didn't want the nuns to have to believe us when they never believed the dumb kids.

⦾

Sometimes we were not above being dumb. The dumbest thing someone could forget is his shoes.

More than once, we were halfway to school when one of the morning slowpokes — Douglas or Charles — noticed they had forgotten to put on their black lace-up uniform shoes. They were wearing only socks. They couldn't even go to church like that so they had to wait at Daddy's store — which was only two blocks from both the downtown church and its block away school — until Jim could run out to the house, a 20 minute roundtrip, for the forgotten pair of shoes. Sometimes one of us ended up in the car with tennis shoes on instead of the uniform shoes. Such shoe lapses, like showing up naked for a history exam, are the kinds of trauma that dreams are made of.

I got out of the car once and started walking up the slope of the asphalt parking lot toward the church with the rest of the crowd of young Ericksons when I noticed I was limping. The foundation of that peculiar gait was that I had only one shoe on. And it was a tennis shoe rather than a uniform shoe — proving, at least, that I didn't make the same mistake twice.

I had wandered throughout the house wearing only that one shoe — eating breakfast, peeing, gathering books, piling in the station wagon — for the entire 40 minutes since I had gotten dressed upon first springing out of bed, but hadn't noticed. Until I looked down to investigate the unusual limp I was experiencing with each step through the very familiar parking lot. I was dumbfounded to discern the shoddy status of my feet.

⑩

We forgot our uniform blue ties so often Daddy finally broke down and bought an extra blue noose which he kept at his store. That worked for a few months — until someone took it home and forgot to bring it back.

CHAPTER 12

The Whore House
On The Corner

Perhaps the most surprising aspect of our so rarely talking about sex when growing up was our unusual proximity to it.

No, I'm not talking about the upstairs bedroom where the parents "slept." I'm talking about the whorehouse two doors away.

Not too long after moving into our "new house" on Glenwood Drive, we became aware of the Glenwood Manor, a small motel at the intersection of our busy crosstown street and an even busier one, McCallie Avenue, which was the main thoroughfare to downtown.

The Glenwood Manor was Chattanooga's, and possibly all of Tennessee's, most notorious whorehouse.

Our near neighbor was built in the 1940s. Just another large house until it was converted in the 1950s to a motor court and raised a neon sign to catch Yankee tourists drawn by the ubiquitous "See Rock City" signs painted on barns and stamped on birdhouses throughout the North and Midwest. A brilliant advertising strategy that brought an endless number of Northerners to Chattanooga, where many of them also forked over money to ride the elevator 150 feet into Lookout Mountain to "See Ruby Falls." What many families saw first, though, was the Glenwood Manor. It was the first tourist court weary drivers met once they came through the Missionary Ridge tunnel and entered the city of Chattanooga. A good place to pull over and rest up for the big day ahead.

The new Holiday Inn and Howard Johnson motel chains quickly made Mom and Pop tourist courts obsolete. Some found a way to repurpose those empty bedrooms.

We didn't learn what the Glenwood Manor had turned into until the Haddocks, a Catholic family, though not nearly as Catholic as we were, moved in next door. They had a son in Eileen's grade school class and a daughter in Cecilia's. We had never spoken to the previous neighbors.

The Haddocks quickly noticed there were an awful lot of men pulling into the driveway of the busy little motel next door to them. Staying only an hour or two instead of overnight. Most with local license plates that started with the number 4.

Chattanooga was in Hamilton County, Tennessee's fourth largest, so all of its plates began with a 4. Drivers out of Memphis, the state's largest city, had plates that began with 1. Nashville was 2. Knoxville/Knox County was 3. Chattanoogans felt bad about being from only the fourth largest city, but cars from nearby counties had much worse numbers. 37. 63. All the way down to 95. The Haddocks were suspicious about all of those sedans whose license plates began with a 4 pulling into the house whose sign offered rooms for the night.

The Glenwood Manor, officially defined in occasional court documents as a "bawdy house," was run by a frumpy woman in her 40s, Naomi Roden, who spent most of the day in a loose-fitting cotton house dress that she wore when she stepped outside to check her mail or collect garbage cans from the curb.

The police weren't very interested when the Haddocks called them to investigate. They already knew about it. Everyone knew about it. This whorehouse was as protected as the city's many bars that illegally served liquor long after the statutory 1 a.m. closing. But one officer the Haddocks implored finally suggested they write down license plate numbers. Some of those numbers turned out to belong to judges, local politicians, and even high ranking police officials. Which explained why she was able to operate so long and so openly. Favors given; favors returned.

Under steady pressure from the Haddocks, Naomi was busted every three to five years. Paid a small fine. And resumed her courtly business.

This was going on right under the nose of a family with 11 boys. But, like everything else related to sex, while it might come

up during the day when Mother was speaking in hushed tones with Mrs. Haddock, it was never spoken of during those kitchen table sessions at night. Indeed, even when it became general knowledge in our household that the Glenwood Manor was a whorehouse, that meant little to the vast majority of the 11 boys who were ignorant as to what whores did. But we were pretty sure it was a sin.

The church steeple poking up from bottom right is a nice touch.

Naomi must have dressed up, or maybe just undressed, at night because court documents said she was one of the two or three women who went with one of the undercover detectives into one of her rented rooms to provide services. She was fined $50. Maybe even spanked, depending on whether the judge was a consort.

The madam sometimes had live-in whores. The only reason we know this is because of the one-armed boy.

The one-armed boy showed up one summer afternoon when we were playing wiffle ball, batting from the opening in the hedge that led to the Haddocks' back yard. You bat from the opening in the hedge across the bricks that constituted our basketball court, badminton court, and parking area into our grassy back yard. He stared at us for a bit from two houses away before bravely walking across the Haddocks' yard to ask if he could play.

We didn't like strangers. But we knew it would be a sin to turn our backs on a kid. Especially one with just one arm. So we let him play. He batted one-handed. He was maybe 11 years old. The same age as one of us. Older and younger than others of us.

He started coming over every day. We didn't like him. Never asked about his arm. Never really talked to him about anything. We even let him go to the park down the street with us one time, because we were going, he had shown up, and there wasn't any way around it.

We didn't know his mother was a whore. If we had, we could probably have refused to let him play with us, trading one sin for another. Our catechisms didn't really cover that situation. Nor did the nuns. But, overall, we knew we were doing the right thing in tolerating, if not exactly "taking in," this disadvantaged stranger.

I'm sure Mom and Mrs. Haddock were as uncomfortable about this kid being in our midst as we were. After two weeks, to everyone's great relief, he was gone. Disappeared.

But what a great story we brushed up against: A one-armed kid raised by an itinerant prostitute. What did he know about his mother? When did he learn? What became of him?

Naomi stayed in business for years and years. It was rumored she had girls from the public high school three blocks away working for her at one time. The judges, councilmen, and police commissioners would have loved that.

We loved being two houses away from Chattanooga's most popular whorehouse. Instead of right next door.

CHAPTER 13

Staircases and Statues:
Tragedy's Ugly Head

Instead of Santa or his elves, it was the Melpomene, the Greek muse of tragedy, and her comedic sidekick, Thalia, who visited our decorated home shortly before Christmas many trees ago, delivering their high and low.

⦿

The big entrance hall off the rarely used front door was the room always most carefully spruced up.

Our towering Christmas tree was annually planted in its green, metal holder — "Check daily for water to avoid fire!" —near the front window of the entrance hall, leaving lots of room for the presents that would soon surround it, and the constant foot traffic that flowed past it in every direction until that slowly arriving day.

Daddy was a wholesale florist, and the Christmas trees were shipped to Chattanooga by one of Daddy's ferns and evergreen suppliers. To show their appreciation for his business, that firm cut each year's tree from their mountains in Oregon, selecting it for the symmetry of its foliage and making sure it would just barely miss scraping our ten-foot ceiling. It often arrived by train a month before Christmas and was kept in cold storage.

Our spruce or fir was as carefully chosen every year as the White House's own Christmas tree. It was deco-rated every year with the same cheap red and green glass bulbs twisted by wire to the bottom branches where little babies could explore without being able to knock them off. But then with beautiful, hand-painted, fragile glass ornaments depicting marvels like churches, asteroids, Santas, and starbursts placed around the upper branches, out of the reach of clumsy grabs.

There were also strings of blinking and bubbling lights, streamers, bells, suckers, lots and lots of tinsel, and assorted odds and ends, but they are not important to this tragedy.

The blinking tree took up most of the wall to the left side of the entrance hall's massive front door. The right side held but a small table on which the Christmas crib scene was displayed every year. The crib set was one of Mother's most prized treasures. Year after year, she warned us that its carefully molded and intricately painted porcelain statues had to be handled with extreme care because they came from Germany. I grew up revering the fact that the crib came from centuries-old Germany more than I revered the touching scene comprised of the Madonna and Child, flanked by Joseph, and wise men, and shepherd boys, a sampling of farm animals, and assorted angels kneeling in the straw or hanging from the rafters of the weathered wood shelter.

There were other decorations in the room. Evergreen streamers and such on the mantle over the fireplace, on the telephone table, and hanging from the broad walnut beams that crisscrossed that room's ornate ceiling. These scented and decorative ropes were nice, and we would never have had them had Daddy not dealt in floral products. But they are not important to this tragedy.

⦾

What is important is that one Christmas many trees ago, a few days before the big event, a couple of little kids (no names, but not necessarily any of the forever Little Kids) were playing ball in the entrance hall.

The best rubber balls for inside are about the size of soccer balls, but much lighter and squishier so they can be grabbed. And the best way to play ball in the entrance hall is to bounce that inflated rubber ball against the staircase that leads up from the entrance hall opposite the front door and near the telephone table. A ball tossed against the flat part of a stair will roll listlessly back down, bouncing just a little as it returns to its kid. Tossing and retrieving such balls is never the goal. Because a ball thrown perfectly against the front edge of the fifth, sixth, or seventh stair up arches beautifully back to its source, who can spear it cleanly out of the air with one triumphant hand. "Aiming for the edges" is the way to  play ball against a staircase. And the challenge is to catch it on the fly.

That's the way it was being done at our house one evening just a few days before Christmas by someone who will remain nameless, but who was probably Little Eileen now that I reconstruct the horror.

I know it was evening because Daddy was home.

I know Daddy was home because he stepped right into the middle of it. And was instrumental in ending it.

"It" began with a faint but easily recognizable crash. The kind of tinkling crash that could be made by only one thing — one of the hand-painted, cherished, delicate glass ornaments falling  from the tree and hitting the hardwood floor, disintegrating into hundreds of colorful, shiny splinters. The person who was "playing ball in the house" — an activity forbidden hundreds of times before — mishandled an exceptionally high bounce off the edge of the stairs and knocked the ball with his or her fingertips into the upper branches of the tree. Into one of the prized, irreplaceable ornaments. Everything in the downstairs of the house came to an immediate standstill as that faint but immediately recognizable crash penetrated our collective consciousness.

The ball mishandler picked up the ball and stood forlornly over the little mass of shattered glass, awaiting the righteous and vociferous indignation she would receive from Mrs. Erickson, whose footfalls indicated she was rushing to the scene from the kitchen.

I know I was there, as were several others, because I remember all the big, quiet, guilty faces. We were all guilty of having played ball in the house since the last time such usually innocent insolence had been banned. We were all relatively guilty and would be severely censured along with the one who happened to be most guilty at this silent moment.

It was much worse than we expected, or we might have swallowed our lingering guilt and run for cover in the farthest reaches of the house.

Mrs. Erickson didn't just reprimand. She ranted. And when she finished ranting, she raved. At the end of which she renewed her ranting.

Mother always walked a tight emotional line in those days just before Christmas. Though her shopping was mostly done during the previous year's after-Christmas sales, she was charged with wrapping two or three rooms full of presents. Plus dealing with the hundreds of special assignments —

The crib was always placed on a table to the right of the front door.

school Christmas parties, extra cooking, visits to Santa Claus, driving to see neighborhood Christmas lights, extra Church services, etc. — that plagued this "holiday." She was always at the breaking point as Christmas neared. And she was coming especially close this one evening while looking at the splinters of her prized glass ornament.

Daddy, who certainly didn't hear the delicate ornament disintegrate, couldn't help but hear the ensuing commotion in the entrance hall. There was no doubt that his wife was near the edge, so Daddy set down his evening paper, got up from the kitchen table, stalked sternly into the entrance hall, and, in full view of a roomful of children, broke her into splinters the size of those shards on the floor.

Surveying the damage, listening to the ranting and raving of his wife and the babble as his children tried to explain yet another "accident," and then seeing the rubber ball, he put it together very quickly. "Give me that damned ball!!" he hissed between his most volatile combination of clenched teeth and pursed lips. He grabbed the ball with the authority of the ages from its crying little holder and began to hiss again, "You kids are just—" That was as far as he got. We kids never learned what we just were because Daddy wasn't such a great ball handler himself. It slipped from his hands at the height of his

A blow up of the crib, from the earlier photograph.

grab, caromed off one of the ceiling beams and bounced hard into the crib on its table under the window, taking one of the beloved, hand-painted, staggeringly irreplaceable, porcelain shepherds with it.

Mother was no more nor less stunned than everyone in the room.

Everyone except Daddy who was quick enough to realize by now that the problem wasn't the kids at all. It was all balls.

So he grabbed the inflated tool of destruction off the floor, began hissing some epithet about "BALLS in the HOUSE!!!" and threw it with great frustration toward the open living room. The colorful ball never made it. It bounded off one thing, and then another, and then another, before finally finding its way back behind him — *to the table with the crib.*

This trip it nailed a rare old wise man who had been peacefully standing there, oblivious to the uproar, just trying to give some myrrh to the Baby Jesus. It took the wise man to the floor where his pieces mingled with the shepherd boy's.

As her life passed before her, Mother came to the recent part about the treasured ornament, reeled on to the first broken irreplaceable crib statue, looked down at the second broken statue, and came, understandably, unglued.

She ran upstairs to cry — something she had been needing to do for several days.

Daddy took a last mean look at the rubber ball which was now resting quietly by the door, between the Christmas tree and the remnants of a crib, took a mean look all around at all of us, then trudged despondently upstairs to go through the futile motions of comforting his wife.

We aimed our big round eyes at the ball, and then at each other. The room, in fact the whole house, was very quiet as we tried to figure out how we could get that vicious, treacherous, murderous rubber ball out of the entrance hall and back to its home in the corner of the closet without anyone having to touch it.

Mostly Pregnant
BOOK TWO

CHAPTER 14

The
"Big Boys Room"

First there were the Big Boys.

The original Big Boys were Harold, Frank, and Allen.

I wasn't there when that status was sealed, but I suppose when they were seven, six, and five years old, they looked a lot bigger to the parents who gave them that enduring distinction than the four-, three-, and one-year-olds trailing after them.

John and David were sometimes considered Big Boys, but that was more a view of the stream of smaller ones crawling in their wake than of the parents or the original Big Boys themselves.

David was always big for his age, which might have caused some confusion. John was always big for his britches.

The Big Boys: Harold, Frank, and Allen. With John and David in the wagon.

Harold, Frank, and Allen remained the Big Boys even after they left for college. And the upstairs room they shared after our momentous move to the "new house" continued to be called "the Big Boys Room" for several years after they had given up their twin beds to lesser lights.

The middle members of the family never had a room even temporarily named after them. Perhaps because they never had a name. This group begins with the half of David that was not even a dissonant member of the Big Boys and includes Philip, Michael, Douglas, and half of Louis.

We who constituted this cluster were the Erickson equivalent of the nameless, faceless masses. Lacking identity, we passed inconspicuously through infancy, childhood, and adolescence. By the time we became college students, the experience was no more unique than having hiccups.

It has only been in the real world, aided by the good name of our respective professions, that we have achieved a semblance of personal stature.

But blossoming in the middle of this nameless, faceless mass was Little Eileen, the first girl after seven boys — and her mother's namesake.

Eileen was momentous. An entity unto herself. A world apart. A rare, precious jewel.

While the rest of us were tentatively grouped together in bedrooms, sorted by size and position, Eileen was grouped singly in her own bedroom. While The Big Boys established a pace of academic and intellectual achievement which all the other boys were expected to follow, Little Eileen was guided into and successfully set a pace of social distinction which all the other girls, should there be such blessings, were expected to duplicate.

Weighing the sociological impact that Eileen imposed on the family, it is hard to believe there were fewer than ten of her.

The girls were collectively a unique caste. But the last two girls were also members of another group. Beginning with half of Louis and extending through Cecilia, Paul, Charles, and Carol, we have the Little Kids.

Most of us — the Big Boys and Eileen being the only exceptions — were "little kids" through the early part of our lives. But that distinction was constantly usurped as even littler kids kept appearing on the living room rug. When this rug finally quit producing its annual crawler, those who then held the designation of being the "Little Kids" maintained that distinction for the rest of their lives. They were never usurped.

The Little Kids. They're the same ones who were never allowed to move from the kitchen table to the dining room table. Never allowed to eat without parental supervision.

The Little Kids: Cecilia, Carol, Charles, and Paul.

15

Harold:
Our Not So Humble Beginning

Dear Nieces and Nephews,

Your Uncle Harold says a fish's eyeball is the best bait.

He's right. I know because I've seen many fish die in my ten gallon aquariums over the years and survivors always go first for the eyeballs.

Even if I didn't know, Harold would be right.

Harold knows all there is to know about life. It's his job. He's a scientist. He is also sort of an apathetic existentialist.

He has determined to his satisfaction that life was just a little accident. That it comes to the nothing it squirmed from. That morality is an interesting, but mindless, social custom.

His favorite movie is "Apocalypse Now." And he has stated, albeit as a means of firing Uncle Philip's hawkish fervor, that the 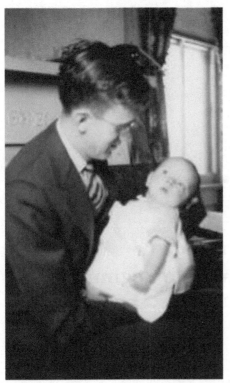 *Vietnam War was good to the extent that it gave us a fine movie.*

Harold, the oldest, gave us all something to shoot for — and miss. He won a scholarship to the Carnegie Institute of Technology. He earned a doctorate from Johns Hopkins. He went on to study a few years at Cambridge where he boosted one of his teachers over a hurdle in that physicist's route to a Nobel Prize. It's in the credits.

Harold returned to the states where he earned tenure teaching and conducting research at Duke. He travels the world filling colleagues in on his ground-breaking work with RNA.

Your Uncle Harold is easy to brag about.

When everyone gathered in Boston a few years ago for your Uncle Charlie's wedding, the accountants and lawyers of the family made a point of discussing enough business to justify their trips as tax write-offs. Uncle Harold topped them by letting Harvard pay for his trip, and for a week of lecture fees.

I shopped at the Harvard bookstore while we were there. They didn't ask me to lecture.

∞ — ∞

Harold applied for a scholarship at Harvard, but never heard from them. Late in his senior year, he and Mother contacted the school. An admissions person explained they filed his part of his application under Harold Erickson and part under Erickson Harold. Dumb old Harvard. "You would have qualified for a scholarship. But we don't have any left. Sorry."

"It would almost certainly have changed the trajectory of my life," Harold acknowledged midway through his successful career. "But I'm in a great position at Duke, so maybe not."

He admits to being especially pleased when fellow scientists approach him at the meetings of international societies and say, "Dr. Erickson, I've read many of your papers. I always pictured you as a much older man."

∞ — ∞

The parents assumed, and we ignorantly accepted their belief, that we would all be as intelligent as this firstborn. It seemed likely at the time that several of us would even excel his mental merits.

There has been some pretty formidable competition within the ranks, but I think I've heard the various brothers claim virtually everything short of, "I'm smarter than Harold."

Harold was a child once; but maybe not like the rest of us.

Relatively yours,
Uncle Rags

Harold Paul Erickson, born January 16, 1940
Married Jacqueline Gonzalez, June 26, 1965, in Baltimore
Jacqueline Gonzalez, born February 20, 1941, Puerto Rico
Rachel Jacqueline, born July 3, 1968

16

Frank: Second In The Still Unforeseeable Line

Dear Nieces and Nephews, and Interested Others,

Uncle Frank. The name has a nice ring to it.

And it fits him well. Just what you want in an uncle or a brother. He'll play you a tough game of tennis or bridge but not so tough that you can't win your share. He doesn't meddle in your problems — unless invited.

Frank is often invited to meddle in problems. Frank saw a lot of life's problems while spending a few years as a priest. He's seen a different perspective as a lawyer.

It was inevitable that a large, devoutly Catholic family like ours would produce a priest. Frank, the second oldest, and John, the fourth oldest, both chose that vocation. John withdrew after six years of study. Frank was ordained and took a long inside look before seeing a different light.

And then there were two.

The whole concept of being a priest changed dramatically from the late-Fifties when Frank made his decision to the late-Sixties, when he changed his mind. The whole concept of nearly everything changed in that decade.

I met the mayor of Knoxville once. He and Frank are close friends. The mayor blurted out in a downtown store where he was campaigning at the time, "Your brother Frank married me."

More accurately, Frank married one of his former parishioners. She has since become a Ph.D. clinical psychologist. She understands the whole family.

As a kid, Frank dazzled his peers and younger brothers with his ability to dislocate his shoulders and thumbs at will from their sockets. He could also wiggle his ears.

Frank was a child once; much like the rest of us.

Relatively yours,
Uncle Rags

Frank Robert Erickson, born May 18, 1941
Married Elaine Scruggs, May 5, 1973, in Nashville
Elaine Scruggs, born April 1, 1950, Nashville
Natali Kristina Erickson, born February 20, 1997

Frank baptizes Harold's child, Rachel.

1 7

Cecilia's
Worm

We have a worm in our kitchen.

It's in the cabinet above the counter where the toaster oven sits in front of a desperately written note that looks more like a sign and warns: UNPLUG TOASTER BEFORE PLUGGING IN TOASTER OVEN. That sign taped above a counter-height plug socket prevents people who don't come home very often from blowing fuses when they try to make a toasted sandwich for lunch.

The worm used to be on that same cluttered counter with the toaster and the toaster oven. But now it's a few feet above the counter. In the cabinet with the plates and coffee cups. On the second shelf. In the front left-hand corner.

It's a rare worm. A rare red worm. Curled up in a little jar about the size of a shrimp cocktail glass. I would say the worm lives in that jar, except that the worm is obviously dead. Encased in formaldehyde.

The worm was a Christmas gift from Harold, the oldest, to Cecilia, who was his godchild. Several of the older ones are godfathers of the younger ones. Mr. and Mrs. Erickson had more children than they did friends and relatives.

⓪

Harold gave Cecilia that little jar full of rare red worm and formaldehyde when he was in his early years of college, and she was about five years old. She had great expectations as to what might be in the prettily wrapped present and was awfully excited when working her way past the ribbons and foil as she opened her present at the kitchen table in front of the gathered family — until she got it unraveled and stared at it for a few long seconds.

Then she squealed, "Ewww! It's a worm!!!"

She held the jar away from her at arm's length. With only her thumb and one finger. For several long seconds, she had given the curled object in the jar every chance in the world to be a ring or bracelet or anything the least bit desirable before finally admitting to herself and then declaring to the world that it was a worm.

We had never had a worm in the house before. Upon passing the jar around, everyone agreed it was definitely a worm. About five inches long. No one measured. The label on the jar affirmed that it was a worm. A Latin worm. Or, at least, a worm with a Latin name.

⓪

That there was a worm in that jar was perhaps the only thing ever stated around the kitchen table that was universally agreed on.

Generally, if someone at the table said it was raining, someone else would walk to the kitchen door, look out, return to the table and correct the errant observer by concluding, "It is only drizzling." But there was definitely a worm in the specimen bottle. It was talked about for several minutes. Some took a second look and enjoyed a second laugh about Cecilia's worm. Then we lost interest — which means we probably settled on something that could be argued over rather than agreed on. As interest in the worm dwindled that afternoon, it was moved off the kitchen table, which is actually in the breakfast room, and placed on the counter in the kitchen where the toaster is. During the next year, the worm got pushed farther and farther back on the counter. For the next two years it occupied a little space about the circumference of a silver dollar and the height of an aspirin bottle in the back corner of the counter, among some stubby pencils and assorted pieces of ownerless change.

Right now, in that very space the worm occupied for a few years on the counter, there is a firecracker.

No one knows whose firecracker it is. It's been there four or five years. When we were young, we were not allowed to have firecrackers. It was even more prohibited to have them in the house. And it was unheard of to leave a banned and illegal firecracker out in the open. But now that we are too old to care, the parents have left a firecracker lying on that counter, back among the pencils and loose change, for several years. I think they are waiting for the rightful owner to recognize it while visiting sometime and take it back outside. Because firecrackers are not allowed in the house.

⑩

After a few years, the worm got moved off the counter — victimized by a rare, particularly intensive cleaning spree.

Cecilia never really wanted the worm, so it would have been unfair to send it up to her room. As a compromise, the worm was lifted three feet off the counter and tucked into the left front corner of the second shelf in the cabinet where the plates and coffee cups live. Cecilia lives in Houston now. She has probably lost track of all the other presents she was given 20 years ago when she was a little girl. But her worm is in the kitchen.

18

Allen: Number 3
Teller Of Tall Tales

Dear Nieces and Nephews, and Interested Others,

Cue the lawyer jokes. We've got one. Not a joke, but a lawyer. The first of five (so keep those jokes handy).

Yes, Frank, a year older, is also a lawyer, but Allen was the first. He was practicing the dark arts of the bar while Frank was still practicing sorcery in the priesthood.

I remember little about Harold's life in the house other than my childish desire to play interfered with his desire to study. He used to bark.

Frank had a girlfriend in high school. Memorable because nei-ther I nor nine of my other ten brothers had girlfriends in high school. And then Frank became a priest.

When I think back to Allen's impact on the house the picture is clearer. I see him stretched across his yellow bunk in a corner

of the Big Boys Room, not bother-ing with his homework because he was that rare stu-dent who could make an A with-out opening the book. Passed the time in-stead with

Three.

paperbacks. It was the late 1950s. So the paperback would be a Steinbeck or Salinger. The Sound and the Fury. *Maybe Camus or Sartre. Nietzsche, on the floor.*

He could absorb their often disturbing messages. But it is not always healthy, little nieces and nephews, to have too much in-sight into Thoreau's "lives of quiet desperation."

∞ — ∞

To Mother's horror, Allen was the first and only Erickson ever suspended from school. He and a few friends skipped high school one afternoon in 1958 and ventured to downtown Chatta-nooga to show their support for Black high school students who were causing a major stir while holding a "sit-in," a popular pro-test at the time, at one of the five-and-dime store's lunch coun-ters. Demanding to be served. The protesters gathered outside to support them were infamously dispersed when assaulted with fire hoses.

The school principal, Father Driscoll, understood Allen and his colleagues were supporting the civil rights movement, but had to make examples of them to prevent their less progressive classmates from skipping class to support the fire hoses.

∞—∞

I remember Allen returning home for Christmas or Easter or summer vacations from the University of Windsor. Windsor was in Ontario. Allen won an academic scholarship to Canada.

He thrilled us impressionable younger ones with tales about life in the land of heavy snows. He said the buildings on campus were connected by tunnels because the snows routinely made foot travel impossible. He talked of bonfires and bobsledding.

We had occasional snows in Chattanooga, but we knew nothing of real winter until Allen came back with the word. And the word was cold.

Allen working on high school newspaper.

Allen liked impressing us with his tall tales. And still does. Mark Twain wrote about a group of steamboat crewmen sitting around one night swapping stories. When one of the taller stories finished falling, a crewman said, "Say boys, let's divide it up. Thar's thirteen of us. I can swaller a thirteenth of the yarn, if you can worry down the rest."

We get to divide Allen's tales into thirteenths as well, but some of them are still hard to swallow.

∞—∞

After returning from his faraway Canadian province Allen worked his way through the University of Tennessee law school.

The first of five in the family to get a law degree. His initial job was with the Federal Trade Commission. Washington wasn't cold enough to suit this ersatz Canadian's masochistic tendencies, so he moved with his wife to her old family farm just outside of Boston. Became a New England lawyer.

The farm is adjacent to the Foxboro stadium so it gets shown off a lot when the crew televising a New England Patriots football game scans the beautiful countryside.

Allen was town attorney for Foxboro and one of the officials at Schaefer Stadium that night many years ago when a bunch of over-indulged fans from Boston turned a Monday Night Football game into a nationally televised barroom brawl. Allen claims it wasn't his fault. I could maybe swallow my thirteenth share of that one.

∞ — ∞

Allen was a child once; much like the rest of us.

Relatively yours,
Uncle Rags

Allen Edward Erickson, born June 1, 1942
Married Edith Persis Brown October 26, 1968, in Boston
Edith Persis Brown, born Feb. 16, 1945, Boston
Clifford Andrew, born August 18, 1970
Kirsten Elizabeth Eileen, born November 27, 1972
Allen Edward, Jr., born July 5, 1978

19

A Case of Budweiser; Two Cases Of Pampers — "Everybody Pile In! We're Going To Missouri."

Mother could just as well have said: "We're going to Mars!" I did-n't know. When you're five years old there's a lot you don't know.

Besides, I was just barely awake. They thought if they kept us just barely awake we'd all go back to sleep as soon as we got in the car. Early morning take off. Crack of dawn. The longer they sleep, the faster we'll get there.

But not me.

I never have been one to sleep in a car. I want to see the truck that's going to mash me. Besides, the vibrations you feel when you rest your head against a car door rattle your teeth. Who can sleep through that? Even when you are more gum than teeth.

⑩

It was one of our trips to St. Joseph, Missouri, home of the Pony Express, home of Mother's parents. There were two such

A photograph that appeared in the St. Joseph newspaper chronicling the visiting horde from Chattanooga.

trips in my lifetime. One in 1953 with the new red station wagon. One in 1957 with the new yellow station wagon. You might say our Dad was showing off . . . and you'd be right. New cars were among life's biggest status symbols and greatest joys in the 1950s.

These new station wagons didn't really belong to Daddy. They were company cars for delivering flowers. But, like the company truck, they lived at our house when they weren't at work.

⑩

Getting from Chattanooga to Missouri was a two-day drive up long, winding, two-lane highways. Daddy was always jumping out into the wrong lane, and flooring it. Activating that little silver

knob under the accelerator. Passing gear. "Just to get around this old slowpoke," he would explain to his panicked wife. Mrs. Erickson, who didn't drive, and who was pregnant at the time, was kept busy trying to push her foot through the imaginary brake on the right side floorboard. Now Daddy, who probably shouldn't be driving at all, is one of those old slowpokes.

⟪⟫

At the end of one full day of passing cars in his new yellow Ford wagon with the big V-8, Daddy had made it as far as St. Louis. On the northern outskirts of that city he began looking for a motel and finally found one that said "Vacancy. Kids Free." The manager changed his mind about that "vacancy" when he saw our station wagon drive up. Turned on the "No" part of that red neon light. There were only ten of us at the time — not counting the parents. Daddy was cussing mad. But we found an opening up the road.

⟪⟫

After that we didn't take any trips. At least, not until Harold got married seven years later up in Baltimore. For that trip we split up. Mrs. Erickson and the kids left early in a friend's station wagon.

Daddy and the older ones took the company's new blue Chevy station wagon and headed up at the last minute. Everyone riding with Daddy was old enough to drink beer so they packed a cooler for the trip. I think this was Daddy's first experience with how much beer his educated sons had learned to drink because he never went on another trip with them.

Rumor has it they were doing pretty good just to get out of Tennessee. Rumor also has it that David proved beyond a doubt that his being blind in one eye affects his vision. He got booed, ridiculed, and menaced in every way imaginable before finally giving up the driver's seat to one of the rowdy beer drinkers in the back of the car.

Daddy said that his older boys were crankier on that trip than they had been as babies going to Missouri.

He threatened to buy diapers instead of beer for the return trip.

20

"An Only Child"
By Harold

My earliest memory dates from when I was only 22 months old.

Knowledgeable people assure me I can't remember anything at that age. But I remember, or have reconstructed, a Sunday afternoon, a typical Sunday afternoon on Kirby Avenue. Mother was taking a nap and Daddy was listening to the radio. "Swing and Sway with Sammy Kaye."

Then the excitement, something happened on the radio, the announcement of the attack. Mother came out and we were all three very concerned. (Just imagine: our family until a few months earlier when Frank showed up out of nowhere, really did comprise Mother, Daddy, and me, an only child.)

We were suddenly excited and anxious about the nation, about war, about an aunt and uncle who were living in Honolulu, which had just been attacked. Obviously, I had no idea what was truly going on, less than two years old, but I do remember the interruption of the standard and peaceful Sunday music.

For the rest of the war I remember our stomping on tin cans (to flatten them for storage, collection, and recycling). Not too many toys, but we tried hard with what we had. I remember oleo (or was that after the war) when it was first introduced. They had a law that it be colored white, so you wouldn't confuse it with butter. It came as a white stick wrapped in plastic, but there was a little bean-size bag of orange coloring inside that you could pop and then squish the whole thing around until the margarine looked just like butter.

And then the end, VJ day, was a big night of celebration. I think I felt a little left out. I knew everything would be better with the war over, but I really didn't know how. Except we could stop stomping on tin cans, but I really never minded that, or squeezing the margarine.

— Harold

2 1

Roller Skates And Scooters
By Allen

Among the early and more pleasant memories I have are of going to the Ridgedale playground. This was during my pre-school days.

We would go to the top of the hill on the playground where they had the sandbox and playing cards. They had only Rook cards instead of regular playing cards because Rook was a simpler game. The playground was a great place for catching June bugs that we would tie to strings so they could fly in circles around us.

By the time I was in the first grade we were getting permission almost every afternoon, after taking the streetcar home from school, to walk down the alley by ourselves and go to the playground. It was basically only a half-block away. I drove by there the last time I was in Chattanooga and I have to say that the hill leading to the top of the playground sure looks small now compared to how it appeared when we were kids. The slate rock wall we used to have to climb over on our way up that hill, well, it's really not much more than a little step.

When Harold was having problems with his left leg one summer our grandparents sent Uncle Paul's old red wagon by rail from St. Joseph, Missouri, so we could get Harold around. Frank and I would take either end of the wagon that summer, one of us pulling

it by the handle and the other pushing it from behind, to take Harold to the playground. I don't remember it as an inconvenience. The playground was fun, and even more so with all of us there.

There was a street with a well paved sidewalk running alongside the playground. It was a steep hill, coming off Missionary Ridge, and ideally suited for breakneck roller skating. After our first few rawly skinned elbows and knees (to say nothing of the less regenerative loss of pants and shirts) Mom passed a firm rule forbidding roller skating on that hill. Her rule made us more careful.

At first we had to stoop. Then, at much greater risk to our appendages, we started coasting down this hill standing up. Before long we were striving to get up enough speed on the downhill swoop to allow us to coast along the level part at the bottom - all the way to the community center building. It could be done with a really good run. But the real trick was to have just enough speed rather than too much. There was a seriously sharp turn that had to be negotiated at the bottom of the hill before any serious coasting could begin, and the whole secret was in being able to maintain control while coming into this knee burner.

Roller skates were bad enough, but hauling down that hill on scooters was its own kind of hell. It never occurred to Mother that she would have to forbid something that stupid.

— Allen

88

2 2

The Ping-Pong Room

Things change. Even the name of the "Big Boys Room" gave way to something newer.

For several years it became known as the "ping-pong room."

This room at the head of the stairs in the "new house" was large enough to accommodate four beds and a full-sized ping-pong table. A row of three twin beds jutting horizontally from the left wall and one flat against the corner of the opposite wall. Its first occupants were the Big Boys. A later occupant was the ping-pong table that dominated its center. It was tight. Required everyone to develop valuable skills playing close to the table's edges.

The table was purchased with Top Value Stamps, which was Kroger's version of Green Stamps that successfully lured housewives to the A&P and other supermarkets in the Fifties. The table was given as a bribe to two of us who were dragging our feet in completing merit badges necessary to earn the Eagle Scout pins that would tie and then set a world record for the most Eagles in one family.

A pederast Scoutmaster undermined Mrs. Erickson's ambitions before those two foot-draggers could fulfill them. The troop fell apart. Leaving more time for ping-pong, a pursuit with its own world of bragging rights — for some of us.

Upon returning home from college, whether for Christmas or the longer summer breaks, we were assigned to one of the beds in what had gradually become known as the "ping-pong room." It didn't matter if the table was put away, the gaping space in the middle of the floor defined the enduring character of that room, and the name itself was a constant reminder that if the visitors just took a few minutes to drag the two green halves of tables out from against the wall behind the beds and then find the net, paddles, and balls, their visit home would take on a life of its own. For the duration of the weekend or holiday the parents saw their visiting sons only during supper and that night's beer runs.

Ping-pong, like nearly every aspect of a young man's life, generates a healthy thirst. Beer. Those waiting upstairs for winners took turns darting downstairs, past the parents sitting at the kitchen table in the breakfast room, and on to the kitchen's refrigerator to load up on a fresh supply of beer for the two playing the current game, and whoever else was in line for winners. Conversation with the parents usually consisted of Daddy's inevitable interrogation: "How many is that for you tonight, Louis?" And the courier's lie, "I've only had two. These are for Douglas, Paul, and Michael."

We might also see the parents for a wave or handshake in the driveway as the visit ended.

Not our nice furnishings. We had four single beds. And a ping pong table. The upper photo, taken from a realtor's listing, shows the carport room's distinctive doorway that opened from the landing. The lower one shows the back windows.

Daddy always took the ping-pong table down as soon as everyone left, being careful to put it behind the most cumbersome objects in the room in his effort to discourage our resurrecting it during the next visit.

Over the course of the next decade, the parents wised up and changed the name of that troublesome room. It took a while, but determined repetition changed it to the "carport room" — so named because of its position above the covered part where our driveway passed by the side porch and where we always parked the station wagon. It might technically have been a *porte-cochère,* but there was no way we could afford one of those. We were lucky to have a carport.

And a "carport room," big enough for a ping-pong table.

2 3

John: No 4
Singularly Impressive

Dear Nieces and Nephews, and Valued Readers,

Your Uncle John is a natural born tyrant.

And a cunning diplomat.

And the family's first millionaire.

∞ — ∞

As he became prosperous John concentrated on overriding his tyrannical nature and is often nothing short of benevolent.

Tyrannical benevolence.

John is bossy. Always has been.

Whenever Mrs. Erickson left the house for an overnighter, which means whenever Mrs. Erickson went to the hospital to have another baby, John, even at age 10, took over. He marshaled everyone younger than him into an annual housecleaning of his design, rather than hers.

Resisting John's tyranny was not an option — not just because of his innate persuasiveness, but also because of the carrots he benevolently waved. Always an opportunist, John cozied up to rich people. He had access to boats, horses, and other exotic amenities the rest of us poor kids could never touch on our own. Waterskiing was our reward for following orders.

∞—∞

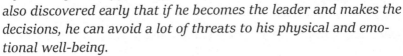

John manipulates as easily as many of us slam ping-pong balls. Those being manipulated rarely resist, because a requisite of that fine art is making sure everyone comes out at least a little ahead. John had two physical characteristics that contributed to his tyrannical nature; he was a bit of a redhead; and he was small for his age.

As a proportionally small first grader, John instinctively realized the advantage of befriending the biggest boy in the class. He also discovered early that if he becomes the leader and makes the decisions, he can avoid a lot of threats to his physical and emotional well-being.

He naturally strove to take over every activity he became involved in. He ran the high school while a student there. He ran the seminary during the years he was studying for the priesthood. Changing vocations, John distinguished himself with RCA before becoming an entrepreneur. His latest acquisition is a quaint little college on a hill overlooking Baltimore he has converted into the largest life care community in the country.

John is the only one in the family who owns a college.

∞—∞

John is an authority on linguistics, psychology, geometry, astronomy, theology, oceanography, photography, history, electronics, mechanics, and carpentry — among others. But we don't know how intelligent he might be. He always dodged taking the standardized tests in order to assure he didn't come in second, or worse.

∞—∞

John was witnessing the birth of his daughter and couldn't help but notice the anxiety mounting within the delivery team as the baby's heartbeat began bouncing up and down on the TV monitor while it was still trying to free itself from its mother's body. He could tell the delivery team was confused, and that they were contemplating surgery to free the baby just in case the problem was as severe as the monitor was warning them.

John with his godchild, Carol, the youngest.

John stepped out to the hall for a moment, thought about what he was seeing, re-entered the delivery room and suggested they attach a new sensor to the top of the baby's emerging little head. He was right. The erratic heartbeat was being caused by a faulty sensor — not a faulty baby. The doctors put their knives back into their sheaths and the delivery proceeded smoothly.

John is that rare person who can tell doctors what to do.

Earlier, while living in San Francisco, he fixed up the home of a casual business acquaintance who was so devastated by the death of his child that he faced bankruptcy if he didn't pay his taxes and address other financial deadlines. After repairing the man's neglected house and pool, John sold it for him, taking in enough to meet the tax bills and give this troubled soul a fresh start. The troubled soul was Howard Ruff, who went on to become one of the country's best-selling financial gurus. Ruff hosted his own syndicated TV talk show, published a highly regarded newsletter, and authored a number of books telling followers how to make it through tough times. It was typical that John had once stepped in and salvaged the Ruff house.

∞—∞

John was a child once; but not like the rest of us.

Relatively yours,
Uncle Rags

John Carl Erickson, born September 6, 1943
Married Nancy Jane Anderegg, March 20, 1971, in Cincinnati
Nancy Jane Anderegg, born January 27, 1947, Cincinnati
Mark Randall, born May 29, 1973
Craig Andrew, born July 11, 1974
Scott Richard, born October 22, 1976
Andrea Cay, born May 23, 1980

2 4

How Impressive?

Dear Nieces and Nephews, and Valued Readers,

Your Uncle John was one dinner away from becoming the family's first billionaire. (Well, maybe the second. There are a few secrets.)

He had a dinner meeting the day after Thanksgiving in 2008. Papers were going to be signed to sell half of his company. Those papers would have made him a billionaire.

Lehman Brothers, a major financial firm, had failed a few weeks earlier and the national economy was in free fall. The buyer showed up that night and told John he had lost so many customers he just couldn't go through with the deal to become a full partner in John's chain of retirement communities. John didn't get to become a billionaire. At least, not that night.

∞ — ∞

When I was ten, The Millionaire *was one of my favorite TV shows. The reclusive John Beresford Tipton directed his man, Michael Anthony, to give a check for a million dollars every week to*  *some surprised man or woman whose life would be forever changed. Because with a million dollars in 1958 you could buy a yacht, a few houses, everything you ever wanted, and still have plenty of money to live on the rest of your life.*

These days, nearly everyone in the family is at least a millionaire. Even me. But it's not the same. Not that anyone is complaining. Except, maybe me. Selfishly nostalgic for those days when a million dollars would buy a mansion and a yacht instead of a tent and a dinghy.

Relatively yours,
Uncle Rags

(This was a 2022 amendment to the 1985 original.)

2 5

A Nagging Toothache
Kind Of Poverty

You have to pay for life's pleasures.

We paid for ours by being poor.

Chronic poverty was reverse compensation for all the games and brains and other natural resources deposited in our old rock-walled asylum.

Ours was not world-class poverty. Not the sort you might encounter in a geography book. It was not even of the back-breaking impossible-to-get-ahead vein. Ours was more the nagging toothache sort of poverty. We could meet life's necessities, but few of its extras.

There were a few kids at our largely middle-class parochial school who were poorer than the Ericksons, but not many. I had one in my class. I never liked that kid. He and I were the shortest in our class. He and I both had the runniest noses. He was a reminder of the side of myself that I most wanted to escape. I never visited him.

I never visited anyone who could beat the Ericksons at either ping-pong or poverty.

When I was at friends' houses, I was always intimidated by their furniture. In front of their televisions, they had big soft, leather-like chairs and brightly colored plaid upholstered sofas.

Furnishings that made one feel settled just sitting in them. And in their bedrooms, they had matching beds and dressers that looked like they actually belonged to someone.

The beds in our house were ones various armies and seminaries had given up on. Our mattresses were so thin you could roll them into pillows.

The house itself was a striking monumental showcase of turn-of-the-century architecture. The furniture inside was about as interesting as a screen door. For character, we had kids.

And for money, we had a money cup.

2 6

The Money Cup

When Harold, the oldest, was a baby, some distant relative gave him a nice, pewter cup.

That cup was promptly wrestled from his sticky little fingers and placed out of reach. Soon after, some loose change had to go somewhere, so it was dropped into the cup which had been set on the shelf of a kitchen cabinet. Ever since, that tarnished pewter artifact has asexually reproduced loose change from its dark corner in the cabinet.

The money cup dispersed 14 nickels a week for the children's individual donations to the collection basket during Sunday Mass. It dispersed additional nickels when annual classroom contests were waged between the boys and the girls to see which gender could generate the most money for the Bishop's Relief Fund.

We each donated a nickel every Friday during the duration of the fundraisings. That money supposedly helped feed starving lepers in countries more disadvantaged than Tennessee. More backward, even, than Mississippi. Scandals in recent years suggest much of the Bishop's money was diverted by secular-minded priests toward investment property in Pennsylvania's famous honeymoon haven — the Pocono Mountains. But the money cup didn't care. It also paid the paperboy, and he brought bad news every day.

The kitchen cup gave up four cents per person per school day so we could buy half-pints of chocolate milk to wash down the sandwiches we brown-bagged from home. Once a week the cup was prone to splurge with an extra nickel per mouth so we could revel at lunch with a bag of Fritos.

The kitchen cup put 14 kids through grade school and continues to this day to meet those nearly extinct home expenses of less than three dollars in magnitude.

A conservative estimate is the cup has circulated $1,500 in just nickels during its bountiful life.

I never once saw it empty.

I never once saw it fed.

Daddy used to always kid Mrs. Erickson — who was never one to be kidded — that, "Like the birds of the air and the lilies of the field, the Lord will provide." She wasn't one to say "Bull——!" so she said, "Poppycock!"

Daddy knew she thought he was the one who fed the money cup.

⦿

Despite its spawning of nickel eggs, the little kitchen money cup could hardly be counted on to meet the larger financial obligations our struggling army incurred while barracked at the house. Those were handled by the Lord, and by Daddy's very stretched salary.

Nor could the cup handle luxury purchases. Those were managed with Top Value Stamps.

27

David: No. 5
Engineered His Way Forward

Dear Nieces and Nephews, and Valued Readers,

David, number five, is hard to figure. Hard because he's probably about as close to normal as anything the family produced. Engineers are notoriously normal.

∞—∞

For a long time, David had the reputation of being slow. The reputation was unwarranted — a repercussion of his being big for

105

his age, and, at the same time, destined to paddle in the wide wake intentionally churned up by his older but smaller brother John.

True to a tradition interrupted only by his two older brothers who chose the seminary, which was a totally free ride, David earned a college scholarship. Breaking with tradition, he chose to stay in the state, to study engineering at the University of Tennessee in Knoxville. He became the first in a long line who would take this easy route (just head north on Highway 58 for 110 miles) to higher education.

The welcoming committee doesn't seem too pleased with this new arrival.

After holding down a few private sector engineering jobs while earning a master's degree, David landed in Washington with the Department of Defense.

His task for several years was the design of windshield wipers for a ridiculously costly submarine that TIME magazine and 60 MINUTES used to poke fun at every few years. No one knows if the submarine was ever completed since the news organizations lost interest in the story after its first decade of cost overruns. When he was finally on the verge of solving the windshield wiper problem the government quickly moved him into an administrative position where he could monitor the annual leave and other paperwork for a whole new team of windshield wiper problem solvers.

As of this writing, David is in an advisory position with the Joint Chiefs of Staff — on the civilian side. His letterhead is easily the most threatening of anyone's in the family. Finding an envelope in the mail from some distant law firm arouses respect, but finding a communication from the Joint Chiefs of Staff commands it.

In a note he sent me once on his Chiefs of Staff memo paper, David mentioned that he had an important meeting coming up with "the Principal Deputy Assistant Secretary." Being so long in the bureaucracy, it apparently did not occur to him that we free-enterprisers talk virtually every day with our secretaries — and seldom have to deal with the person who is the main helper to the person who helps one's secretary's assistant.

∞ — ∞

With so many lawyers and accountants in the family, few of us ever get around to actually paying any taxes — but we never fail to give David a good portion of grief for living off us taxpayers. Still, I believe him when he says he has saved the country several million dollars several times over during his career by doing something right when it could just as easily have been done wrong a few times first.

∞ — ∞

Off his job, David presents an imposing picture. He is not only financially secure, but is personally secure. Secure enough to admit he has insecurities. And, it turns out, David is very intelligent. Enjoys taking college courses on a wide variety of subjects. He was always one of the more mechanically adept siblings, but has developed an in-depth understanding of science and medicine, so he's a welcome resource whether you're trying to fix the knocking of a motor, or knock down a lingering pain.

∞—∞

David was a child once; much like the rest of us.

Relatively yours,
Uncle Rags

David Anthony Erickson, born August 16, 1944
Married Janet Furman August 7, 1971, in Clifton, New Jersey
Janet Furman, born January 7, 1948, Passaic, New Jersey
Michael David, born April 15, 1975
Kevin Furman, born October 15, 1978

2 8

Holding His Breath
Until He Passed Out
By Mother

During the War years everybody improvised, making do with what was available.

We didn't have many ornaments for the Christmas tree, so we decorated it with pinecones and I bought candy suckers, covered them with colored cellophane, tied a ribbon around them, and hung them on the Christmas tree. Every afternoon each of the children got to pick a sucker off the tree and eat it. It was a special treat because even suckers were hard to come by in those years.

Unfortunately, David decided that if suckers were good to eat, he would try some of the other ornaments. He gave us a bad scare when he bit into one of the glass ornaments. We did not know whether he had managed to spit out all the pieces, or had swallowed some slivers of glass. Luck was with us. After a couple of nervous days we decided he was going to be okay.

John was sick so much as a baby that he definitely had to have special attention and special food. He also developed one very bad habit. When he did not get his own way, he would start screaming and hold his breath until he passed out. This always managed to scare the other kids, especially when he fell on the ground or the floor in one of his tantrums. Of course, once he passed out, he would start breathing again. Still, it was a rather terrifying episode to watch, and things reached the place where the others would give in to keep him from pulling it.

One hot summer day when John pulled a breath-holding tantrum, I was drinking a glass of ice water. Just as he started to hold his breath, I threw the ice water in his face. The results were spectacular. He drew a perfectly normal breath, and started whimpering. The next time he started, I grabbed the bottle of ice water we kept in the refrigerator and gave him the same treatment. And that was that.

I won that round, John, but you won plenty more.

— Mother

29

Philip: No. 6
The Four-Eyed Accountant

Dear Nieces and Nephews, and Patient Readers,

Your Uncle Philip was the first of three accountants. And the first and only child in the family to wear glasses.

It rained a lot in Tennessee. It was particularly grating to play tennis with Philip during light drizzles. He stopped every few points — but only the points that he lost — wasting a lot of time wiping his glasses.

The reason I mention Philip's spectacles is because children wearing eyeglasses are assumed to be brainier than

111

children sporting baseball gloves. Television commercials regularly exploit this stereotype. If we are agreed that eyeglasses indicate intelligence, I'll wrap this introduction up by noting Philip's contention that among his many credits is the fact that he has the lowest IQ in the family.

He says he's seen all the IQs and that the parents used to speak in hushed tones whenever they would talk to him about such prospects as good grades and bright futures. I don't really believe he's seen all our IQs because I can't remember having ever seen mine. But I'm not a picky sort of person — so I'll accept Philip's argument that he's the dumbest in the family.

Yearbook photo.

As you might expect, there's a catch: Philip hasn't been going around all his life claiming to be stupid. He only started that the past few years. And it's not just a coincidence that during that same stretch of time he has been sitting down in Naples, Florida, making all kinds of money with his own CPA firm. And it's no coincidence that if you give most people the choice of being either smart or rich they'll quickly take the money.

∞ — ∞

All of you nieces and nephews are probably pretty familiar with Naples, Florida. The new family seat.

After finishing school at the University of Tennessee, Philip moved to that quiet little resort town on the Gulf of Mexico. It wasn't quiet long because he was dumb enough to open his comfortable waterfront home to any of us game for a trip to the beach. That became a pretty popular game.

A lot of Ericksons decided to save gas by just moving down to that once quiet little resort. Paul used to escape Knoxville's cold drizzle by spending his winters helping with tax season at Philip's firm. And moved in full time once he finished school.

Carol got her degree in accounting and decided she would just as soon squabble with Philip as squabble with any other bosses.

And Louis reasoned that if dumb ol' Philip could get by with working only a few hours a week as a CPA and make money in the process that it would be good pickings for a young attorney.

It was just a matter of time before the parents were finally persuaded to sell the old house in Chattanooga and move their routines to the new family seat.

∞—∞

Philip was the first of the older ones — though he's really just a middle one — to take an active interest in sports. He was good at back yard football and basketball, and was serious enough about tennis to become a tournament player.

The coaches thought we were all too smart to play sports in high school, but we were pretty much forced to play in the band since we were the only thing holding it together. Before we gave up and let the band die, Philip played an aggressive trombone. Among his favorites, or at least loudest, were the popular John Philip Sousa pieces like Stars and Stripes Forever and The Washington Post March that all bands of that era played. Going into his senior year of college, the

113

bespectacled former trombonist married a charming little Italian named Rosemary Sousa, who was a direct descendant of John Philip.

There is no telling who Philip would have married had he taken up the harp.

∞—∞

Philip was a child once; much like the rest of us.

Relatively yours,
Uncle Rags

Philip Andrew Erickson, born November 7, 1946
Married Rosemary Sousa June 22, 1968, in Orlando
Rosemary Joanne Sousa, born February 9, 1948, Bellerose, N.Y.
Christopher Brian, born April 30, 1977
Jessica Marie, born March 31, 1979
Marcia Rose, born April 19, 1981
Deanna Rene Erickson, born January 14, 1987

3 0

The Bear In The Mountains
By Philip

We were early users of convenience stores.

How many times did we go from the 12th street house to the little Glaze's corner market to pick up a loaf of bread? It's surprising that we could be trusted with $1.19 for a loaf of bread and two pounds of hamburger at such an early age.

The Ridgedale community center was a major part of our early lives. Three comments about the community center: 1.) People running down the street leading to the center screaming, "It's a BOY," or, "It's a GIRL." Not an everyday occurrence, but it did happen more than occasionally. 2.) Football games with some of

Frank's high school classmates and an introduction to basketball and ping-pong (not to mention sandboxes with especially sticky summer sand). 3.) John and one of his early business enterprises — a Kool-Aid stand at a night softball game; risky, but he turned a profit.

The older ones regularly returned home for visits, even after getting married. After a two-day hike to Spence Field in the Smoky Mountains with Harold and his new wife, Jacquie, we began a pre-bedtime discussion about the dangers of storing food in the back of our tents. Michael and I were brave enough to agree to store the food in our tent; however, prior to bed we asked our near adult leader and natural scientist, Harold, about a course of action if we are approached by a bear in the night. His suggestion was to scream at the top of our voices. This scream should scare any reasonable bear.

At about two in the morning, the worst happened. I looked up into the door of the tent and saw a silhouette in the sky that was lighted by a full moon. The silhouette was a large brown bear that was about to, with claws extended, begin walking across my face on his way to the food in the back of the tent.

Seeing the bear, I followed Harold's advice and proceeded to let loose a loud scream which broke the silence of the night. The scream was very effective. Michael, who was sleeping next to me, jumped about six inches high. Not an easy task while lying on your back. And you should have seen the bear as it . . . reached down with its right paw and . . . slapped me on the shoulder and said "Philip, be quiet or you will wake up everyone in the camp, and please hand me the insect repellant." Well, the camp was awake and Jacquie, Harold's wife, took the insect repellant back to her tent.

— Philip

3 1

So What, It Was Only
A World Record

We were almost famous once.

We were famous several times but once we just barely missed and were left with being "almost famous."

This was many years ago. Back when we were trying to break a world record for the most Eagle Scouts in one family.

⊙

All the older brothers joined the Scouts at an early age and began ambitiously earning merit badges. If a Scout joins early enough and has an interest in merit badges — rewards for showing an interest in subjects as varied as knot tying, stamp collecting,

117

canoeing, electronics, archery, etc. — he can hardly fail to reach that ultimate of honors: Becoming an Eagle.

Becoming an Eagle back in the 1950s and early-1960s was considered a major accomplishment. It was noted on television and in the newspapers that famous men like astronauts and senators were Eagle Scouts. As all of the other ambitious, honest, self-righteous Eagle Scouts around the country read that a famous person was an Eagle they said to themselves and their wives, "Me, too!" It meant that as teenagers, they had developed an expertise in and earned merit badges in 20 different subjects. Good for them.

Erickson Eagles Four Eagle Scouts in Notre Dame; and John, 15, sophomore at Notre one family is the record Dame. They have 85 merit badges among them. set by the Harold A. Erickson family of Chat- The boys come from a large family. "We have tanooga. Left to right are Harold, 18, a fresh- enough for a football team and three cheer- man at Carnegie Tech; Frank, 17, senior at leaders," says the father. There are 11 boys and Notre Dame High School; Allen, 16, junior at three girls.

The Big Boys were great Scouts. They could build 10 different kinds of fires. Dig five kinds of holes. They could tie every knot that had a name — as opposed to we whose knots just hold things together. They could find north after being spun in circles, in the wilds, on a cloudy day, with only a turtle in their pocket. And they could tell how high a tree stood by measuring it against the length of their thumbs and the shadows of the sun.

As each in turn received his Eagle award, Mr. and Mrs. Erickson sat proudly in the audience. Seeing that this could go on for a long time, Mr. Erickson gave Mrs. Erickson, who was pregnant at the time and suspected there might be yet another Eagle soaring out of the hangar soon to accept the world's laurels, a large silver pin. On this silver pin she put the first three little silver eagles that had already been awarded to the parents of the Scouts who achieved this milestone.

The proud parents of other Eagles usually noticed Mrs. Erickson's shiny pin as she walked not-so-humbly into the awards ceremonies. Their first glance was tinged with curiosity — then they gaped awestruck as they comprehended the combined achievements her relatively young pin, with just three Eagles, represented.

Harold was an Eagle. And Frank. And Allen. Then John. Then David. That made five Eagles. After David got his, someone from the local Boy Scouts of America headquarters looked things up and found that the most Eagles ever in one family in the whole world was six.

Lots of pressure came to bear on Philip and me. Philip could be the record-tying Eagle Scout of the whole world. Then I could set the new record.

With Douglas, Louis, Paul, and Charles — who had all descended to earth by the time of David's rise to its top — waiting in the wings, we could obviously set a record that would stand for a long time.

There were a couple of problems, though. The main one being it was fun for Harold, Frank, and Allen to get their Eagles and do all the things that Scouting offered because no one had ever done them before. They were out, as usual, playing in new frontiers.

The frontier had long been settled by the time John came through, but it was easy for him to get his Eagle anyway. John was inherently so over-qualified in all aspects of Scouting that the merit badges piled up on him. He was also a natural born leader and Scouting offered ample opportunity to flex some of those skills. Without either his merit badge or leadership skills, John could have made Eagle easily enough by just walking down to the local headquarters and talking them out of a pin.

David had a difficult time getting his Eagle, but he managed. Then Philip and I inherited even harder times.

The reason it was difficult for David and very trying for Philip and me was that Troop 75, which we all in turn belonged to, began falling apart. I suspect one reason it was disintegrating was that John did such a good job of running it while he was moving through the ranks that, after he gave it back, the old Scoutmaster was reluctant to do anything with it again.

The old Scoutmaster solved his problems by dying of a heart attack, and the new Scoutmaster was far more interested in watching his little Scouts swim naked at the YMCA indoor pool than teaching them how to become Eagles. It's likely he didn't want his Scouts going into the homes of the men all over town who were experts in various fields who had to test and sign off on those seeking merit badges. Didn't want his Scouts blabbing that all of their weekly meetings were spent swimming naked at the YMCA.

The only one trying to keep the train rolling was Mrs. Erickson. She wanted that world record. She was always reminding Philip and me to get our merit badges and become the Eagles we were cut out to be. She understood that the troop was falling apart. But she also knew we could work around that minor obstacle if we really wanted to. We didn't really want to. In fact, what we really wanted to do was play basketball and continue exploring some of the new ground we had found for ourselves in that over-populated world we were growing up in.

To her credit, Mother pushed Philip and me all the way up to Life Scout — which is only one step from Eagle. To accomplish that, though, she resorted to bribery. She acquired a ping-pong table for us by trading in some of her Top Value Stamps. The ping-pong table was supposed to be given in *exchange* for our Eagles. Mrs. Erickson learned through that experience to never pay in advance. In fairness, Philip and I have always suffered pangs of guilt while playing at that table.

Douglas and Louis, meanwhile, were working their way up the Scouting ladder as well, but their route was even more hindered. Douglas was another natural born Scout — there being a merit badge for everything he was interested in. Yet, even he could not advance within the deterioration.

⦿

The new Scoutmaster got caught in the backseat of his car with one of his naked little Scouts. Fortunately, not one from our family. And the troop never met again. Even Mother never mentioned Scouting again after that horror.

But culture was the real villain standing between us and the world record. Scouting was a socially redeeming activity in the Fifties. But as the Sixties wedged in, it was considered by everyone, fellow students and the sponsoring Knights of Columbus alike, an embarrassment that only clods pursued.

⑩

Time won, and we lost. Philip never tied the record. I never broke it. And Louis and Paul became the first Ericksons to letter in sports while competing for city championships in tennis and wrestling.

⑩

Philip actually got all the merit badges, passed all the special tests, and did everything that was required to become an Eagle Scout. The troop, however, was in such decay at the time, and Philip was so disinterested in this routine achievement, that the local Boy Scouts headquarters never got around to giving him his world record-tying medal.

I never made it past Life Scout. Life Scout, according to the manual, is quite a milestone and something a man will be proud of the rest of his life.

I am not at all proud of my Scouting. My ping-pong skills? Oh, yes. But not my Scouting.

3 2

Michael: The Seventh Son.
The Fortunate One?

Dear Nieces and Nephews, and Much Appreciated Readers,

And then there's the miserable, heart-wrenching story of your wretched Uncle Michael.

Yes, me. "The seventh son. The fortunate one."

Michael is also known as Uncle Rags. A name Uncle Allen's daughter, Kirsten, tagged Michael with many years ago because his pants and shorts were all frayed and torn. And because his tennis shoes flapped. Because his sweaters had holes in them. And his shirts were so worn at the elbows that his bony arms poked through.

But let the raggedy Uncle Rags explain: Jeans cut to become shorts are meant to be frayed . . . old tennis shoes are the best tennis shoes . . . sweaters don't mind having holes, and the holes don't let many drafts in . . . and Michael's shirts don't live long around the elbows because he types a lot and his sharp elbows are always pressed against the arms of his chair.

Besides, he's so skinny that most clothes don't fit him right and when he finds something that wears well he tends to wear it until it's gone.

And, besides that, he likes old clothes.

And, to be completely honest, he's very, very poor.

∞—∞

He's been rich a few times. At least, comfortable. But Michael has spent most of the years since graduating from college mired in chronic poverty. He's one of those rare people who, if he had it to do over again, admits he would make a real point of doing it differently. Though, he would probably still come out poor. And ragged.

Understand: Michael dove off the highchair at the age of two and has never been the same. All the peanut butter and jelly sandwiches in Chattanooga could not put him back together again. Would he lie to you, little nieces and nephews? No. Why lie when the truth hurts even more. That is why you can believe him when he stipulates life has dealt your Uncle Michael a brutal hand. If he were to discard some of those fives and sixes, life's deck would just replenish that hand with threes and fours. If he were a game of Scrabble, he would have no vowels. If he were a shower, there'd be no towel. But do you think this pathetic relation ever complains about his dismal fate?

∞—∞

Aside from not being able to make money, Michael is unduly frustrated with mechanical things. Things like cars. And women.

∞—∞

On the positive side, he's a good athlete.

But no killer instinct. Give him a commanding lead over an inferior opponent and he will intentionally miss enough shots in whatever game he is playing to ensure the opponent catches up. He's the rabbit who sometimes plays it too close and loses to the turtle. But get this: he claims to have gone five years, twice, without losing a game of chess.

∞—∞

Michael had a miserable time in high school. He wanted to play sports. But the freshman basketball coach cut him from the team during tryouts because the freshman basketball coach was a dull young man who had been a classmate of Harold, the family scientist, and was as sure as all the nuns and priests and other coaches that Ericksons were too smart to play sports.

A summer intern with
The Chattanooga Times.

Michael's only distinguishing achievements in high school were quitting the altar boys, quitting the Boy Scouts, and quitting the band. But, the summer before starting college, he managed to land a fortuitous internship with the local newspaper.

College was where your Uncle Michael came into his own. He discovered enduring friends, joined forces with the political and cultural revolution, and even became a temporary big shot on a campus of 20,000 students.

Michael and the days of long hair, faded jeans, and Led Zeppelin were made for one another. But all was not wine and roses, because it was in college he became addicted to the twin evils of cigarettes and women.

During those college years, Michael was a journalist and worked for two of the state's leading newspapers. After college he played at public relations, did well in advertising, and kept stabbing at writing. He was a consummate beer drinker, but finally had to stop when the beer began consuming him.

Michael was married once. She was a lovely girl, and it's too bad none of you will get to know her — but marriage wasn't one of his better sports.

∞—∞

Michael was a child once; much like the rest of us.

Relatively yours,
Uncle Rags

Michael James Erickson, born August 14, 1948
Married Carla Chappas December 31, 1972, on a riverbank in Mullins Cove, Tennessee
Carla Chappas, born July 25, 1953, Baltimore
(Reminded her to take her birth control pills, then years later:)
Married Lorraine (Lori) Frances Serfas,
October 21, 1995, in Baltimore, Maryland
Lorraine Frances Serfas, born November 25, 1960, Baltimore
Lauren Frances Erickson, born Dec. 10, 1985
Michael Sheldon Erickson, born Dec. 8, 1997

3 3

The End Of The Line

Dear Nieces and Nephews, and Valued Readers,

After me, there were no more.

End of the line.

Finished. Kaput. Over.

∞ — ∞

Mrs. Erickson had a miscarriage before the birth of Harold. The doctors thought she might never bring a baby to term.

She had another miscarriage eight years later, in her pregnancy following the birth of her seventh son. The doctors told her she shouldn't get pregnant again. It was too risky.

Mr. and Mrs. Erickson took the doctor's warning very seriously and doubled down on their practice of birth control. But it was, evidently, the same birth control technique they had used the previous eight years.

It's always been our guess that, being devout Catholics, they practiced the rhythm method. Defined as "the calendar-based method promoted by the Roman Catholic Church as the only morally acceptable form of family planning."

But then there's also that definition of rhythm: "A strong, regular, repeated pattern of movement."

Hmm.

Relatively yours,
Uncle Rags

The seven sons.

3 4

Eileen:
The Second "Firstborn"

Dear Nieces and Nephews, and Valued Readers,

Well, maybe there were a few others.

And so, it's time to violate all standards of decency and propriety by telling you about your Aunt Eileen.

∞ — ∞

The first girl after seven boys caused quite a stir.

A psychiatrist told me I was among those most stirred.

There was immense privilege accorded with being the first girl. Little Eileen was programmed to enjoy all the social distinctions that Big Eileen, Mother, was forced to abandon when the Great Depression yanked her from college, where she was, naturally, excel-

ling academically and socially, and turned her into a department store clerk. For Little Eileen, there were ballet lessons . . . tea parties . . . summer lunches in department store restaurants . . . friends . . . birthday parties . . . cheerleading . . . beauty contests . . .

To some degree, Little Eileen was an innocent victim of the pressure. On the other hand, she never fought for equality. She was content to enjoy the privilege that came with being a girl, even when well aware she was benefiting at the expense of long-standing traditions of superiority by seniority. Just little things. Like who gets to sit in the front seat, or even the back seat by the window. Or who might fill the limited capacity of a car going on a trip. Little things, though, are what much of life is made of. At least that's what my psychiatrist says.

∞ — ∞

Eileen was a winner. She was pretty. Sophisticated. And smart. Smart enough to keep showing her slip instead of her brains.

Like everyone else in the family, she worked her way through college. She worked two summers at Sears in Chattanooga, one summer at a dress shop in San Francisco, then at a department store in Cincinnati. When she graduated with one of those "home ec" degrees nice girls used to get, she passed on a career as a buyer and

began flying with Eastern. She turned down marriage offers from lots of hotshots including a renowned physicist and a rising star in the FBI before settling down with a good ol' boy developer whose family had been taking its time selling bits and pieces of its vast Atlanta farm, otherwise known as Buckhead, to the press of newcomers.

She still flies. Not just for a living, but also to Aspen for skiing. Or to Europe where she might dine with royalty in a centuries-old castle.

Eileen is prone to act very shallowly, which helps her move fluidly in society. But whenever we spend more than just passing time with her . . . once she has caught us up on the glamour of where she has been and who she mingled with . . . after she has thrilled us as to how she spilled a drink on the President's chief of staff, but didn't notice if he was high on cocaine . . . after she has finished gushing then we can become re-acquainted with this globe-trotter and appreciate her actual depths.

∞—∞

Eileen was on a return — non-working — flight back to her riverfront home in Atlanta one afternoon and couldn't understand why everyone was making such a fuss over a well dressed Black man riding in the first class seat next to her. Between the steady demand for autographs she finally asked, "Who are you?"

"Hank Aaron," the man said.

She reflected but the name didn't mean anything. "What do you do?" Eileen asked.

"I play baseball."

"Are you any good?"

"I'm okay," the legend told her — just two weeks before establishing his immortality by hitting his 715th home run and breaking Babe Ruth's record. Then Hank excused himself to visit the restroom because, as he explained, he always gets stoned on flights. When he returned, he wondered if this Eileen-girl might join him for dinner when they landed in Atlanta. Typically, she had to decline because she already had plans.

∞—∞

Eileen was a child once; but not like the rest of us.

Relatively yours,

Uncle Rags

*Eileen Louise Erickson, born
May 28, 1950
Married Beverly (Bo)
DuBose September 21, 1979,
in Atlanta
Beverly (Bo) DuBose, born
Nov. 25, 1940, Atlanta*

3 5

Toys And Red Cars
By Allen

When looking back on those early years, I see them as having a natural dividing line: before Eileen, and after Eileen.

Her birth was viewed very sarcastically by her older brothers. Mom and Dad were really happy to finally have a girl, but we — I guess we older ones were in the nine, ten, and eleven range at the time — did not show the same appreciation. We kept talking about how there was a queen in the house. Frank made a paper crown for her.

During the war, and just after the war, they were not making any toys. But somehow, for my fourth birthday, the parents managed to come up with this cardboard milk truck. It was black and white, mostly white, and made of a hard press-type board. It also came with maybe a dozen little glass milk bottles that fit inside it. It was a great present, made even better by coming after such a long drought. Frank, though, didn't see it that way. His birthday had been just a few weeks earlier, and they were not able to come up with anything for him. We were outside on the night of my birthday catching lightning bugs in the yard and putting them in the little finger-sized (a child's finger) milk bottles when Frank's anger finally burst and he started smashing my bottles against the bricks on the side of the house. After that outburst, anger was, of course, strictly prohibited.

I have this vague memory of Dad's 1938 Pontiac, but probably my first vivid memory is of what seemed to me to be a very interesting argument between the parents over that old car. This was probably around 1945, and I would have been three. Dad had the car painted. It was gone for a few days while it was being painted the maroon color they had chosen. But when he finally drove it home one afternoon, it was fire engine red instead. And I remem-

ber Mom simply exploded. The reason I remember so well is that I couldn't imagine it looking any prettier than that sparkling bright red, and I couldn't understand what Mother could be talking about as she kept saying it was so horrible looking.

No matter how I pieced it together, there was no connection between what she was saying and what I was seeing. Daddy sold the car about three or four weeks later. He took the streetcar to work for maybe the next nine months until he showed up one day in the '46 Chevy. It was tan and brown, and only the second new car that had made it to Chattanooga when they started making cars again after the war. I remember Mom and all of us jumped in as soon as he got home and we drove downtown. Everybody was pointing at it as we passed by, totally captivated by our new car. About a month later we drove it to Missouri. And driving new cars to Missouri immediately became something we always did.

— Allen

3 6

Pregnant, Again
By Mother

At various times in life when things started stacking up the wrong way, it seemed that the tunnels got awfully long. While you might hope that there was a light at the end, only an incurable optimist could pretend to see it.

After having the first five boys in four years and seven months, we managed to get two years between David and Philip, Philip and Michael, and Michael and Eileen. So I was more than a little chagrined when I realized that I was pregnant again when Eileen was only about five months old. Pregnancies were to be endured, but they were not supposed to interfere with our normal life, so along with getting other things ready for Christmas, I was baking my usual Christmas cookies to send as gifts to all the teachers at school and as part of the Christmas treats for the family. I made fancy cookies back in those days — flowers with colored petals, Christmas trees, camels, and doggies . . .

139

Mrs. Erickson with Baby Eileen, Michael, and Philip. Pregnant with Douglas.

Probably there was no relationship between standing there making cookies and having a miscarriage, but I landed in the hospital, hemorrhaging rather badly. The doctor decided that it was necessary to do a D&C immediately. Since it had only been a few hours since I had eaten lunch, a saddle block was preferable to a general anesthetic. Everything went along just fine, and they did not even give me a blood transfusion because I always had a quite high red blood cell count and built up my own blood pretty well by the next day. I spent the day after the operation in the hospital.

The next day, the doctor dismissed me and l was ready to go home. I mentioned that morning that I had a little headache, and the doctor said it might be from the saddle block, but was probably just strain, so home I went. By that night, after I had tried to be up and around during the day, I had a giant-size headache. I got the doctor on the phone and he decided that it probably was a spinal headache because they did occur sometimes if there was a slight imbalance in the spinal fluid as a result of the anesthetic. Theoretically, the pain and nausea would go away as long as I lay flat on my back, and it would probably only last a couple of days. If I needed something for pain, he would give me some codeine. I had tried codeine in the past and, instead of relaxing me, it had me climbing the walls. I chose to try to get by without it.

Three days passed, and then four, five, six, and Daddy is getting desperate. He persuades me that an osteopath or chiropractor might help by giving me an adjustment. He brings one out to the house That almost finishes me off, and makes the headache much worse. Poor Pop. He is trying to get the last minute things for Christmas. He is stuck with gifts to be sorted and a tree to be put up. I finally tied a tight band around my head and got up to put the lights on the tree, but that was as far as I could make it. I can remember lying there on Christmas Day, trying to help put a toy filling station together. I had now been out for ten critical days.

The day after Christmas the doctors realized that I was going to have to get on my feet some way, so they decided that if I took codeine for pain and then phenobarbital to counter the hyper effects of the codeine, I might be able to manage. That night, loaded to the hilt with drugs, I made it to the back room when the older ones were getting ready for bed. Harold, Frank, and Allen were comparing notes and checking each other out for little spots. Mama took one look, and, on her first night up, discovered that she had three cases of chicken pox on her hands. Inevitably, it would spread.

It is bad enough to cope with three kids who are sick with the chicken pox when you can hardly stay out of bed yourself, but knowing you face five more is excruciating. In rapid fire succession, we had three, and then five cases of chicken pox, and then a round of three-day measles, and pink eye. So when Harold broke out all over with a rash that April the only thing I could think of was scarlet fever. It turned out to be a violent allergy of some kind, and I was so glad, because at least allergies were not contagious.

The headache finally got better, but I spent months kicking things out of the middle of the floor because I could not bend over. And I couldn't remember things, even telephone numbers and things I had just been told. And, oh yes, I was pregnant again. Douglas was born the next September.

— Mother

37

Douglas: No. 9 — It Took A While To Find A Doctor

Dear Nieces and Nephews, and Valued Readers,

Doctor Doug.

Yes, finally a real doctor.

Not one of those quasi-doctors. Not a Ph.D. "doctor." Not a "Doctor of Divinity," or a pompous "Doctor of Jurisprudence." Or even a mere "doctor of words." A real doctor finally emerges from the fecund brain trust.

∞ — ∞

Uncle Doctor Douglas was the first in the family to sprout blond hair. We blackheads concluded he was delivered by the milkman.

If anything, it was the iceman. Like the occasional superstar athlete who remains stone cold no matter what is erupting on his field of play, Douglas seems forever distant from everything he is part of. Always has.

Driving through the country, we used to wonder what the cows were thinking — what they saw that nurtured such deep disinterest. We used to wonder about Douglas, too.

He could spend hours watching the dryer drum tumble round and round in the lonely upstairs laundry room. We never knew what the spinning meant to him, and he used to pass days at a time sitting alone in an upstairs bedroom, riding the rocking horse. We never knew where he was trying to go.

We began to wonder if all blond-haired babies were abnormal. Then Charles showed up and proved it.

∞ — ∞

It was a relief when Douglas finally started school because he demonstrated beyond a doubt that he was brilliant. That's good,

since he was never much of an athlete. We used to waste the first 30 minutes of each valuable afternoon of play harassing and insulting him until he would reluctantly join us. We wouldn't have bothered except that you can't play three-on-three football or basketball with just five kids. We needed Douglas a lot more than he needed us.

And that's still the case. Douglas drifted up to the school in Knoxville for a year like four of us before him, but had the good sense to transfer via scholarship to Duke. He went on to become the family doctor. He's our first, and least expensive, source when we need to know why our noses run. Or why our legs don't.

Douglas knows as much as anyone about the body. Maybe the mind, too. He says bad memories should be suppressed rather than dwelt on. Maybe the dryer taught him that.

∞ — ∞

Douglas doesn't get to share his knowledge with many of his patients. He is a pathologist. It's a quiet world — that of the dead. But a quietly compatible one.

∞ — ∞

Doctor Doug lives in Macon, Georgia. Moved there after finishing a residency at Vanderbilt in Nashville. Of all the things he used to think about, I doubt he ever thought he would end up living in Georgia. The position there was the second best of many outstanding partnership offers. The best required moving with two babies to Switzerland.

But it doesn't much matter where Douglas lives. His bovine nature is so alien to any environment that he could be just as content in a valley as on a mountainside, in a desert as on a beach.

Douglas was a child once; almost like the rest of us.

Relatively yours,
Uncle Rags

Douglas Joseph Erickson, born September 26, 1951
Married Tanya Clarke July 5, 1974, in Durham, N.C.
Corrine Leigh, born June 29, 1980
Natalie Lane Erickson, born June 21, 1982
Jocelyn (interestingly, no middle name), born May 14, 1985
Married Patricia Marie Bernier, in Bandera, Texas, Sept. 4, 2005
Patricia Marie Bernier, born November 3, 1951, Binghamton, N.Y.

3 8

Louis: No. 10
"Play Ball!"

Dear Nieces and Nephews, and Patient Readers,

Lawyer Lou, the third to find his way to the bar, was a little more than a year younger than Douglas, but quickly surpassed the frail blond in both size and athletic skills. Douglas's resistance to sports was likely rooted in his younger brother being bigger, faster, and more naturally talented.

Though Uncle Douglas ultimately grew to a respectable 5'11" and ranks tall enough by statistical standards, "Large Louis" — as some softball buddies used to call him — broke the six-foot barrier and stands tallest in the family at almost 6'2".

Douglas, lest you get the wrong impression, is not a push-over in any sport. But Louis developed into one of the family's two premier athletes. Like his older brothers, he was excluded from school sports, so he settled for being one of the best non-playing football, basketball, and baseball players to ever pass through Notre Dame. A left-hander, his amateur play at first base is legendary. And his tournament-caliber tennis skills allow him to swat that fat softball to any part of the field he chooses. Tennis players are always great at nailing the much larger softballs.

If any of you little nephews get involved in sports, you're going to have your hands full when certain uncles come to visit. We'll be well past our prime, but we'll have the advantage of experience. One of the first things you learn from experience is to do your drubbing of younger players before they hit their prime.

Instead of just trekking up Highway 58 to the degree factory in Knoxville, Louis ambitiously went after the same scholarship his third oldest brother, Allen, had received several years earlier and attended the University of Windsor in Canada. Louis was not the

glutton for punishment Allen was, so he stayed in those cold hinterlands during summer quarters and plowed his way out of college in three years — anxious to get back to the sunny South.

Motivated by the fact that several of his old high school friends were working on advanced degrees, Louis quit the real world after a year's vacation from school and made the pilgrimage to Knoxville to earn his law degree. He graduated at a time when many attorneys were surviving off their real estate licenses. But Louis beat the odds and his Naples law practice turned him into the kind of materialist that local car, truck, and boat dealers would like to see cloned.

He is formidable in the courtroom or at a negotiating table where he takes full advantage of his inherent, narrow-minded stubbornness.

∞ — ∞

Louis was a child once; much like the rest of us.

Relatively yours,
Uncle Rags

Louis Stephen Erickson, born January 31, 1953
Married Barbara Sue Partello, November 26, 1988, in Naples, Fla.
Barbara Sue Portello, born July 28, 1952, Madison, Indiana
Anthony Jenn Partello, born April 26, 1976
Debra Lynn Erickson, born January 14, 1981

39

Gold Letters:
Adding A Shine To Science

Louis was standing on a football field one Saturday afternoon participating in a punt-pass-and-kick contest.

It was a sport. It was fun. It was short-lived.

He was at the University of Chattanooga's football field and made the mistake of casually glancing through the chain-link fence behind one end zone. He had a quick laugh at the expense of some egghead-type kids carrying posters and card tables and electronic paraphernalia from their cars into one of the university's halls. "What a dumb way to spend a Saturday," Louis thought as he eagerly waited for his name to be called again in the punting competition.

But as he thought for a few more seconds his spirits sputtered, then collapsed. Those tables and posters and contraptions were science club exhibits. Those eggheads carrying them were winners of their respective schools' competitions. This was the afternoon contestants were required to set up their displays for the city-wide science fair.

Louis very reluctantly remembered that he, too, was an egghead. He had won first place at his high school, and now he had to immediately abandon the pleasant football field, get home, and spend the rest of a once-promising Saturday lugging his ignominious science club exhibit over to the university.

Painful. Shameful. Louis was tenth in succession. Winning anything that smacked of academic recognition was considered a trespass, an infringement on his right to be an individual. Louis preferred kicking footballs to understanding the universe.

⬤

The bulk of the work at science fairs, of course, is done by the parents of the exhibitors. Usually it's the father — an engineer or frustrated inventor. In our household, it was Mrs. Erickson who stepped in after her natural-born exhibitors (Harold and David) graduated. She not only came up with most of the ideas for the projects but often drafted and then lettered the posters to save us from crippling her good ideas in our confusion.

The ideas came easily. We, innocent fools that we were, thought things would happen only once and never again. She, experienced in the ways of the world, knew that "annual" meant every year. She knew that no science fair was either the first or the last. Throughout the year whenever she heard us pose a difficult question, she scared us by answering how that question might make a good science fair project.

Then, without any more warning than the word "annual" might mysteriously convey, there came that time of the year when we were forced to put together a project. We always whined, "But

I can't think of anything to do it on." And she always answered by quoting back, one after another, the many questions we individually posed to her during the previous year. Questions she had scrupulously left unanswered.

⦻

I remember she tried every way possible to explain to me how magnets work when that became my project one year. She led me to all the research material, even drew elaborate diagrams on my display's poster boards. But it was like trying to tell a desert cactus what it feels like to take a bubble bath.

Her efforts were not totally unrewarded. We won several ribbons from judges who were impressed with her simple explanation.

⦻

With the deep scars Mrs. Erickson suffered during The Great Depression, she was probably quite undone when she and little Harold showed up for their first science fair — rocked by the expense other parents had incurred to enhance their children's exposés of bugs and sparks.

For future science fairs, she initiated the extravagant tradition of buying clean white poster boards. She squandered even more money on a bottle of India ink.

A forerunner of the magic marker, India ink is like a heavy black paint. It was used by virtually all exhibitors to fill the white poster boards with neatly printed descriptions of wonderment. Headlines and body copy blackly proclaimed what the jars and cages and electric shock machines were doing on their card tables.

Only two things were known about India ink. We knew it was from India — that land of snake charmers and beds of nails. And, adding to its mystique, we knew India ink was *indelible*. We were

warned year after year not to touch it or get any on our clothes. "That's India ink!" we were told. "It's indelible! It will never wash off or wash out!"

The real problem with touching it, of course, was that it would indelibly smear our posters.

⦿

Mrs. Erickson, tough competitor that she was, went the other parents one better than just India ink. She used gold letters.

The gold letters ranged in size from one to three inches. They were an elaborate Old Roman typeface. And they were gummed on the back. They could be pasted down one at a time to form headlines and subheads. Mother did most of the critical letter work, the rest of us being a bit slow when it came to licking, pasting, projecting widths, or otherwise gaining maximum benefit from the outrageously expensive 30-cent sheet of white poster board.

The gold letters came from Daddy. He sold them in his wholesale flower business to florists who affixed them to ribbons, sashes, Styrofoam hearts, and other decorations. All their lives,

the gold letters had said nice things like "I Love You" or "Happy Birthday" or "Miss Mineral City." (I don't think the splashy gold letters were used in the funeral end of the business. "Sorry" does not look sincere in gold.)

Mrs. Erickson came up with the idea of letting those fancy gold letters shout new messages. Messages like "Effects of Residual Centrifugal Force" or "Exteroceptive Delineation of Ionophobic Light Refraction."

The nuns who did the judging were duly dazzled. They had never seen such messages shouted so reverently in gold. Those early exhibits got exceptionally high marks for clarity.

The gold letters were fine, but, like everything else that anyone in this obsessive-compulsive family ever did, they quickly became an institution. Year after year, the Erickson exhibits were characterized by white poster board with hand-lettered India ink body copy, topped by glittering gold headlines.

What we lost in the way of creative impact with the judges, was more than made up for as they recognized the gold letters — all judging being done with the exhibitor's name concealed — and awarded the display a ribbon simply because it was another in a long line of those traditionally well-conceived Erickson exhibits . . . even by the time these science projects were being turned in by aspiring athletes instead of aspiring physicists.

40

Cecilia: Our Second Princess — The One Who Kissed A Frog
(Sorry, George, I Couldn't Resist)

Dear Nieces and Nephews, and Valued Readers,

No doubt contributing to the spoilage of Little Eileen was the rapturous omen of her birth. This package, containing such an astounding rarity, a baby girl, arrived just one day after its bearer's own birthday. Big Eileen had turned imperceptibly 36.

The fact that your Aunt Cecilia showed up in the same vainglorious month, May, might have afforded her some special attention as well. But being only the second girl amidst the brood of nine brothers already qualified her for all the attention she would ever need.

Cecilia was encouraged to do all the things Eileen did. She tip-toed around in ballet shoes. She twirled batons. She was a cheerleader.

She even did something Eileen had not quite managed: She was voted homecoming queen. Eileen's girlfriends were a little jealous of the way she ignored so many in her own class while enjoying the attention of boys who had graduated with her older brothers. No matter how deserving, a girl can't become homecoming queen without the support of her classmates. Cecilia's classmates and girlfriends came through. But Cecilia never actually got the homecoming crown because the nun who tabulated the ballots arbitrarily decided to let the girl who had finished second in the voting become queen because that girl was Black and . . . well, it seemed like a pretty decent gesture.

One of Cecilia's girlfriends happened to overhear the nun discussing this vote tampering with another nun. Cecilia cried a little but did not make an issue of it. Underneath that facade of God, nuns, after all, are just people.

∞ — ∞

Cecilia stuck with tradition and headed up Highway 58 to the University in Knoxville, but transferred after a year or two to the small, high school-type college in Chattanooga so she could be close to her boyfriend when he returned on weekends from the University of Georgia. When she got her degree, she moved to Athens with him. She taught school during the day and tutored her boyfriend at night because whenever she whined, "George, I think we should get married," he whined back, "I don't think we should get married until after I graduate from college, Cecilia."

George almost set a record for staying in college, but Cecilia finally tutored or tortured him out.

After graduating, George still managed to postpone the wedding a year or three but ultimately ran out of excuses.

Because of his unique stature, to say nothing of his truly warm and engaging personality, George was "a good catch."

∞ — ∞

George's unique stature can be summed up in one word: Money. Bottomless wealth.

Though it is not tasteful to talk about another person's money, it would be dishonest to not bring this up since it is Uncle George's most fascinating facet. And I, for one, can't help but be intrigued by money — much as a turtle would be intrigued by pole vaulters.

George's money is particularly interesting. His great-grandfather was one of the partners who took the recipe for Coca-Cola out of an Atlanta drugstore, literally bottled it, and turned it into the world's single most recognizable product.

When George's grandmother, the daughter of that original bottler and a matron respectfully referred to in Chattanooga as Mrs. Coca-Cola, died, it took pages of classified type in the nosy evening newspaper just to list her stock holdings. The largest will ever probated in the South.

And if you've ever traveled in the South and been fortunate enough to taste one of those uniquely sensational little Krystal hamburgers, you were biting into George's stepfather's 250-store enterprise.

It took Little Cecilia a full two years of marriage to adjust — first to the reality that she had somehow become unfathomably rich, but then to the complementing reality that she and George are more comfortable letting sleeping dogs lie, which they do by maintaining a surprisingly modest lifestyle.

Her primary career in the years since their marriage has been being his mother, sister, and wife. For his part, George worked from seven in the morning until seven at night in a middle-management position with the family bottling company in Houston before pursuing something that truly interested him from early in his still young life: Music. George isn't a musician, but he admires them, and has helped many very talented artists make waves in the world by adding them to his Texas-based record label, New West Records.

∞ — ∞

This charming couple met back in high school. Cecilia was a cheerleader and George, who attended one of Chattanooga's prep schools, was wrestling Cecilia's boyfriend. As insecure then as he is now, George couldn't understand why the girl to the side of the mat was cheering every wrong move he made. In an act of inexpli-

cable brazenness, he challenged the ponytail for an explanation after he had lost the match. Cecilia explained the boyfriend angle, and George, growing bolder by the minute, saw a chance to best his opponent in love if not in war. The handsome boy and the pretty girl got together. Just like in the Coca-Cola TV commercials..

Before you accuse little Cecilia of gold digging, it's important to know that neither she nor anyone in the family knew for a long time about George's storybook wealth. We knew he was rich, because he lived on the mountain. Lookout Mountain. But the family was used to dealing with rich mountain folk. Lots of them sent their kids to Notre Dame. And there's a lot of distance between rich and wealthy. It was several years before anyone learned that this new sports buddy Cecilia had dragged home owned a sizable share of the world's liquid assets.

Because of his interest in playing and watching sports, George quickly became a fixture around the house. He enjoyed escaping from his mansion on the hill to slouch in the beanbag chair in the living room of our home in the valley where he could drink beer and argue football with the Little Kids. By the time he ran out of excuses and had to set a date for the wedding, it was hard to tell if we were dealing with a marriage or an adoption.

Cecilia noted once that whenever contemporaries tried to intimidate her by talking about international politics or medieval philosophy or other intellectual drivel she hadn't taken an interest in, she comforted herself with the thought, "I don't mind coming across like a dumb girl because I've always known that if everyone else in the family is so intelligent, I must be pretty smart as well."

Indeed, as years have passed and motherhood has brought its own predictable challenges, Cecilia has become the go-to expert among her friends when it comes to their own kids' fevers, sprains, stomach disorders, and the far more intricate matters of physiology and psychology.

∞—∞

Cecilia was a child once; much like the rest of us.

Relatively yours,
Uncle Rags

Cecilia Ann Erickson, born May 19, 1954
Married George Rawlings Fontaine, November 20, 1978, in Chattanooga
George Rawlings Fontaine, born March 30, 1954, Chattanooga
George Rawlings Fontaine, Jr., born April 25, 1981
Ryan Thomas Fontaine, born December 10, 1983
Cartter (a family name, not a typo) Lupton Fontaine, born January 15, 1988

4 1

That Catholic Horde
By George

I have been associated with the Ericksons for 15 years now, but it seems like just yesterday that I was parking in front of the house on Glenwood Drive and hoping that I would not have to come inside to get Celia and be confronted by that Catholic horde.

That fear, coupled with the fact that Celia didn't show much enthusiasm in her kissing of me, led to an 18 months hiatus, at the end of which I decided that Ericksons couldn't be any worse than having to go to Signal Mountain for a date, or having to carry on meaningful conversations with Preacher Blevins while he created religious artifacts out of clay.

163

I made up my mind to be a big boy, park in the driveway, and deal with the masses. It came as a real surprise how easily Mr. and Mrs. Erickson accepted me, even though I think Mr. Erickson thought I was Douglas a good part of the time. Not long after I began venturing into the house, I became a regular at the kitchen table for "Ericksons After Hours" — easily the best and most exclusive club in town.

What seems so incredible is that two people were brave enough to raise 14 children during less than stable times, and have lived to look back on it so many years later. The only thing that saddens me a little is that there are no longer any Ericksons living in Chattanooga. Glenwood Drive represented Chattanooga to me, and it is just not the same going home now that no one is there.

— George

4 2

Paul: We've Made It To No. 12 Meet Everyone's Good Friend

Dear Nieces and Nephews, and Valued Readers,

Paul has an outie.

Everyone else in the family has those typically gnarled but indented belly buttons. Only Paul's poked out. It looked much like the nubby little air valve tied off at the end of an inflated balloon. We frightened him by coming at him with scissors, threatening to clip it off. We told him he would go whizzing around the room bouncing off walls and ceilings, until all the air was out. Then he'd land all flat and shriveled on the floor.

He used to keep his shirt on. Not only around us so we wouldn't think to say things like that but also around classmates and strangers. He was self-conscious about having an outie until he discovered in high school that girls were intrigued by such things. Paul doesn't wear shirts much anymore.

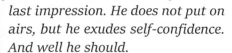

The fourth attorney and second CPA, Paul is the most personable of all the Ericksons. Everyone he meets likes him at first and last impression. He does not put on airs, but he exudes self-confidence. And well he should.

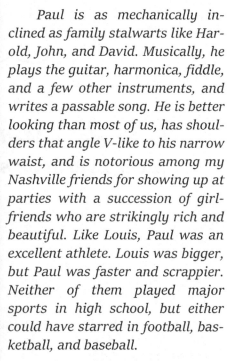

Paul is as mechanically inclined as family stalwarts like Harold, John, and David. Musically, he plays the guitar, harmonica, fiddle, and a few other instruments, and writes a passable song. He is better looking than most of us, has shoulders that angle V-like to his narrow waist, and is notorious among my Nashville friends for showing up at parties with a succession of girl-friends who are strikingly rich and beautiful. Like Louis, Paul was an excellent athlete. Louis was bigger, but Paul was faster and scrappier. Neither of them played major sports in high school, but either could have starred in football, basketball, and baseball.

When Louis graduated from college, he spent a month in Chattanooga managing Paul's successful campaign for student body president at the high school. As a joke, they ran Paul on a "student power" platform. He promised that, if elected, he would resign if the school administration refused any of his demands. Paul won in a landslide.

His first demand was turned down. So he resigned almost immediately. Mother was not very proud. Especially when the next issue of the school newspaper proclaimed in headline type with each letter about the size of a hamster: "Erickson Quits."

∞—∞

Though never considered exactly brilliant, Paul got through the University of Tennessee well enough, passed his CPA exam, then abandoned accounting after a couple of years to return to Tennessee for his law degree. It looks like a bright future. Corporate tax attorneys, which is what he is qualified to be, make almost as much money as Florida drug dealers.

∞—∞

There is more to Paul's story. Much more.

I'll get to it later.

For now, it's enough to note that Paul was a child once; much like the rest of us.

Relatively yours,
Uncle Rags

Paul Lawrence Erickson, born July 22, 1955
Married Mary Earl Wilder August 6, 1983, in Corbin, Kentucky
Mary Earl Wilder, born January 25, 1959, Corbin, Kentucky
Corbin Andrew, born July 17, 1990
Chase Wilder, born January 10, 1992
Laura Beth Zhongyuan, born Dec. 29, 1999, Hainan, China

*Eileen, Michael, and Philip stand behind
Douglas, Louis, Cecilia, and Paul.*

43

"It Just Broke"
By Paul

Louis, as a child — and it certainly strains the imagination to think of him as a man — was quite the scientist and philosopher.

He professed rules are made to be broken, or bent as needed, and was determined to discover if this was an empirical rule of nature.

He went through a stage of about five years while in elementary school during which he ruthlessly tested this theory on the objects his younger siblings viewed with affection: Our toys. The "rule" he seemed determined to prove was: "That which doesn't

169

bend, breaks, and that which does bend, if bent back and forth in the same focused area for a long enough period of time, will also break." Pencils or long sticks, like those belonging to our Tinker Toy set, would find their way into Louis's hands. The Tinker Toy would begin sweating profusely, straining to survive, as 10, and then 20, seconds ticked off the clock. Suddenly, there would be the familiar SNAP, and it was all over. Louis would then announce in a startled, almost despondent, voice, "It broke."

Enraged, one of his siblings would yell at him "You idiot! Why did you break that?" Only to hear the same, so often repeated response, "I didn't. It just broke. I guess I should throw this broken piece away. "

— Paul

44

Charles: No. 13
"Let's Salt That Wound"

Dear Nieces and Nephews, and Valued Readers,

Uncle Charles, the last of five attorneys, is the one we really try to contend isn't a brother.

There's pretty good evidence for this claim. He's left-handed, an ignominious imperfection that only Louis and Allen were afflicted with before him.

And he's got blond hair, the only blond other than Doctor Doug.

The chances of there being a left-handed blond-headed Erickson are about the same as your being around Charles for more than three minutes without getting drawn into an argument.

He argues as naturally as poison ivy itches. He should do well with his law degree.

Before enrolling at the University of South Carolina law school, Charles made a few frustrating fortunes in computer programming. I can see him hunched over his green-tinted cathode ray tube, keying, "The answer is 8.41," and viewing, "Sorry, it's 12.8," and punching back, "You're wrong, you electronic imbecile! It's 8.41," and reading, "If you'd just recalculate you'd see your error," and, warming now to his user-friendly adversary, "You're a mindless misfit with an obviously defective chip. And you're so stupid I doubt you even know who's going to win the pennant." "Which one?" "The National League." "Houston." "With their hitting? You're crazy. It'll be Philadelphia." "It's a pitcher's game this year." "You don't know what you're talking about." "That's because you programmed me." "No. It's because you weren't paying attention." . . .

∞—∞

Charles and Paul both came to Nashville one weekend for a party Louis and I and our softball buddies were having. One after another, my friends took me aside to confide, "Hey, Michael. I really like your brother Paul, but I might just come to blows with that Charlie before the night's over." Charlie was busy buzzing around the room bragging about how he was better at everything than any of them could ever hope to be. He was stepping on lots of fragile toes. We managed to get through the night, and the next day we played a lot of sports — giving Charlie a chance to prove to everyone's satisfaction that he is just a lot of hot air. They got along with him very well once they learned the trick. The trick is not to pay attention to anything Charlie says.

That trick only works, though, when Charlie is bragging about himself. When he's picking on your favorite pro or college team everything he says is a fully-loaded fact. He knows the weaknesses of every team and every player and just waits for someone to speak highly of a sports entity so he can take a few swipes. He's got the same knack when it comes to politics or religion or any of those other conversation pieces. Even the weather. Just mention a sacred cow in front of Charlie and he'll don his brass knuckles to start the milking.

∞—∞

As though he doesn't have enough faults, Charles is incredibly intelligent. When he was at the University of Tennessee with Paul and Carol he was a constant aggravation for, among countless other trespasses, the way he spent every night bicycling to a bar or over to the gym for some basketball and still made straight As. When he transferred to Duke, he stayed home more often — but only to watch the ACC basketball games that were televised nearly every weeknight. He graduated magna cum laude and would have made it summa had they credited his Tennessee grades.

The ones who grew up with him have developed the veneer of an immunity to Charlie's basic nature. They had to. He has the natural tenacity to pester the buzz off a sweat bee. He and George, Cecilia's very affable and gracious husband, are seldom on speaking terms because of Charlie's inclination to be for whomever George's team is playing against in whatever sport happens to be in season. If Charlie's team loses, he dismisses it with, "Well, they're really not much better than your team, anyway." But if it goes the other way — which it does half the time — and George's team gets the short end of it, Charles gets out his salt shaker to start dressing the wounds.

Since he was a little kid, we've made a determined effort to give Charles away. It's only recently that we've found a taker. His

Paul, Charles, and Cecilia.

wife. A sweet Catholic girl, she won't have to stay long in purgatory after spending a life with this scab picker.

∞ — ∞

Charles was a child once; but not exactly like the rest of us.

Relatively yours,
Uncle Rags

Charles Patrick Erickson, born September 5, 1956
Married Kathy Pavlovich May 25, 1980, in Boston
Kathy Pavlovich, born in Wilmington, Mass.
Married Jill Garvin, November 5, 1990, in Lake Tahoe, Nevada
Jill Garvin, born January 27, 1952, Cuyahoga Falls, Ohio

P.S. Charlie, coincidentally, was born on the same day as Daddy. Daddy turned 51 that year. His hair started hueing gray almost immediately.

45

The Toe Grabber
Strikes Again

Harold, Frank, and Allen — the Big Boys — were altar boys.

Their decision to become altar boys was just another of the cruel legacies they saddled us younger ones with.

I wish I could say it was noble and honorable to have been an altar boy. But former altar boys don't lie.

All being an altar boy meant to me was that three or four times a year I had to get up at six in the morning for a solid seven-day week and go downtown to serve 6:30 Mass. That wasn't so bad during the school year because we always began the day with a Mass anyway. Albeit the eight o'clock one. During the summer, though, that two-week stretch of serving — one week of 6:30 Masses and one week of eight o'clock Masses — was as pleasant as stepping on a roach barefooted.

The Ericksons always served as teams. Harold and Frank were a team. John wasn't a good team player so sometimes he was teamed with Allen, with whom he didn't get along, and sometimes with David, with whom he didn't get along. John knew early on he should be saying the Mass instead of serving it. The nuns and priests also knew that. They were pleased when he entered the seminary. "A natural-born bishop," they all said.

Philip and I were a team. Douglas and Louis were a team. Paul and Charles were the last of the Erickson altar boy teams.

⦿

Mrs. Erickson always ignored my complaints about how I didn't think it fair that we all had to be altar boys. She said it wouldn't hurt us.

As always, she was right. It didn't hurt. In fact, hanging around the inner sanctum of the priests and nuns and serving several times a year at their highly ceremonious rites gave us a lifelong insight into the hocus pocus that had built up in the Church since the Middle Ages. We were a part of history. A fading part, since we were involved in the last of the centuries-old Latin Masses.

◍

The three most painful aspects of being an altar boy were having to go to Mass on Saturdays during the school year. Having to go to Mass at all on weekdays during the summer. And — most painful and memorable — the way Daddy woke us at six in the morning to serve those 6:30 Masses.

He would sneak quietly into the room so as not to disturb the other three sleepers, locate his victim then grab that unfortunate child by a big toe and start shaking until its owner sprang violently awake. This was his way of waking us for all early morning duties. It assured we started the new day silently cursing the cruel old world in general, and its cruel old toe grabber.

One of life's truly great joys stemmed from the toe grabber's twice-a-year errors. Sometimes he woke the wrong toe — and there is nothing more satisfying than the moment that toe's startled owner realizes he does not have to get out of bed and curse life. The toe's owner informs the toe grabber who the correct victim is, listens while that unfortunate sibling is stunned into brutal consciousness, then falls peacefully back to sleep. No late morning dream could ever top that reality.

4 6

Burrs On The Stool
By Charles

Saturday Morning. We would generally be rolling around playing football or something near the helicopter tree in the Haddock's yard when the first call came blasting from the kitchen: "DOUG-LAS!!"

The calls always came in order, oldest first. There was a time when Doug was considered the oldest. He would go off. Fifteen minutes later he'd be back, but before he returned to the field of play there would already be the next call: "LOUIS!" After Louie came the "PAUL!!" (Girls were excluded.) And I was next in line. It didn't matter that Louis and I were on the ten yard line (Michael substituting for Paul. We never got that close when Paul was in the game). Sure enough: "CHARLIE!!" And off I have to go.

The stool always sat in the middle of the kitchen. It never looked secure enough to hold a kid, much less an almost grown-up. Four shaky aluminum posts on an aluminum seat. Rocking backward was never even considered on this stool. On the floor surrounding the stool was a mixture of straight brown, straight black and curly black. If Michael had been called and not Philip, the curlies outnumbered the straight. Black always outnumbered the brown, but I'd help to even that out. Of course, no one but me ever noticed this contribution, because I was always last.

Today's style is the burr. The burr was in vogue for many years running. A perfect, consistent cut that looked equally good on curly heads and straight heads. Any problems relating to cow-licks were easily remedied by wearing a cap made from an old pair of nylon stockings to bed at night. Ten minutes after balancing myself on the stool, my burr would be complete. Philip used to watch a lot of times. Mom said he kept my attention and helped me sit still. It was always a little hard to sit still while she thrashed my head with a pair of electric clippers that must have been purchased and first used on Harold. I think, more than being helpful, Philip just liked watching me trapped on that stool with a hot piece of plastic pinned around my neck and sticking to every pore of my body.

It always felt good to get that plastic off so I could hurry back to the helicopter tree. But sometimes they would have moved whatever game they were playing to the hand-grenade tree during those insufferably long Saturday morning minutes I spent on Mom's wobbly hair-cutting stool.

— Charles

47

The Mostly Friendly
Ghosts Of Glenwood Drive

About the time Carol was born and Harold left for college, we moved into "the new house."

Carol isn't so old, but that still seems like a long time ago.

The house, in fact, is much older than Carol.

It was built in 1917, two years after Mrs. Erickson was born in St. Joseph, Missouri. The house took three years to build. Carol only took nine months.

The house, unlike anyone in the family, is made of rock. The first floor, anyway. "Chert," they call it. The only one of its kind in Chattanooga. Maybe elsewhere. It had a matching rock-walled outbuilding — a three-car garage with a servant's quarters on the second floor. We stored our old science projects on that second floor, and let the servant sleep with Daddy. We never encountered another house like it in Chattanooga. Nor another family like ours.

Our house was lined by hedges on two sides and a chain link fence on the other two. The hedges ate a lot of balls that were kicked, thrown, and batted into them over the years and never heard from again. Daddy put the fence up just before we moved in. It was his first home improvement. It kept a long succession of little Ericksons from toddling out into the instant death that thrived on the streets.

Our "new house" was on the corner of a very busy intersection. A kid who was given a bicycle instead of a fence was killed there two months before we moved. Over the next 15 years, kids on bicycles were run over — but never killed — five times. We saw some of them, before and after, while playing inside our fence. We were not allowed to have bicycles. But we used to walk a lot to other play areas in the neighborhood.

Two or three times a day there would be blood-curdling screeches as motorists tried to avoid hitting each other on our fronting street, or get their three-thousand pounds of steel to a full stop after rolling down the steep intersecting road that descended from the ridge. Mother would race to the side window

The old house." Tight quarters for parents and their then 13 children.

three times a day, her hand over her pounding heart, to make sure. . . . It never was one of us.

We were very careful. And lucky.

⨀

The new house was also haunted.

One of the ghosts used to watch television with me late at night. Channel 12's *Creature Features*. Actually, he sat in the adjacent room, the entrance hall, and made me watch those scary movies alone. His chair creaked whenever he got up or down. He was there for a whole summer.

A few years earlier, Mother and her crew of babies were all upstairs taking their afternoon naps

when the television downstairs began blaring at almost full volume. She ran down, turned it off, and noticed that some lights had been turned on as well. No one could have entered the locked house. It was just a lonely ghost hoping to see *Topper* on television while waiting for the babies to wake up. A hard of hearing ghost.

⦿

One year John was putting a new medicine cabinet into the downstairs bathroom and discovered an empty room when he pulled the old medicine cabinet out of its hole in the wall. it was more of a hallway than a room, measuring about five feet by twelve feet. Discovery of the abandoned room was cause for at least five minutes of excitement as we raced madly through the house trying to find a flashlight that worked. We hoped to find buried gold in this sealed off room. We dreaded finding a body. We found only a lot of dust once some light was shed on the discovery.

I guess one of the house's previous owners found the gold. And buried the body.

48

Carol: No. 14 — Pizza Princess
And The End Of The Line

Dear Nieces and Nephews, and Much Appreciated Readers,

Carol was the littlest person and the biggest brat to ever pass through the house. She is still little. Admirably thin. But she is not quite the brat she once was.

∞ — ∞

Carol was and is and always will be the youngest. Raising the youngest was probably as traumatic for the parents as bringing up the oldest. Most families don't have such extreme extremes.

I'm sure the parents would have spoiled her had Carol not taken control of the situation and so generously spoiled herself.

I easily remember her sitting at her front corner of the kitchen table eating supper with the rest of us. But I can't remember her ever eating what the rest of us were picking off our plates that evening. From the day she was the last to graduate from the oak high-chair polished by years of diapered, little buttocks from each successive milk spiller — everything was special order for Carol Erickson.

At age ten she discovered how to prepare a Chef Boy-Ar-Dee pizza mix on her own. From then until she started college, Carol ate cheese pizzas for lunch and dinner — and cold pizza leftovers for breakfast. She survived well enough, but all those pizzas left her flat-chested.

When she wasn't eating pizza, she was whining. Life, especially its Ericksons, seemed full of offense. Most of us refused to have anything to do with her for about ten years — and she whined about that as well. She mellowed when she started high school, but it was still several years before we spoke to her again, suspecting at first that she was probably just up to another of her little-girl tricks.

Carol was so tolerable by the time she made that two-hour drive to the University of Tennessee that Paul and Charles let her live with them in the big apartment they were renting. They taught her to cook staples other than pizza — difficult dishes like tacos, spaghetti, and hamburgers. She, in turn, let them fall in love with her girlfriends.

∞ — ∞

Carol graduated with a degree in accounting and passed every section of the CPA exam on her first effort. Neither of her certified older brothers had accomplished that.

She had problems in the real world, though. Her first position was with one of the "Big Eight" accounting firms, a firm that de-cided an attractive and talented female would make a nice display in its regional office. She did not adapt well to its rules — rules

Charles, Carol, and Paul.

prohibiting such activities as riding a bicycle to work, or lunching with one of the secretaries. Carol moved from there to a smaller firm where the wives of the partners soon ran her out of town *because of her assumption of equality (not with the wives, but with her male colleagues).*

After that rough start, she settled into a prosperous career in Naples culminating in running her own accounting firm. Along the way, nearly every client she worked with, from small businesses to large banks, tried to hire her away with the hope she would take over and run their business with the same efficiency and insight she applied to their tax and growth issues. From time to time she took up those offers, but kept returning to accounting once she got them over various humps.

Carol is my example of the ideal liberated woman. She assumes equality rather than fights for it. And she doesn't try to keep cheese on both sides of her pizza. As a child, she wasted a lot of years and tears seeking both the equality of being one of the Ericksons and the privilege of being one of their girls. She was ostracized for her efforts. She finally began playing down being one of those girls so it could be held neither for nor against her. And, by attending college in Chattanooga for her last couple of years and staying there for that first year of work, she learned what few limitations there are for a smart, ambitious woman from one of the true masters —
her mother.

∞—∞

Carol was a child once; much like the rest of us.

Relatively yours,
Uncle Rags

Carol Elizabeth Erickson, born October 8, 1957
Married William Daniels, November 24, 1979, in Chattanooga
Married Peter Louis Girardin, January 16, 1988, in Naples
Peter Louis Girardin, born March 7, 1942, Fort Myers, Florida

49

All I Inherited Was Everyone Else's Rules
By Carol

I was going to make a list of the brattiest things I did while growing up, but it would take too long.

Instead, I'm just going to remember some things.

Like having to go to bed first.

After a lot of arbitration, a plan was worked out: My bedtime was 8:30, Charlie's was 15 minutes later, at 8:45, and Paul's 15 minutes after that, and finally Cecilia at about 9:30. But I didn't like the plan. I pitched a fit. Every night. None of us ever went to bed until 9:30 because I could cry and carry on at least that long. It wasn't any fun going to bed first. But now I go to bed at nine. Eight, when I can.

There were a lot of unfair aspects to being among the youngest. For reasons we still don't understand, we were not allowed to take showers. We took baths for years after we had learned all about how to stand up, and how soap works.

The older ones gained the right to start drinking Cokes at night. We younger ones were promised a sip if we would run to the kitchen for them while they watched TV, fill a glass with ice, and bring them their Cokes. Not much fairness there. Then we negotiated terms by which we were allowed to pour exactly one-fourth of the Coke for ourselves. Chase down two Cokes and you earn a whole half, but it still wasn't fair. And they could eat Fritos whenever they wanted. We got Fritos only on Friday nights. And boy were they ever dished out sparingly.

I don't know who it was who chose the snacks we would have each afternoon for "milk and candy." But I'm sure it must have been some of the older ones. They would go to the wholesale candy place and chose whatever they liked, then we would have to eat it because there sure wouldn't be another trip until we had finished every last piece of the stock in the pantry. Fig Newtons were among the worst. All I know is I was never once invited to go down to wherever it was and take a look at the choices.

We used to have Kool-Aid on summer afternoons. But it was almost always lime. Maybe Mother thought it was a vegetable since it was green. Does anybody remember ever seeing real vegetables on our kitchen table? Or fruits?

Paul and I discovered that if we invited friends over for dinner we could eat with them in the dining room, which gave us a chance to run outside during the meals and dump our mashed potatoes and apple sauce into the bushes. My friend Pam Martin actually loved apple sauce, so when she came over, which was pretty often considering her assets, all we had to dump off the porch was our mashed potatoes with lumpy gravy.

I wonder how long it will take for Mother to speak to me again after she reads this. I know, Mom, that when you read the next one, it'll be even longer.

— Carol

5 0

If One Is
The Loneliest Number

After Carol, there are no more. She was and is and always will be the last.

"Last" sounds diminishing. But, really? How about "sixth"? Or "ninth"? Or "twelfth"?

At least last is more than just a number.

(Not, to paraphrase *Seinfeld*, that there is anything wrong with being a number.)

What was the flow like? To my way of thinking I see the births as coming either one or two years apart. But I've been around enough women to know they think in the more concise terms of months. The flow, with my way first, based on entry and graduation classes in school, and theirs in parenthesis is:

Harold, followed in a year (16 months) by Frank, followed in a year (14 months) by Allen, followed in a year (14 months) by John, followed in a year (11 months) by David, followed in two years (27 months) by Philip, followed in two years (21 months) by Michael, followed in two years (21 months) by Eileen, followed in a year (16 months) by Douglas, followed in two years (16

Standing: Harold, Frank, John, Allen, Philip, and David.

months) by Louis, followed in a year (16 months) by Cecilia, followed in a year (14 months) by Paul, followed in a year (14 months) by Charles, followed in a year (13 months) by Carol, followed by a vacuum. . . .

⟲

For purposes of play and sleeping arrangements and jurisdiction of such things as bedtime rules, we often paired off. Harold and Frank constituted the first pair with Allen allowed into their world depending on what their world involved at the time. John was such a disruptive influence that he did not pair well with either Allen or David, leaving David, more so than Allen, to fend for himself. Philip and I were virtually inseparable as children and once he lunged awkwardly into puberty — a state I still had to wait a while to inhabit — I reached down past soul-searching Douglas and grabbed at Louis to keep me entertained. Louis and I devoted ourselves to thousands of hours of various sports. Except for my meddling, Douglas and Louis were a natural pair, as were Paul and Charles, the two who were most isolated by those bookends called sisters on either end of them.

The pairs, of course, fought as routinely as they played. I fought with Philip (though he, an unusually aggressive child, was always the antagonist). Douglas and Louis were quick to find fault with each other. And Paul and Charles set the record for years of ongoing squabbling.

⦿

As much as I might fairly contend that the three girls were privileged, they — like the rest of us — paid their own way through the last years of high school and through all the years of college. Even in a world that refused to pay its females the same wages it offered males, these girls still made it on their own.

⦿

Daddy's only complaint with the first draft of this book was that it portrayed him as a poor provider. He pointed out something he had never bragged about: That he took great personal pride in achieving a five-figure income, $10,000, when fewer than ten percent of U.S. households had crossed that threshold. Not bad for someone with no formal education, who taught himself to read, write, and master business math, and whose daily donning of white shirts, ties, and suits solidified that look of the 1950s-'60s American businessman.

Though he hung his jacket in the closet and sometimes loosened his tie, Daddy never changed out of his white dress shirt and suit pants after work while eating, sweeping the kitchen floor after supper, carrying out the garbage, giving baths, and then for an hour-and-a-half of reading the evening newspaper. At 9:30 he traded this uniform for pajamas.

Out of respect, which is the only way anyone in the family has ever viewed this modest man, I'm correcting the "poor provider" record here. Still, while Daddy's denominator might have been a big and impressive number, so were we numerators.

We survived those thirty years of child-rearing by sticking to the premise: "There is barely enough money to meet necessities, and anything above that needs to be saved for emergencies." It's possible we were not as impoverished as I thought. But, if "you are what you eat," maybe, also, "you are what you spend." We never spent anything that wasn't pinched first. There was never a time, not a single time, when the parents took us to a restaurant. Fortunately, we kids didn't care, and were probably even grateful since we wouldn't have had any idea how or what to order.

When the older ones were home from college, we might send someone out for a late-night pizza pickup. If so, the cost was calculated to the square inch, and everyone paid his or her share. Sometimes we generously covered Mother's two slices, but other times she pinched her 85 cents from the pewter Money Cup.

From left: John, David, Paul (foreground), Douglas (behind him), Allen (rear), Frank, Cecilia, Louis (behind her), Michael (behind him), Carol (foreground), Eileen, Philip, Jacquie, Charles, Harold. Circa: 1966.

Mostly Pregnant

BOOK THREE

Book
Three

Book Three introduction from the original 1985 spiral bound printing.

CHAPTER 51

Spilt Milk

Take an ordinary glass of milk. Tip it over. It spills.

Science recognizes only two ways of spilling milk. Intentionally or accidentally.

But since the day milk was first extracted from a moo cow's gland and served at a growing family's dinner table, children have been spilling it a third way: Inevitably.

Sit a child at a table and he or she will spill milk.

Not every time, of course. If more than just a few children spilled milk every time they came near it, adults would long since have abandoned procreating. No. Children spill milk only often enough to prove to their parents they are incapable of mastering life — that they will take their own good time learning how mean ol' Mr. Gravity works.

A child's fearful look as the milk forms a river on the table and then begins a waterfall to its lap says instantly that he or she did not do it on purpose. Of course, it's usually apparent to everyone else at the table that it couldn't have been just an accident. You can't accidentally turn a glass of milk slowly to its side — even if you didn't mean to do it. To the child, though, Mr. Gravity, like God, works in mysterious ways.

⦾

I grew out of the milk spilling stage at about the same age any reasonably awkward child would. But I had the misfortune of spending the next several years experiencing Eileen, and then Douglas, then Louis, then Cecilia, then Paul, etc., discovering to their individual little capacities to be endlessly surprised by the phenomenon that when you knock a glass of milk over the contents spill across the table.

Our eating arrangements around the kitchen table were tight, to say the least, so the bungler spilling the milk seldom suffered the wet, sticky aftermath alone. Usually two or three of our laps would be targeted by the panoramic waterfalls. Mrs. Erickson, who was pregnant nearly all the time, sat at the end of the table nearest the kitchen and closest to the nasty old dishrag she used for cleaning up spills. Daddy sat at the other end where he was helpless to do more than growl and hiss through his teeth at the culprit — often as not hissing at the wrong toddler.

Eileen, Douglas, and I would sit along one side of the table, with Philip, Louis, and Cecilia facing us from the other; Louis always being at an appropriate end position to accommodate his chronic left-handedness. Paul, Charles, and/or Carol would be in the highchair at Mother's right, depending on which of them was currently dirtying diapers. Whoever was presently

Front row milk spillers: Eileen, Douglas, Michael, Philip, baby Cecilia, and Louis.

occupying the highchair, and thus frequently distracted by bowel movements, was expected to spill milk. The rest of us were supposed to know better. I hardly understand why. It seems that if Harold, Frank, and Allen didn't know better at a particular age, then Louis, Cecilia, and Paul should hardly be the wiser.

Regardless, spilling milk was an intolerable offense punished by a series of loud grunts and sighs from Mother as she swabbed it up and by Daddy's excitement at the commotion and his fear of a change in his pregnant wife's disposition. As his hissing and mean looks began to wear down, Daddy would usually grit his teeth to convey the tone of a shout and demand from the visibly shaken offender, "Now why did you do that!?" The teary-eyed ne'er-do-well would always stammer, "I-I-I was j-j-just trying to d-d-drink it."

Often there were two or three of us in various stages of milk spilling. Getting milk dumped onto your lap was almost worth it if the bungling dumper happened to be an older brother. Made you feel like it must not be so stupid to spill milk after all. And when the spiller was younger, you were allowed to sit there and gasp loudly like Mother, hiss between your teeth like Daddy, and even stand up or shift frantically in your seat to add to the commotion and the seriousness of the crime.

It was fair for the older ones to ridicule the crying perpetrator. "Good gosh, Douglas! You're such a ba-by!" "Yeah, Douglas!! When are you going to grow up!?" "Douglas isn't ever going to grow up. When he goes to school he'll be carrying a rattler instead of a lunch box." "He'll be the only kid in his class who has to wear a bib." "Yeah, Douglas is always going to be just a little b-a-b-y!"

There was nothing we string of babies hated more than to be called a baby. Worst of all was for a big baby to be called a "little ba-by." "I am *not* a little baby!" we would cry whenever accused of such depravity. "Then why did you spill your milk?" the prosecution would retort, always laughing loud enough at its own wit to drown out the whimper of, "I was just trying to drink it."

Milk was spilled at least every third night. Sometimes every night for a week, by which time every baby at the kitchen table was too traumatized and superstitious to drink. The high points came on those occasional instances when two glasses of milk would be spilled during the same meal. Sometimes this could be accomplished by the same little ba-by. A few times a year one glass of spilled milk would cause someone else to jerk out of the way and spill his simultaneously. Daddy, trapped against the wall at his end of the table, was visibly devastated, his life flashing quickly before him in an attempt to discern how it came to this, by those two-milk spills.

As though cramming from six to nine fledglings around a table wouldn't cause enough spilling on its own, the parents greased our miscreant conduct by having the older ones, the Big Boys who ate at the table in the dining room, serve themselves buffet style from dishes placed every night in the middle of our crowded little table. This meant that if you were one of the babies the older ones were always balancing plates of hot gooey food over your head. No matter where you sat, an arm or two would be reaching in between you and your neighbor scooping something out of the middle of the table.

You might notice a stringy clump of hot macaroni and cheese or a glob of cold applesauce ready to drop off David's serving spoon, angled directly at your little bare forearm. The Little Kids spilled gallons of milk trying to protect themselves from the carelessness of the Big Boys. The Big Boys were known to personally upset a glass of milk on occasion with their own carelessness and immediately cast a blaming look at the little one below who would be so shell-shocked by the white-washing that he could not muster a convincing defense. The guilty Big Boy always denied any involvement, loudly testifying as an expert witness to the innocent baby's long history of similar "accidents." They were usually specific as to just how the "ba-by" spilled his milk in this instance and were quick to support their evidence by recounting said baby's frightening inability to grow up.

⦿

There is a classic piece of film in which a drop of milk is magnified about one hundred thousand times and captured by slow motion as it falls into a puddle of milk. The drop creates an art form that can inadequately be described as a cross between a volcanic eruption and a blossoming tulip. A solid wall rises around where the drop landed and then breaks at its crest showering a circle of new little drops onto the milk's surface. My theory is that if you magnified just one of those little drops falling from the first drop's crest, it would create the exact same volcanic tulip as it in turn splashes down. And each of the drops created by its shower would create the same effect. *Ad infinitum.*

Yes, to infinity. Each little drop is still creating ever smaller drops which are still creating even smaller drops. "The Spilt Milk Theory of the Universe."

Somehow, hard as it would be on Daddy if he should get his head around this theory, all those tumblers of milk we spilled over all those years are still out there infinitely cascading away.

The original 1985 version of this very slightly revised book.

52

Daddy's Downtown Toy Shop
By Charles

Somewhere in Chattanooga, Daddy has a shop.

Not a flower shop where roses are cut and mums picked one petal at a time or shaken till they shatter. No, this shop is different. It's a toy shop.

It has a bazooka gun that can blow a delicate church ornament off a Christmas tree from 25 feet. There is an old, camouflage-colored tricycle that had a broken wheel when I last saw it. It's probably the centerpiece of the shop. But it's not just broken toys that become candidates for Daddy's shop. In fact, most of the toys taken there seemed to work just fine. But Daddy had

205

a real nose for discovering basic design defects. Guns that shot too far or too hard, electric football games with noisy vibrators, and dolls that cry or pee — these were all candidates for the shop. Daddy was much better at spotting these basic flaws than his kids were.

It's hard to estimate just how many toys Daddy has in his shop. No doubt he still has occasion to add a toy or two. I think Philip's daughter Marcie's toy puppy might have made it just last year. It seems the puppy's voice was a bit too raspy. Although he might have planned for growth, by and large, Daddy's shop must be getting pretty full. Marcie's puppy has the honor of being the first battery-operated toy admitted into the shop. We were never allowed to have toys with batteries because they wore out and new D-size batteries were expensive. Daddy was selective enough to limit his impounding to the many toys laying around the house.

You won't find any bicycles in Daddy's shop. No bicycles at all since we were never allowed to even bring one of those killer machines into the house or yard.

Someday I might try to find that shop and get all those toys back into the hands of kids. But I won't bother giving them to my nieces and nephews. They would just wind up back in satellite shops opened by John, Philip, David, Allen, Cecilia, and Douglas.

— Charles

53

John In The Box
By David

It all began one day when Mom had a new refrigerator delivered to the house. "It" is the one event everyone in the upper third of the family associates with the side yard at the house on East 12th Street.

It was very unusual that we got anything new, especially something the size of a refrigerator. We probably got a new one because the old one died, but I like to think it was purchased to provide us with a new toy, and perhaps the best toy we had ever had. Not the refrigerator; they're dangerous. Our great new toy was the box it was delivered in. This toy came with no official directions, but that was not a major problem since we were all practiced at inventing rules.

The most imperative problem was determining who was going to play with it, and in what order. Hollers of "First!" then "Second!" then "Third!" and then a "Next" or two started us on a foundation, albeit shaky. Hearing the commotion outside, Harold set aside his electric motors and came out to see what was happening. Detecting the confusion, he, being the oldest, took control and resolved our immediate issue. Since he was not present for the turn calling the only sensible solution, he pointed out, was to take turns according to age. This, of course, made him first; but, according to Harold, that was his God-given right.

I think it was a very large box that we were trying to turn into a toy, but it might be just that we were very small. Anyway, having resolved the order of play, we were left with only one nagging problem: What were we going to play? We chose the obvious. Harold, Frank, and Allen would test the idea of using the box as a clubhouse. They would test this application for one hour, they agreed, and if the test was successful they would then turn it over to John, myself, and Philip to play in. After an hour the report came back to John and me that it wasn't a very good clubhouse. So everyone had to start all over finding and testing a new use. John and I did not necessarily agree with this determination, but then Harold, Frank, and Allen were older than us and were not particularly interested in our opinion.

By this time it was around one o'clock and Mom (still "Mommy" to all concerned) was taking her nap. This is important because when she took her nap we were free to engage in more physical activities, such as tackle football. However, there were definite restrictions with nap time play. We were not allowed to get hurt, or to wake her up with noise, or for that matter, we were not allowed to wake her up for any reason.

The new game we settled on was a simple one with just a few rules. Simply put, the box was placed near the bottom of the side yard. One person would get in and the box would be closed.

Everyone else would start at the top of the side yard and on a count of three would charge down the little slope and plow into the box with maximum momentum. The objective was to see how far we could knock the box before it came to a stop. The first time down the hill was fun for everyone. No one knew exactly what to expect, so the feeling was somewhat like riding a roller coaster for the first time (not that any of us had ever come close to riding a roller coaster). At least three of us hit the box, and we rolled it a good six feet on down the hill. Not bad for the first try. Harold crawled out and confirmed what we all suspected — that it was a lot of fun to be inside the box. It sounded great to me, and I could hardly wait for my turn inside. Frank was now in the box and we charged again. This time we hit it a little better and knocked it even further down the hill. Frank came out, confirmed that it was great, and we were off for the third run. I could see my turn coming closer and closer. Just Allen, then John, then me.

Allen's turn went quickly and now John was in the box. John was a new challenge. He was a lightweight, and provided us a new opportunity to really set a good distance record. As I was slightly heavier than John, the next opportunity for a record would be Philip. However, Harold was already losing interest, which might mean the loss of our largest knocker, and we also realized Philip was probably too young to hit full force. So the distance opportunity was definitely John.

At this point, I should note that John was not always the favorite among us. Because of that, there was more than just the record behind our charge down the hill. In fact, John always seemed to know we had these baser feelings and usually avoided placing himself in such vulnerable situations. Indeed, I was surprised to see John out there at all as the afternoon wore on. To quote my former boss, Ronald Reagan, popping John good would "make my day." All of us kind of felt that way, and it made the day for all of us as we charged into the box with John inside and sent it sailing for a new family record.

To me, the fact that it was now my turn was almost as important as the distance record we had just set. If John would just hurry up out of the box, we could be on our way for the next round before Mom woke up or people started to quit. But John didn't get out.

He was carried out.

John, the victim, on the left. Then, standing, Allen, Harold, Frank, and David.

I don't remember whose job it was to wake up Mom, but someone did as the rest of us carried limp and unconscious John into the house.

I was not particularly concerned about him because he frequently fainted just to gain attention. My far bigger concern was the fact that the game was stopped by Mom and I never got my turn. As I think back on the incident, however, I wonder now if John maybe orchestrated that sensational bit of unconsciousness just to end the game before my turn. It would have been just like him.

— David

5 4

Potato Chips
Are The Best Vegetable

I should talk about food for a minute, because pretty soon I'll be talking about boils — and the two don't mix well.

Except for breakfast, which was something we handled with toast and eggs, bacon being far too expensive to waste on kids, our house could have served as a clinic on how-to-not-eat-right-but-live-to-complain-about-it.

Our greatest peculiarity was that we didn't eat vegetables. Virtually never. With the turkey dinners that traditionally interrupted our football watching on Thanksgiving and

211

Christmas, we were required to shovel down a forkful or two of those ugly, little green peas while so willingly stuffing ourselves beyond reason on Mother's incomparable gravy-bathed turkey and dressing.

So, Thanksgiving, and Christmas — that makes twice a year that we had vegetables. Mandatory vegetables. And sometimes when Daddy was out of town on business — about once every three years — Mrs. Erickson, as likely pregnant as not, celebrated her freedom by serving us Dinty Moore beef stew for supper. That canned stew came laced with potatoes and carrots that were disguised well enough within the tangy sauce to make them edible. But from what people tell me about my current eating habits, vegetables in canned stew have the nutritional value of bath water.

Ten one-inch potato chips offer the same nutritional value as an apple. That's a dubious food fact found in the Department of Agriculture's enlightening "Guide to the Nutritional Content of Foodstuffs." We ate a lot of potato chips, few apples — and only the very rare true vegetable.

Vegetables were on the table when we were growing up, but we weren't required to eat them.

Green beans would show up in a little serving bowl in the middle of the table, and they would be avoided like a puddle of spilt milk. Spilt milk was a regular feature on the kitchen table. But never broccoli. Never asparagus. Never collard greens — that foul-smelling oiled grass that I gag on sometimes as I'm passing it in a cafeteria line during one of those efforts to eat my monthly dish of vegetables. I usually choose broccoli, if it has enough cheese sauce to negate the aftertaste, and fried anything. Fried okra, if you can imagine something so horribly gooey turning crisp when battered and then splattered by grease, is the best of all the vegetables. If I ever have a garden, I'll plant plenty of fried okra. Our table was never blessed with this delicacy I was introduced to in my twenties by a friend's Southern mother.

About once a month, Mrs. Erickson would diligently cut up a carrot and leave it on the table. Carrots are said to be good for the eyes, but I think if you've seen one carrot you've just about seen them all. Once a month we would hurt a carrot's feelings with our callous disregard.

Twice a year we had corn-on-the-cob. We younger ones wasted a summer afternoon shucking the corn near the garbage cans outside the kitchen door. Then got in trouble that evening for spinning the corn in the butter dish. Hot corn cuts a noticeable groove into a quarter of cold margarine. Spinning it in margarine was one of those harmless, victimless crimes — like playing basketball in the house — that was forbidden on principle.

Corn-on-the-cob leaves annoying bits of residue between the teeth, so I ignored it as easily as I ignored any other vegetable that might make it to the table. No great loss. According to the Department of Agriculture's guide, corn has the nutritional value of thumb-sucking.

⦿

We got by for the most part with simple meals. In fact, we got by for the most part with just one simple meal: round steak with mashed potatoes and applesauce.

On our birthdays, we chose our favorite meal, so long as it could be purchased at or less than the going rate for hamburger. The other 351 days of the year, with the exception of Fridays, we ate Daddy's favorite meal, fixed the way he liked it. He liked round steak, mashed potatoes, and applesauce. And he liked his round steak cooked hard and dry. Every ounce of juice would be burned out to be used in making the deep brown gravy he favored for his potatoes. Sometimes I could read the entire evening paper chewing on just one bite of that round steak. When I finished the paper, I would pull the gray pulp from my mouth and hide it somewhere on my plate.

On Fridays, fried fish sticks or some other kind of Catholic food replaced the little cut of round steak on our plates. Everything else stayed the same. Mashed potatoes and applesauce.

Sometimes a dry, burned hamburger replaced the little cut of round steak, but everything else stayed the same. Even pork chops occasionally showed up in place of the round steak, but everything else stayed the same. It was always meat, mashed potatoes, and applesauce — sometimes garnished by a passing glance at a vegetable.

A dinner in the old house staged for a newspaper photograph.

55

Learning Book Buying From The Master
By John

The task of re-working my oldest son's school schedule and getting his books was assigned to me one year. While negotiating with the principal and department heads to move Mark into the higher math section, and changing him from Spanish to French, and finally getting his books together — I recalled with horror those pre-registration days at the old Notre Dame High School. It gave me a shuddering glimpse of Mother's phenomenal stamina and thrift.

First she had to judge the intellectual acumen of each of us and then lobby with the various teachers and staff to see that each was placed in the appropriate section — always an upward move to keep us better challenged. Ericksons were not to be afforded the luxury of loafing in the "C" section. The nuns seemed determined to eliminate us from the upper level math or science class, so every year Mother would confront Sister Thomas Aquinas who, under pressure of just trying to get the school year started, would finally acquiesce to our much touted brilliance. Harold was first, and very smart; a fact Mother reminded the nuns about for years on end to win her positions. Although the rest of the Ericksons certainly never measured to this standard of achievement, it took at least a decade for the nuns to realize they had good standing to argue our lesser performances. In the meantime, Mother had pushed us to higher levels, whether we liked it or not.

After these polished negotiating skills came one of the most intense bargain basement purchasing efforts you might ever encounter. Mother had to buy books. Her book-buying efforts actually began at the close of the previous school year as Mother targeted and then negotiated scrap prices from families no longer able to make "hand me down" use of their textbooks. Sometimes this backfired as the nuns had a tendency to change editions in subjects like literature and science and she might be stuck with an abandoned edition. But, she learned quickly enough, except for a few page numbers the new editions were essentially the same and could be renumbered to match the newer version. Besides, out of date books were even cheaper than scrap paper. One trick she learned early was that girls always kept their books in better condition than boys.

By the time I negotiated Mark's schedule, all the used books of previous female ownership were gone and I was stuck with $154 of new purchases. Maybe next year I'll get Mother to visit Palm Beach over our book-buying weekend.

— John

5 6

The Year Of The Boils

Dear Nieces and Nephews, and Valued Readers,

Once upon a time . . . a time long forgotten by all who weren't there to suffer through it . . . a time whose final passage was hoped and prayed for by the stoutest of man and child alike . . . yes, once upon a time . . . We. Had. Boils.

I hope, for your little sakes, that you don't even know what a boil is.

And if you do know what a boil is, I hope for your mental and physical well-beings that it's because you studied them in science.

217

Or, if you have been subjected to even more personal experience, I hope it has come from seeing them on the trembling physique of an afflicted classmate — rather than as a putrescence on your own tender membrane.

∞—∞

Boils were invented by Moses.

In the days of antiquity, this cruel old man cast his shepherd's staff at the Pharaoh's feet and plagued the kingdom with festering boils. The boils, which only hardened the Pharaoh's heart, were known as a staff infection until the Middle Ages when a Jesuit monk, his mind addled by too much drink and too little carnal knowledge, misspelled this particular plague while quilling a new translation of the Bible, and boils have been known ever since as "staph" infections.

I don't know why there is a "p" in "pneumonia," (As an irrelevant aside, the reason you can't hear a pterodactyl relieve himself is because the "p" is silent.) But silent p's aside, I understand completely why Pharaoh's heart was hardened by the misery cast off by Moses and his staff. I, too, suffered boils.

We, nearly all of us, suffered boils. Incestuous boils.

∞—∞

The dictionary tastefully describes a boil as "an inflamed, painful, pus-filled swelling on the skin, with a hard center." That's putting it mildly.

Maybe you've played sports or done mechanical work with someone who appeared to be all thumbs. Imagine that person, his body a lush garden of nice fat thumbs, afflicted with an all-encompassing case of thumb screws and you can get a slight feel for what our boils were like.

They visited one summer — and that was their only redeeming value. They wiped out a good part of our vacation, but had they struck during the school year our physical anguish would have been aggravated by the mental humiliation of having to take our boils to school. It was bad enough having to take our snotty noses to school as bad colds worked their way toward pneumonia. It was bad enough taking our poison ivy to school when that blight was at its gooiest. It would have been unconscionable to take our boils to school where we would have been cast away from our cleansed classmates like the lepers we had become during the reign of the boils.

Thank you, boils, for the single consideration of being a summer plague.

∞ — ∞

John, who didn't have boils, said they were "TV boils." He said we got them from sitting on our butts watching too much television.

We got them on our butts, but not from sitting on them. They had spread to everyone's every part. Everyone but John, who was spending most of that summer at the suburban home of an older couple he had met through working at the church.

John's status in the family was always unique. But it took an even more pronounced turn when he was adopted. Not into the family, but out of it. Never officially, but as John reached high school age he took up with a childless couple he had met while doing volunteer work for our downtown church on weekends. He became the perfect son they never had, and began trading off his perfect son-ness (exchanging lawn work and other home maintenance services) for their suburban rewards of grilled steak dinners and the use of their boat, their horses, and country club pool. Neither John nor his new family was taken advantage of by this remarkably compatible relationship.

John shared his new upper-middle-class life with those of us willing to adapt to its many rules. The big stumbling block was that Tommie Pachoud, the suburban housewife around whom this lifestyle cycled, insisted that any Ericksons who came to visit had to eat their vegetables. Horseback riding and water skiing are tempting little morsels — but we all thought eating vegetables was a pretty steep price of admission.

219

Though John became more and more a part of the Pachoud household, having what evolved into his own bedroom in their new rancher with its central air and wall-to-wall carpeting, he remained, by his strong nature, a considerable force in the Erickson household as well. Even as he became less and less a tangible presence.

It was because he was not home very often that summer that he was spared our curse of the boils. I guess he was probably punished in other ways for what Eve had done to Adam back in the dark days of Eden. Maybe John suffered

Philip taking advantage of one of John's horses.

blisters on his hands from too much water skiing. Or maybe Moon Shadow, his shiny black stallion, slobbered on him. But John did not suffer the insidious, incestuous boils.

∞ — ∞

I was a skinny little kid of 13 when the boils plagued us. That makes Charles only four, and I was thinking that both he and Carol, a year younger, must have been spared or else they surely would have succumbed. But I asked Charles once if he remembered the boils. His face turned pale — almost ashen — and his eyes glazed over with one of those far away looks. After a couple of preliminary gags, he muttered weakly, "It was a long, long time ago. . . . Ohh, the pain! . . . That white stuff. . . . The pain!! God, Michael, why did you have to remind me!?!" Charles apparently did suffer boils. And just barely survived.

David, Philip, Eileen, Douglas, Louis, Cecilia, Paul, Charles, and Carol have all tried to suppress that summer from their memories. But I dwell, because I despair.

∞ — ∞

I remember that during the worst of it — and, trust me, the least of it was Dante's third circle of Hell — I had four raging boils on me at the same time. Four shiny, red, tender swells the size of half-dollars. Right elbow . . . left side of neck . . . right thigh . . . and, like everyone else, one on my butt.

Mother, bless her heart, tried every possible home remedy in her efforts to eradicate the boils. Weeks into it, she even sent one of us to the doctor. Nothing worked. Not even the exceedingly foul tasting little pink penicillin pills the doctor prescribed. Those pills effectively poisoned nearly everything God's perfect design saw fit to let corkscrew its way into our bony little bodies, but they had as much success against our case of the Pharaoh's boils as a parakeet with emphysema would have trying to blow out California's annual forest fires.

Mrs. Erickson decided that if she couldn't eradicate the boils she could at least pop them into submission.

A futile but exceedingly painful exercise.

Every night she called us one at a time into the kitchen. For surgery. It was her contention that bursting the hard white core of each boil would somehow subdue the inflammation. Professionals fight fire with fire — so why not fight pain with pain?

Her surgical kit included a blackhead popper — which, when applied to these monster boils was like trying to stir paint with a toothpick — and an assortment of stainless steel implements that were actually designed for pitting the kernels from walnuts.

Blinding pain! Believe me, you little children of such sheltered lives, that the bursting of a boil is blinding pain! And the bursting of two or three boils in a row on countless nights in succession. . . . The horror!!!

One would think, even hope, the senses would flee in shock, but these boils defeated even the natural inclinations of the pitiable human neurological design. The pain was blinding — but not totally senseless.

Poor little us. Had we been so fortunate as to have been born back in the days of leeching, we might at least have died soon and been spared.

We moaned a lot. We cried a lot. We all sat sideways on our chairs while eating. The rest of the time we didn't sit at all. We entertained ourselves as much as was possible under the harrowing circumstances by ridiculing the size and locations of each other's boils. And by reminding each other throughout the long days how horrendously the other person's swollen infections were going to hurt that night when Dr. Mrs. Erickson began pinching and probing and mashing at them with the weapons in her arsenal, especially with that gruesome eye hook . . .

∞ — ∞

We prayed hard every night for God to come down and take His nasty boils back — or at least pass them on to someone more deserving. A Russian. Or a local Protestant. Never had the nightly family Rosary been recited so fervently.

We practically quit watching television on the outside chance John was right and they really were "TV boils."

And then John came to our rescue. Weary of our incessant complaining about how awful life was and how it was getting worse with each passing day, he finally called the family doctor on his own to talk boils. Ever so competent, John pieced together what he had learned on the phone with what he already knew about the way life is, and tracked the infection to the soap dish in the down-stairs shower. The shower every one of us used every night.

Ever so mechanically capable, John scrubbed the soap dish and, overnight, eradicated those incestuous boils.

Relatively yours,
Uncle Rags

57

Revel In
The Absence Of Pain

Dear Nieces and Nephews, and Hopefully Healthy Readers,

I well remember one night long ago when I was trying to get to sleep in the downstairs bedroom I shared with your Uncle Philip. I remember how the boils were so tender and my skin so tight in those swollen areas that they hurt plenty enough just on their own. And I remember how they hurt so much more whenever I brushed them against anything — even if it was just the well worn summer sheets.

I remember it being the fifth or so night in a row that I was so tender and so blighted that there was no way for me to lie on the bed without some part of that wretched body of mine screaming for me to lie on some other part. I remember thinking how nice it would be sometime in the future — assuming I might survive — when all the boils would be gone, and when no gooey or crusty poison ivy would be in their place, and when there would be no fresh injuries to my elbows or knees . . .

I remember thinking how nice it would be sometime far in the future when I might be entirely healthy and I could enjoy my bed, choosing to lie on my back at will, or curled to either side, and not hurt at all. I remember thinking how easy it is to curse the nights when you go to bed hurting. And how difficult it is for us to celebrate those routinely healthy and painless nights — the ones we take so much for granted. I remember thinking as a 13-year-old festered with boils how I should make a point in that almost un-foreseeable future of celebrating those healthy and painless nights that surely must exist in the upper chamber of my ever-trickling hourglass.

And I remember, little nieces and nephews, how on so many trouble-free nights in the ensuing 20 years I have stretched out on my bed, stretched and curled my appendages to their bones' delight, and have thought about those nights back in the days of the boils and have rejoiced in the good fortune of my good health . . .

Enjoy your comforts. . . .

Relatively yours,
Uncle Rags

5 8

The Family
That Prays Together

The family Rosary was worse than the family boils.

That's a terribly irreverent thing to say. Almost sinful. But so true that I'm going to say it again:

The family Rosary was worse than the family boils.

⓪

The Rosary was not as brutally painful as boils. Not so insufferably inhumane. But where the boils were there one day and

225

gone maybe a month or two later, the pain of the family Rosary was interminable. A nagging, insidious discomfort that struck every night of every week of every month of every year for what seemed like the better half of eternity.

Every night until long past the day that I left for college, the cry would ring out loud and dooming around the big old house: RRROOO-SSSAAA-RRRYYY!!!! Douglas delighted in crying that chilling alarm. After him, Charles was probably the chief antagonist, it being so much his nature.

There is really no nice way of letting everyone know that they have to drop whatever they're doing, hurry to the dining room, and fall to their knees for several minutes of mumble grumble. But some ways, differentiated by just a slight change in the inflection, are crueler than others. Those were the ways that were mastered.

Mrs. Erickson's internal clock told her it was time for the "family Rosary" about the same time every night that her hands finished with the dishes. We ate every night at 5:15, finished at about 5:17, and Mrs. Erickson, who was mostly pregnant, would be through with the dishes at 6:15 or 6:30, depending on how hard that night's mashed potatoes stuck to the plates.

I guess the family Rosary, which was started long before my knees even existed, was supposed to accomplish something. If it was intended to drive most of us away from the church, it succeeded.

A family Rosary is a nice idea. All of our Catholic textbooks — geography, history, math, etc. — managed to recommend it. But I had the feeling we were the only non-immigrant Catholic family in America that actually knelt down every evening and said a Rosary together. The only sheep bleating that much ballyhooed nonsense.

Like nearly everyone in the family, I was very religious for a long time. Perhaps, more so. I even had visions — a phenomenon usually reserved for more modest saints.

Saying a Rosary on our own was sometimes sublime. But none of us got any semblance of a spiritual salve, much less a spiritual awakening, out of the intrusive, compulsory, nightly family Rosary.

This photograph of Ericksons holding their individual Rosary beads was staged in front of the fireplace for a Catholic publication. (Note the small altar over Daddy's left shoulder. Great Catholics!) We actually gathered for each night's Rosary around the dining room table, not at the fireplace, kneeling over the thin cushions of its chairs. But on the same penitential hardwood floor.

In case you don't know what a Rosary is, it's the worrisome "string of beads" you might have seen Catholics praying on in old black-and-white movies. A long series of prayers meant to uplift or console. Fifty *Hail Marys* spaced ten at a time between six *Our Fathers* and five little known Catholic prayers called the *Glory Be.*

Mother always led the first half of each prayer, and we prisoners then raced through the last half. The *Hail Mary* is a prayer cleverly designed for halfies, the chorus coming right after the head bowing that accompanies the uttering of "thy womb, Jesus." Catholics are instructed to always bow their head upon saying or hearing the word "Jesus."

Mother's lead was always well-paced, distinctive, and reverent: "Hail Mary, full of grace, the Lord is with thee and with thy spirit. Blessed art thou, amongst women, and blessed is the fruit of thy womb, Jesus— " Our cue to cut in quick and race through our mumbled monotone of an answer: "HolyMaryMotherofGodprayforussinners-nowandatthehourofourdeathAmen."

Sometimes all of us were so busy reading there would be no answer to Mrs. Erickson's deliberate chant. When that happened — about once a month — she began ranting instead of chanting. She screamed, "If you kids don't want to say the Rosary then we'll just quit saying it!!!" We would all pretend we wanted to say the Rosary and act quite contrite for our misbehavior. Tempting as it was, and nervy as we were, we never once had the courage to call her bluff on that, "If-you-kids-don't-want-to-say-the-Rosary..." routine.

As anyone familiar with the beads knows, there is no part of the Rosary that involves reading. But we discovered the next best thing to getting out of saying the Rosary — by being in the shower or by being Eileen and on the phone — was to kneel against a chair across the dining room table from Mrs. Erickson with well-chosen reading material spread across that dining room chair's cloth seat. Her view was blocked by the top of long table. If we were discreet — which we all were — we could even turn the pages of *Time* or *Sports Illustrated* as we concealed those weeklies on the chair seats.

No one is discreet enough, though, to turn a full-sized newspaper page without drawing attention, so if all the unread magazines were already taken the next best choice was the wordy editorial page of the evening paper. That page had no advertising and might get a slow reader through half of the Rosary. The evening paper, however, was a conservative rag so steeped in fundamentalist religious philosophy that reading its editorials and letters to the editor was hardly any better than reading the Bible, which, at the time, was only slightly more appealing than reciting all those *Hail Marys* and *Our Fathers*.

If there were four or more people reading among the eight or so kids saying the Rosary, we had to be careful to mumble on the cue of "Jesus" or risk answering with one of those telling silences. The very young non-readers could never be counted on to not be daydreaming.

①

We did manage to develop some loopholes over the years. Loopholes that could get us out of the Rosary.

When Douglas or Charles or maybe one of the sweet little girls rang out with the excruciating cry of "RRRROOOO-SSSSAAAA-RRRRYYYY!!!!!" there was a mad dash. Not for the dining room where we knelt around the table, but for the downstairs bathroom where whoever got in first and locked the door was allowed to quickly turn the water on and cry out — as though he were actually lathering up the bar of Ivory — "I'M IN THE SHOWER!"

Philip and I discovered that loophole. Philip and I always raced hardest from the basketball court in the driveway, or from wherever we might be playing, to the downstairs bathroom. Philip was a bully. Brutish. He would push and shove if we happened to arrive at the bathroom door in a tie. He was not above committing the venial sin of "hitting" to secure his place behind the locked door where he could pretend to be in the midst of showering.

We discovered this "out" quite innocently. One night one of us was actually in the shower when Mother's clock told her it was time for the Rosary. Usually she postponed it a few minutes if someone was tied up, but this night she didn't delay her torture. She said the Rosary without the showering soul.

Too good to be true. The nightly showers were never much to look forward to, but they became an immediate blessing with this precedent that a shower could be taken during, and in lieu of, the Rosary. "Cleanliness is next to . . . "

No shower from that day on was ever started *before* the Rosary. But there was always one beginning just as the rest of us knelt to pray. We didn't consider exposing this sham because, though the competition for the shower became intense as Douglas and Louis began fighting for it with Philip and me, there was always a chance that one of those stuck with kneeling in the dining room would be fortunate enough to win the race to the shower the next night. It was something to pray for anyway.

Occasionally, Mrs. Erickson would hear the claim that someone was in the shower and she would relay through her mordant messenger that she was going to wait until the shower was finished. When this message was gleefully shouted through the door to the person just now taking his clothes off but cautious to have water running at full blast, that person would angrily shout back, "Okay. Everybody can wait. But *I'm-washing-my-hair*!" "I'm washing my hair" was colloquial for "I'm going to stand under the water until hell freezes over." The message would get back to Mrs. Erickson, losing much of its credibility in the tone of the provocative relayer. She would heave that great sigh of hers and call everyone on down to begin the Rosary without the hair washer.

◍

There were only three other excuses for getting out of the nightly agony: (1) If you were not at home, you did not have to say the Rosary. (2) If you had started college you did not have to say the Rosary. (3) If you were Eileen and were on the phone, you did not have to say the Rosary.

I suppose Eileen was on the phone one night (in reality, she was on the phone every night) and easily convinced her mother that this particular conversation was too important to be interrupted. Mrs. Erickson was easy prey for Eileen — especially when it came to sparing her from our socially handicapping customs. So the Rosary went on without her one night and it went on without her practically every night thereafter. We were all jealous of this special treatment. Especially because we couldn't take advantage of the same loophole. We didn't have any friends we could talk with on the phone. All of our friends were there in the room saying the family Rosary.

Little angels that we were, we never complained to Mrs. Erickson about the below-the-belt nature of Eileen's exceptions. And we let younger and other brothers cheat us out of showers that were rightfully ours.

We let everyone get away with any device he or she could come up with to get out of the family Rosary and never considered exposing those obvious shams. We were dubious proof that the family that prayed together stuck together.

Nightly Prayers

Another of those many, many, many rituals: Our nightly prayers.

They got longer and longer as time, and pregnancies, went on. But we got faster and faster.

Kneeling on the hardwood floors in the upstairs bedrooms, elbows on the thin mattresses of our single beds, the last thing, after that last drink of water and that last trip to the bathroom, we did was make the sign of the cross and then recite aloud our nightly prayers.

The three or four sharing a room, somewhat in unison, praying with tiny voices: "God bless Mommy. God bless Daddy. God bless Harold, Frank, Allen, John, David, Philip, Michael, Eileen, Douglas, Louis, Cecilia, Paul, Charles, and Carol. Amen." Wrapped with another sign of the cross, and then into bed. Each of us would insert a "me" in the place where our names lined up. "God bless Harold, Frank...me...Eileen, Douglas.... Amen."

But what we really said in going to bed every night was more a mumble jumble of "God bless Mommy. God bless Daddy. God blessHaroldFrankAllenJohnDavidLouisCeliaPaulCharlesand-CarolAmen."

Occasionally, at a family gathering, we'll compete to see who can race past Carol and blurt out the first "Amen."

It's always very close. Rarely a clear winner. We're all equally good at blasting through every name in the family as though it's just one long polysyllabic word.

God, who had heard those same prayers countless times before, was probably pleased that we didn't waste his time dragging them out. Surely he had better things to worry about than enunciation.

59

Bubble-Popping Swordfights — Penises At Play

Penises are little rubbery extensions that form on the front base of the body's trunk. They dangle between the legs.

Everyone has one.

Everyone but girls.

Since girls were so rare in the household, I'll stick with the premise that everyone has a penis, though we called them "dinkies." "Dinky" means "something small; insignificant." Freudian? No. Just the condition of the land mine one baby boy after another starts off with.

A clever entrepreneur seeking fortunes in the toy world might do well to engineer a little rubbery noodle-type apparatus about one-and-a-half inches long that could be attached by a suction cup to any part of a child's body. A great toy that would offer hours of solitary and/or group fun. It would be just like a "dinky," which I can state for a fact is fun to play with. I state that as a fact not because I ever played with mine or knew anyone who ever played with his. I'm so certain they're great fun to play with because it is so absolutely forbidden.

That no one should play with a dinky might be the only thing parents, siblings, nuns, Methodists, Marines, cowboys, Indians, Communists, Republicans, and even zombies would agree on.

If someone made a toy that flopped around just like a little penis, it would certainly be a big hit among both boys and girls.

⬥

Dinkies on little boys are innocent, yet heavily regulated, almost forbidden, novelties.

Forbidden, I guess, because they inevitably grow into the penises of supposedly-matured men.

I don't need to comment about those because the plethora of books documenting the awesome forces of destruction and creativity . . . of strengths and weaknesses . . . of spiritual cleansing and damnation . . . of joy and sorrow . . . of pleasure and pain that stem from this manly weapon-tool already fill your city library.

Little boys don't have to worry about all those things.

All they have to worry about is not touching their dinky.

But certain circumstances of life unavoidably require exposing and touching the forbidden noodle. Going to the bathroom is one.

In the civilized world, bathrooms afford privacy. In the Erickson house, they were minor war zones.

Until the time they reach puberty, older brothers felt free, sometimes compelled, to charge in on a younger brother busy peeing and nudge him to the side of the toilet so the elder can issue a really important stream of pee. The older brother's peeing is more important because it is of a larger volume, inherently more profound, and discharged without the slightest hesitation since it is backed by so many years of experience. And the older brother understandably has to hurry up and finish so he can get back to enterprises far more critical than the younger ones could ever imagine. Older brothers did it to me for years and I, in turn, subjected younger brothers to the same pecking procedure.

We had three bathrooms in the house. The main upstairs bathroom was used almost exclusively by the parents and the girls. It was a barge-in-free zone. The other upstairs bathroom, adjacent to the Big Boys Room, was used mainly by those waiting their turns during ping-pong marathons. The convenient downstairs bathroom was the primary relief station. It stayed very busy. Doubling and even tripling up at the toilet during breaks in play or before meals was not at all uncommon.

I should add for the benefit of any readers who happened to not be little boys at one time in their life, and contrary to what those same non-dinkied among us might contend should they evolve into housekeepers, that dinkies provide excellent aim (when just one foot from the rim). So there was little chance of spraying or otherwise fouling someone peeing beside or across from you.

In fact, a little boy's aim is so good it was inevitable these organic water guns would be adapted to the further enjoyment of life. Aiming at bubbles is, quite literally, child's play. Bubble-popping competitions were a natural outflow of seven- and eight-year-olds targeting their foamy discharge into the same toilet. Taking out the largest bubble before the other can get to it, and then the next largest, unless a new, larger target arose to the yellowing surface, is the essence of this precursor to many video games. Hand-eye coordination was essential during that anomaly when one is allowed to touch his otherwise forbidden penis.

Sword fights were the more advanced game.

In swordfighting, the two, sometimes three, little pee-ers stand alongside the receptive toilet and attempt to cross each other's spray. I can't ethically divulge the secrets, but if you cross the competitor's spray in a certain manner he might get hit with a slight splash. Even the smallest splash — when you are not absolutely certain that it's your own urine — is dismally distressing.

Michael, the slayer, and Philip, the slayed, shared many gunfights, and too many swordfights.

You can cross one another's spray maybe five or six times during an average little boy's non-beer-influenced peeing. Scoring is purely subjective, but one of the combatants almost always declares himself the loser by scouring his hands and wrists, perhaps even applying soap instead of just running water from the faucet, before leaving the bathroom and getting back to whatever game had been interrupted by nature's call.

6 0

The House
Of Noise

When real people look back on their childhoods, there are distinct sounds that bring fond memories. Sounds that trigger pleasant, secure feelings. The hollow tocking of the hallway's grandfather clock . . . dry maple leaves rustling in the breeze . . . the melodious doorbell . . . wind chimes beyond a bedroom window . . .

Ericksons never had those kinds of sounds.

Ericksons don't have those kinds of memories.

Instead of a bell, our two main doors, thick, towering blocks of 50-year-old walnut, were equipped with heavy metal knockers. If those knockers ever said "tap . . . tap . . . tap" instead of "WHACK! . . . WHACK! . . . WHACK! . . ." we knew it was a stranger. Not a welcome sound.

We had no need for strangers. Those whose visits were welcome knew enough to pound out three solid whacks, and knew that even those first three might not be heard over the noise that lived inside the big old house.

Instead of sounds, that's what we had: Noise. Clamor.

The only breaks in the commotion at our house came from about seven until ten at night during the school year. Homework hours. Even the preschoolers were muffled during those sacred hours. Anyone raising a ruckus would be castigated by Mother from her station in the kitchen. She would demand to know why that particular noisemaker wasn't studying.

"I don't have any homework tonight," never carried much weight. None of us, we were assured, were either so smart or so dumb that studying couldn't improve us.

⦿

The preschoolers were usually in bed by eight, but their last hour had to be peaceful or one of the Big Boys would excoriate them for interrupting his weighty studies. If that older brother's scathing exhortation failed — Carol, for instance, was never one to let an older brother prevail — Mrs. Erickson would be called in to castigate the trespassing party. We all grew up with castigation complexes.

But there was a healthy side to the way we four-, five-, and six-year-olds were constantly being called to the carpet — the living room rug being a relatively quiet and acceptable place to play — for interfering with the importance of studies. It made us long for reaching the upper grades so we could join this respected ritual. It was even common for the younger ones to *play* like they were doing homework, which seems about as much fun in retrospect as it would be for me to spend a holiday afternoon *playing* like I'm stuck in five o'clock traffic. Everything is relative.

Mother wasted years trying to keep the noise around the house at a reasonable level during those many hours we were allowed to play at full force. She didn't succeed. She wasn't mean enough. And as her belly continued churning out new little noise-makers, she resigned herself to the foreseeable fate. Daddy lost his hearing.

To give a faint idea of how much noise there might be at any given time, here's a typical afternoon:

Harold, Frank, Allen, John, and David are in the Big Boys Room playing ping-pong. This game requires active stomping and shouts of pleasure punctuated with cries of pain at the end of each

239

bitterly contested point interspersed with very loud, vehement arguments between many volleys over alleged technical infractions ("Your paddle touched the net!!" "Did not!!!") involving both participants and witnesses.

Twenty-one very hard-fought points constitute a game. About 20 very hard-fought games constitute an afternoon. Lots of shouting and stomping, even diving onto the floor up in the Big Boys Room. While waiting for winners, John drifts to one of the other upstairs bedrooms to practice Sousa marches on his trumpet.

Philip and I are seeing who can jump from the higher step and land in one piece on the uncarpeted entrance hall floor. We start on the fourth step and advanced up the stairs one new step at a time, usually chickening out on about the seventh or eighth. Every year we, like the younger ones to follow, might grow another step. Each landing on the hardwood floor below resounds through the house with a thud that sounds like someone has just fallen from the ceiling and broken his neck.

Eileen, Douglas, Louis, and Cecilia are racing from upstairs to downstairs and through every available room firing their loudest possible mouth-driven shots while simultaneously shouting at each other in an intense game of cowboys and cowgirls. This game requires a lot of diving through and behind furniture, and elaborate death-like screams and falls whenever a young cowperson is momentarily killed.

Paul, Charles, and Carol, the eternal babies, are crawling or tumbling just their way of running in those early days — across the living room rug. Perhaps one or two are still in the wooden, barred playpen, intermittently crying and bawling and — with what little vocabulary they have garnered from us elders — earnestly accusing one another of some benighted trespass.

To escape from the noise, one of the older ones, encouraged by the sound of John practicing his trumpet, drifts to the downstairs bedroom to wait for his next turn at the ping-pong table by banging on my drum set.

The drone of the unattended black-and-white television set keeps another downstairs room from feeling left out.

Mother is in the kitchen, wearing her damp apron, skinning potatoes for boiling, before opening a new gallon can of applesauce and then burning that night's round steak in her paralogical efforts to keep all the noise alive.

6 1

Naples — The Hot Vacation Destination
By Rosemary

I suppose that for anyone coming into the Erickson family the first encounter with the whole group is somewhat traumatizing. Even more so for someone coming from a one-sister family.

Since Philip had only advised those at home that he was coming into Chattanooga (from Knoxville, where we were in school) to pick up his bicycle, and that he was bringing a friend, and waited until the day we were going to arrive before giving them even this much information, there was no time for fanfare, which suited me just fine. Philip had been giving me all the particulars about each person in the family for weeks. I felt I knew everyone's characteristics without once seeing even a picture. And he had done a pretty good job because I recognized Celia, Charlie, Paul, and Carol before they were introduced. I had also memorized all the names and their order of ages.

Charlie's first summer away from home, during which he vacationed at our house in sunny (Did someone say "hot"?) Florida was enjoyable, and uplifting for all of us. I'm sure Charlie just loved going to the laundromat with me. One is never too young to find out what life is really all about.

I also remember all the spring breaks people spent with us in our humble two bedroom apartment in our first years in Naples. At one time people from both sides of the family converged and we had eight adults sleeping in that little place. Literally wall-to-wall people.

A visit from Paul and his college friend while my cousin Larry was staying with us also sticks in my mind. Unfortunately, Larry was having a hard time dealing with all these extra people taking over "his house" and "his" use of our old Falcon car. Paul and his friend planned to stay just a few days, but they had a little leeway before they really had to be back at school. Each night Philip and I would talk Paul into staying just one more day and one more day, until Larry feared to come home from work and have to ask, "Are they still here?" It became such a joke that a good friend of mine gave me a plaque inscribed, "Weekend Guest." It says, "If we get to drinking Sunday afternoon and start insisting that you stay over 'til Tuesday, please remember: We Don't Mean It."

We've enjoyed so many great visits over the years from what has to be the most casual and easy group I could ever have hoped to feed to our Florida mosquitoes.

— Rosemary

6 2

Late Nights At The Kitchen Table
By Cecilia

When people sit around and talk about their family and then start asking about mine, I feel as though I'm on one of those old E.F. Hutton commercials. Everyone shuts up and listens to my childhood and teenage experiences. They are amazed that we had our own softball, kickball, and basketball teams. Of course, we also let the Pospisils play, because weren't these girls from two houses down numbers 15 and 16?

When I think back I remember the hours spent in the dirty garage playing square ball, and the nights of Red Light. We didn't

245

play Red Light like most kids. It would be 90 degrees on an August night but we would run to the carport closet and put on stocking hats and the old Notre Dame jackets to disguise ourselves so we could charge back to home base. If whoever was "it" couldn't call you out by name, you were safe, "home free."

Then there were the Sundays at Camp Columbus. Being one of the "four little kids" we couldn't go until after Mom's nap. I'll never forget the day I decided to swim. I don't know how Mom and Dad knew which ones could swim and which ones couldn't. Anyway, I was labeled as one who couldn't. But after watching my brothers I figured out how to do the dead man's float. Daddy saw me and ran in with his shoes and socks on to save me. Needless to say, Mom taught me to swim soon after that.

The one thing all of us have great memories of is "late nights at the kitchen table." Think of all the Fritos, Cheetos, and Black Label beer that was consumed there. To this day George swears that Black Label has more alcohol than any other beer. One never could leave a well attended night at the kitchen table with any prospect of feeling good upon waking up the next day.

My all-time favorite kitchen table night was probably the Christmas Eve in the mid-'70s when we started singing Christmas carols. We had found out years earlier when they changed the Mass that none of us could sing, but we found out this night that none of us even knew any but the first few words to some of the most basic Christmas songs. They were especially disappointed with me, insinuating that since I was a teacher at the time I should know the words to seasonal standards.

We finally settled on one carol whose tune we liked. It was *Oh Christmas Tree*. Unfortunately, though we knew the melody well enough, those were the only *words* we knew, so we sang them as every line of every verse. With great energy and enthusiasm. After about an hour of this refraining, we were close to having worn the words out when someone suggested that we should take our song to the streets, that we should go caroling around the neighborhood. This was about 2 a.m. So we sang our way — "*Oh Christmas Tree, Oh Christmas Tree, Oh Christmas Tree, Oh*

Christmas Tree, Oh Christmas Tree, Oh Christmas Tree" — down to the Pospisils' house and caroled there for the few minutes it took us to realize no one was home.

Cecilia, Charles, and Carol at the legendary kitchen table.
Before their singing days. Note Daddy is in his uniform shirt and tie at
three o'clock on what must have been a Sunday afternoon,
there being no other afternoons he was ever not at work.

247

Of course, we all felt terrible on Christmas Day, but this was becoming an Erickson tradition. And that morning I realized what a pest we "little ones" must have been to the Big Boys at 7 a.m. on those Christmas mornings when they had first started spending long nights at that sticky table.

My last story is about the time Daddy went up to George and asked him what he was doing home and told him to get a hair-cut. At this time George was still a little gun-shy of Ericksons. It wasn't until George started saying "Yes, sir" that Daddy realized it wasn't Doug he was talking to. I'm sure the only reason Daddy figured it out so quickly was that none of us have ever said the word "sir" to him. That is something I want to thank Mom and Dad for. There has never been any stiffness in our family. We have always been able to express our opinions without any fear, and believe me, we did. I only hope I can instill the same respect and openness in my children.

— Cecilia

6 3

Did Someone Say "Ouch"

Little Cecilia, at age six, was bouncing on her bed trampoline-style when she lost control of the situation and bounded into the wall. She was so out of control, however, that she missed the wall and hit a window.

Cecilia broke the window without cutting herself. All she did to herself was break her collarbone. In the confusion over the tragedy, which required racing to the hospital, it was hardly noted that she had violated three rigorous rules: one forbidding bouncing on beds, another forbidding breaking windows, and also the one forbidding breaking bones.

Still, there was considerable sympathy for her broken collarbone. The first significant injury ever to one of the three treasured girls, and so serious as to require an overnight confinement at the hospital conveniently located one mile from both our new and old houses. Convenient, because this is where Mrs. Erickson, who was pregnant at the time, always went to be delivered temporary relief from that chronic condition.

Actually, Cecilia didn't break a window. On this spring day, it had been raised. And there was great relief that Cecilia had not bounced right on through the flimsy screen standing in its place, which was all that kept her missile of a body from hurtling through that second-story maw.

We analyzed the accident many times. Our conclusion was always the same: Had her guardian angel not intervened, she should by all known laws of physics have broken right on through the thin screen and into a 15-foot fall which could only have ended by her being splattered on the ornate circular part of the front yard's concrete walkway.

That we were sure of.

No matter how out of control she was at the time, she would certainly have landed on the concrete if the flimsy old screen hadn't been strong enough to break her collarbone.

When she got home from the hospital and was sentenced to serve three days in that same bed and another six weeks in a cumbersome bandage, Cecilia could hardly agree that she was lucky. She admitted, though, that she was fortunate to have broken something other than the window. Breaking it would have warranted a severe scolding.

⟪⟫

We didn't have near the number of injuries we deserved. The boys knew they would get a stern "I warned you!" instead of sympathy from Mr. and Mrs. Erickson alike for all reported sports injuries, so we played our back yard athletics with a care above and beyond the call of the game. Still, David broke his arm when he got rolled out of bounds and onto the street while playing football with friends in high school in someone else's yard. Daddy was more upset about him landing in the street than he was about his broken arm. We were *never* allowed to play *in the street*, and were expected to have sense enough to not play where we could be rolled onto it.

I dislocated a little finger once in one of our family football games. Most memorable because the Novocain shot pumped into my disengaged digit was far worse than the injury. It took the doctor three hard plunges, the needle filling with sickening blood on each pull back, to get 3 ml of purported pain killer into the bottom half of that 5 ml little pinky. The numbing hurt far worse than merely pulling it back into place would have. Many years later, I dislocated another finger playing volleyball on a grass court 40 feet from a hospital's emergency room doors. Rather than enter, I pulled.

Paul destroyed both knees playing pickup football in college, but this was after he had left home and it was his problem, not the parents'. They were right in adopting this distinction. The scarred knees that Paul lugs around with him and that have a hard time finding their momentum in most sports are definitely his problem.

⑩

Frank and Douglas led the list of major at-home injuries.

Frank started the rich tradition of scaring Mrs. Erickson to death by coming pretty close to that outcome way back when he, Harold, and Allen were about the only little Erickson angels who had traded in their little angel wings for bones.

The way the dragons tell this story, Allen dropped a sack of bricks from the top of the back stairs at the old house right onto Frank's fuzzy little bony head. The sack of bricks wasn't visibly damaged. Little Frank was not so hearty. Something about the way he didn't move and couldn't open his eyes convinced Harold and Allen that they better inform Mrs. Erickson, who was definitely pregnant at the time, what the mean old sack of bricks had done to Frank.

Frank recovered well enough — although his nose appears to have been styled at Madison Square Garden — and went on to break the family's first bone when he landed wrong while making a routine high-flight leap from the back yard swing.

The only other reported case of pseudo-malicious unconsciousness came between Frank's two accidents. He, Harold, Allen, and David were playing in the side yard of the old house with a large box. They had conned John into thinking it would be fun to ride in the large box, then combined their forces and took out a few years of frustration built up against this crafty, but weak, younger brother as they rolled the box accidentally hard into an oak tree.

It was awful quiet in the box after the leaves had finally settled. They looked in, then dragged John out into the open so they could get a better perspective. Lying there in the yard much like Frank had after being hit by a sack of bricks, John didn't look so good. Which meant they had to call for Mommy again and stand by guiltily while she commenced with the frantic sighing, gasping, and running back and forth necessary for bringing children back to life.

After what they did to John, Mrs. Erickson, who was pregnant, made a rule against knocking each other unconscious. It never happened again.

I discovered a loophole in that rule shortly after taking my number in life. The rule didn't prohibit knocking ourselves unconscious so I dove out of the highchair headfirst onto a concrete basement floor. The doctors couldn't find any visible damage, but warned the parents not to expect much from me for the rest of my life. Not ones to heed a doctor's warning, they continue to ask from time to time when I'm going to get a job.

⦿

Douglas tried a variation of that same loophole years later when he was old enough to be little. He tried knocking himself out but, little kid that he was, he failed.

He was playing by himself — not uncommon for this strange blond-haired edition — in the corner of the back yard at the old house where Daddy had long ago ambitiously built a large barbecue pit out of towering red bricks. Douglas managed to pull a whole side of the pit (the equivalent of a small brick wall) onto himself. He was not only decently injured, he was also pinned.

Mrs. Erickson, who was, of course, pregnant at the time, struggled to get him free, then rushed him to the hospital. He was patched up and returned home that night, just in time to hear Daddy angrily hissing a ban on playing around the barbecue pit.

Several years later Douglas managed to do something inconceivable. He slammed both of his hands into the heavy back doors of the panel truck Daddy used in his business. I slammed one of my hands in a truck door just a few years back when I was supposedly grown up and trying to hurry brothers Louis and Paul down to the beer store to pick up a fresh keg for a Labor Day party.

I had to exhibit extreme clumsiness to pull that off so I admire the degree of difficulty demonstrated by Douglas's feat of slamming both hands at once.

Fingers on both hands were cut to the bones. There was a grand mixture of blood and flesh. We all felt really bad looking at his little flailing extremities that day, and for about the next two months. It's a good thing that, as a pathologist, most of Doctor Doug's surgery today is done on people already dead.

Ⓜ

Ⓜ

Ⓜ

Ⓜ

And then there was the day Paul died. Yes, little Paul. Little Paul the super athlete. Little Paul the guitar picker. Little Paul the accountant. Handsome little Paul, who ranked so high on everybody's list of people they liked best.

And then there was the day Paul died. He was twenty-five.

Ⓜ

Sure, we had talked about death some. We knew it was out there. But knowing it and seeing it are such different sides of the coin of life.

Sure, there were times over the years when a bunch of us would be sitting around the kitchen table late at night drinking too many of Daddy's cold beers and the subject of a death in the family somehow raised its ugly head and we'd all look hard at our beers, looking hard for the humor, because humor or, at least cynicism, was how we were conditioned to deal with anything and everything. Anything and everything but a death in the family.

A death in the family. Yeah, we knew that there would come that night when we would be gathered again around that kitchen table — only someone would be missing because it wouldn't be a wedding that had brought us together. A death in the family. We knew it would happen because it would have to happen because life is so intimidatingly terminal. We knew that. And we also knew that if there was one thing in life that we did not know it was how we would deal with a death in the family.

What would we laugh about over those kitchen table beers when we had gathered for a funeral? We knew just about everything, Everything except the answer to that. . . .

I was at a friend's house in Nashville one Saturday evening in the spring of 1979. Three of us, three long-time college buddies, were playing Scrabble and talking basketball. NCAA tournament time. Tennessee was playing Notre Dame in a tournament game the next day. Big doings in our little worlds. And lots of anxious excitement that night as we whiled away the hours playing Scrabble. Chess was mentioned. And I told the story I rarely tell about chess — about the time a couple of years earlier when I was in the vise-grip of a nervous breakdown while living in Florida, and how the only thing going my way was that my good brother and good buddy Paul happened to be staying with me when the nervous breakdown struck. . . .

+

Paul was working with brother Philip's accounting firm in Naples during that basketball spring of 1979. He was working that same Saturday that my friends and I had gathered in Nashville. He could have been watching the afternoon tournament games on television, but Paul preferred working to loafing. He called his girlfriend, Jackie, just before leaving the office late that afternoon to tell her he was heading home. She was going to meet him at the house he shared with Steve — the other member of Philip's CPA firm. They were going to grill steaks. Moose steaks. Steve's friend had shot a moose and given them some cuts.

+

. . . And it was the week before Christmas. 1977. Not a very good year. And not a very good time of the year to be toying with a nervous breakdown.

Christmas, I found out, is the big nervous breakdown season. To get into a hospital that week, you have to have made reservations in August. The symptoms were there in August, but I had not read them very well. Had not made reservations.

I had spent August talking to God. And He talked to me. But somehow I had missed some of what He was trying to say. And then His birthday came, and I was in trouble. Whitewater trouble.

+

Paul arrived home, stopped at the utility room, set his briefcase down, and decided to retrieve a box of soap from behind the clothes dryer. The box had fallen a few days earlier when he was doing some laundry. He knew Steve was planning to wash clothes later that night, and Paul was never the kind of person to make anyone pick up after him.

+

So Paul was babysitting me over that stifling Christmas in Florida as we tried to guess what to do about my falling ever more apart. Neither of us had any experience with that sort of thing. We both wanted to do what was right. What we finally did was call John — ever-competent John — who was also living in the area at the time. Paul in Naples, John and me near Clearwater. And John quickly solved the immediate crisis by getting me an appointment with a slightly famous psychiatrist. Famous for having treated a Kennedy, or two. John can fix almost anything.

+

Jackie, Paul's girlfriend, must have arrived just a minute or two behind him. While walking to the back door, she heard a noise from the utility room. She stopped to look. Saw Paul's legs draped over the dryer. The rest of his body tucked between the back of the dryer and the wall. He was gasping in his hiding place behind the dryer. She thought he was trying to scare her. She said, "Quit joking, Paul."

+

And the story I was telling my friends in Nashville that Saturday had to do with how I was sitting there on the second or third morning of my falling apart and Paul was babysitting me by playing chess and it was all I could do to keep from falling out of my chair as my over-anxious nerves pitched and rolled, again and again. And I was smoking maybe two or three cigarettes at once and life could hardly have gotten much worse but then all of a sudden it got much worse because Paul trapped my queen and took her out of the game. But crazy people can think clearer in many ways than normal people so I responded to the loss of my queen by surrounding myself with a nice new batch of cigarettes and getting a firmer grip on the chair I was teetering in and turned as many channels of my quaking mind as possible over to the issue at hand. I came back and won that game because I just had to win because I had another of my three-year winning streaks on the line and I just had to win because it was so important to still be good for something.

257

And when we were finished, Paul let me get back to the roiling degeneration he had so effectively distracted me from.

+

When Paul didn't answer with anything more than another couple of gasps, Jackie got scared and said again, "Come on, Paul. This joke isn't very funny." But he just gasped a few more times. He was wearing shorts because it's hot in Florida. She touched one of the legs sticking out from behind the dryer — and then realized that Paul was not joking. His leg was clammy. The gasps were awfully real.

+

I can't say much about the nervous breakdown. Not because I don't know, but because it goes on forever. And when I was telling the story that Saturday night in Nashville, I left out almost everything about it because no one ever wants to hear about someone else's journey through that very dark side of life. But I hit the key point that I owed no end of fun and debt to Paul. And my two friends, who knew Paul from the times he and Charles had come to Nashville to play basketball and softball and football with us, both said the same thing. They both said, "You know, I really like Paul. He's one of those people you just really enjoy being around." Yes, I knew that. We all knew that we all liked Paul. What we did not know was that Paul had died and that he had maybe died while I was telling that story.

+

Jackie screamed for Steve who was in the back yard already grilling the steaks. Steve used to play football for the University of Florida. A big guy. It was easy enough for him to pull Paul — his roommate, his co-worker, his close friend — out from behind the dryer and lay him on the driveway. Steve had seen a lot of death while touring Vietnam. It was easy enough for him to see what was happening as Paul finally quit gasping, turned gray, and died there on the driveway.

+

While we were warmly remembering him. . . . A thousand miles away. . . .

+

Steve's frantic attempts at mouth-to-mouth resuscitation and heart massage could not get Paul's pulse going again. Jackie had called for an ambulance, which arrived quickly because the station was nearby. But just as the paramedics thought they were maybe reviving the dead boy in the driveway, they ran out of oxygen. They had brought a nearly empty tank.

+

But then a doctor, a plastic surgeon, stopped his car at the house. The doctor just happened to be driving down that dead end street on a Saturday afternoon to pick up a fishing companion. The doctor just happened to have a tank of oxygen in his car. Not that many doctors will stop as they pass an accident. Even fewer doctors — almost none — carry oxygen in their cars.

The good doctor got Paul breathing, and got his heart beating again. Before turning him over to the paramedics for the race to the hospital, the good doctor pointed at some little burns on Paul's chest and a massive burn on Paul's elbow and explained to Steve and Jackie that their young friend had been electrocuted behind the dryer. He said Paul would make it to the hospital. But warned them not to get their hopes up. Told them that people, even healthy young men, don't survive electrocution.

+

. . . When we finished the long game of Scrabble, I called my brother Douglas — completing his residency at Vanderbilt University Hospital — to see if he would still be able to get together with me the next day to watch the Tennessee-Notre Dame game. It was a big game. "No," he said. "Michael, I've been trying to reach you," he said, "I've got some bad news." His voice was strange. Serious, but impossible to read. I didn't say anything and waited for the bad news.

259

A flat tire can be bad news. A broken air conditioner. I had no idea what kind of bad news he was going to give me.

"Michael. Paul's been hurt. Hurt bad." Well, I mean to tell you that there's bad news and there's bad news and what Douglas said to me on the phone in those simple little words — "Paul's been hurt. Hurt bad." — was the all-time winner in the world of bad news.

There's this thing, you see, that had been going on between Paul and me for maybe four years. I don't know how it got started, but I knew it was there. For several years, we had made a practice of greeting each other after every absence with a warm and friendly handshake. The same warm and friendly handshake was a part of every fond farewell. There were a lot of greetings and departures over those years. Lots of handshakes. The handshake was some kind of an inside joke — or maybe an inside recognition. Neither of us ever knew or bothered asking. It was just something that said something about the special way we felt about each other. If I had to guess, I would say that it stated for us that we were more than family — we were friends; that we were more than friends — we were family. We were close. Close enough to touch.

And when Douglas said so gravely that Paul had been hurt, my mind reeled — yes, minds will reel — and I saw Paul and I saw him going down in a boating accident out in the Gulf of Mexico and I saw him bloodied by a car accident on a straight Florida highway and I was trying to imagine what had happened but my first question was, "Is he going to live?" And Doctor Doug who deals in death said simply enough, "I don't know. It looks very bad."

And then he told me as much as he knew about what had happened and how all he knew was that Paul was still in the emergency room and that Philip was going to call him back from Naples as soon as anyone knew anything else.

+

... *My friends were still in the room talking basketball or books or something very, very small when I hung up the phone and walked out into the spring night and knelt under a big experienced tree and asked God to see if He maybe couldn't reach down and spare one of the best kids in the universe. I mean, what can you say? "Let him live, God. Please, let him live. I've asked for a lot of things in the past, God. Things having to do with girls or money or jobs or success — but now I see that those are nothing, God. And now I'm not just asking for anything — I'm begging for everything. Let him live God. Please-let-him-live."*

+

... *When I walked back indoors I lit a cigarette and sat quietly for a few minutes before interrupting the conversation by saying to my friends in a voice they had never heard me speak from before, "That phone call . . . I just heard the worst news I've ever heard." And I told them about Paul and they were as sad about it as anyone could be because they knew me and they knew Paul and they knew almost everyone in the family, and they knew what was going down.*

+

... *And so I drove back to my apartment and it was a short drive but, wouldn't you know it — because I knew it was going to happen — that in just a matter of the four minutes it took to do that drive the radio managed to play the one five-year-old song that touched the situation more than any other song possibly could. It's a song by Elton John and that's important because it was Paul who had convinced me many years earlier that Elton John was more of a talent than a freak and it was Paul that I always thought of whenever I heard that early song by Elton John about how he thinks he sees his dead brother: "God it looks like Daniel, must be the clouds in my eyes." That song. That night.*

+

. . . And the night was strange, because life is strange. And life is even stranger when there is death in the air. The lights, the traffic, the lively people driving by in their cars, headed somewhere that doesn't matter and isn't important, and it doesn't even matter that it doesn't matter because they can laugh and talk and laugh as they go about their business and even the birds and the crickets — the ones tied so closely to nature that they're almost real — just go right on going on and even they don't seem to notice that the world is supposed to stop because the earth is being shaken by the loss of a favorite son. No, life goes on. But it's a very removed life that pulses when death is in the air.

+

I called the hospital in Naples when I got to my apartment, but there was no news. Philip said it was still a matter of just waiting — that Paul had been taken up for a brain scan. That he, Philip, had made it to the hospital in time to see Paul reeled past on a stretcher on his way to the brain scanning, and that it was . . . well, that Paul was unconscious and convulsing and that his eyes were open but there was nothing there and that . . . well, that it looked very, very bad. . .

So I joined the game of waiting.

+

Two girls stopped by. They wanted me to go clubbing with them because it was Saturday night. But the way I told them "no" prompted one of them to quip, "You act like you're going to a funeral." Someone in the family called and the girls overheard the phone conversation, so I explained to them what was happening. They knew Paul from his occasional visits to Nashville, like everyone seemed to know Paul, and they were as sad as everyone. They left me alone, because that was what I needed. I was learning fast how to deal with life's other side.

+

And as the night wore on I realized that I had no choice but to catch the first flight to Naples. It left early the next morning. Jumping on that flight was the kind of thing I hadn't been able to do for the two years since the onset of the nervous breakdown, but jumping on that flight was my only choice. If Paul was going to die, I had to be there to say goodbye. If he was going to live, I had to be there to shake his hand.

When I got there the next morning, little had changed. He was breathing and his heart was beating. They thought he might actually live. But, his brain, the doctors said, would be severely damaged because of the time he spent dead on that driveway.

+

Paul was tied to a jungle of machines in intensive care.

It was almost two days before he came out of his coma. I was there at the time. His brain was a mess but he finally recognized me through the fog, broke into a smile, and, straining the intravenous life support system, reached out his hand.

+

"Hey, Paul. Welcome back," I choked, clasping that hand more than shaking it. All he could do was mumble through the tubes wedged into his mouth and down his throat. But his dopey eyes smiled brightly.

Because he suffered from amnesia for the next few days and could never gain a steady reference in time I got to see that hand reach out and that bright "Haven't-seen-you-in-a while" smile three or four times a day. And the greeting once he began talking, "Hey, Michael! Wha's happ'nin'?"

Others were there. Had flown in during those two days. They were the younger brothers and sisters he was used to seeing during those fragments of time in the past that he would settle

263

into whenever he woke. Seeing Carol was not such a big deal because he was waking to a day four years earlier when he and Carol were sharing an apartment at the university. Seeing Charles was not such a big deal because he and Charles were also together a lot during those days.

Seeing Mother, however, was disturbing. She and Carol had flown together from Chattanooga that same morning that I arrived. Mother quit visiting him at the hospital during this stretch because it was obvious her presence scared him. He would wake, look around the room, place himself at some time in his earlier life, smile brightly when he saw me or another brother to one side of the bed, and then tremble when he saw Mother at the other side. Mother was a very busy person, and there was no way she was going to be in a hospital room with him unless it was something very serious. Paul would collect himself enough to ask her, "Mommy, am I going to die?"

Mother quit visiting because that question was too hard to answer.

+

Yes, Paul, you are going to die.

Not that time, but sometime.

And sometime we are all going to die. That phone is going to ring 16 times in the years ahead and 16 times it is going to melt our core. . . .

6 4

Life Has Its Winning Moments

Dear Nieces and Nephews, and Hopefully Healthy Readers,

Paul not only lived, he didn't suffer any of the brain damage the doctors felt sure would have set in during the minutes he was dead. It was, by all accounts, a miraculous survival and a miraculous recovery. One that could never have happened had Paul not been in perfect physical condition before the accident.

His will to live was so strong that Paul ate his vegetables. Between the two subsequent life-threatening bouts with surgeries

265

he underwent during the next two weeks (orthopedic and plastic surgery to repair what was left of his electrically fried elbow), almost bleeding to death before our very eyes after one surgery because he had the wrong mix of anti-coagulants, Paul ate every vegetable the hospital delivered. He understood that he had to regain whatever bits and pieces of strength he could get his hands on as his energy kept getting sapped by setbacks.

His various brothers and sisters had enough vacation time stored up to work shifts in maintaining the 24-hour watch for those first two weeks. We broke every rule the hospital had, but we kept him from climbing out of bed and killing himself while trying to

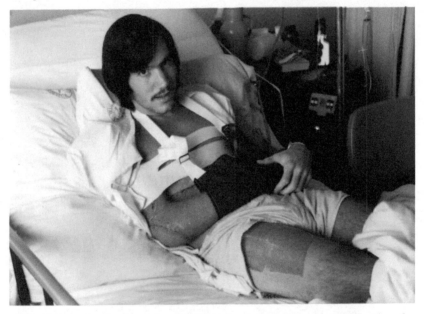

stumble to the bathroom. Paul had a hard time remembering he was incapacitated. The nurses were glad we were around to remind him. And to make sure he ate those vegetables.

⊚

He passed his CPA exam a few months after the accident. That was a great moral victory for him since he had failed two sections of that exam prior to suffering whatever brain damage might have set in. He later won a sizable lawsuit because of the faulty dryer and used that money to pay his way through law school.

Ⓜ

A year after the accident, when Paul was pretty much through his remarkable recovery, I was visiting him in Naples. Carol and Louis were there as well. Everyone was joking and carrying on and I was just sitting back thinking to myself how incredible it was that Paul was sitting across from me — alive and as bright and entertaining as ever. I was thinking about how extremely fortunate we were to still have Paul with us, when he looked up at me and said, "You know, Michael, you were so mentally wiped out a few years ago that Louis and I talked about how it was too bad that we had lost you. I remember telling Louis, 'I don't think Michael will ever be the same. He's really gone.' And Louis agreed. And we talked about how we had at least shared some great times with you before it all happened. And I was just sitting here thinking how incredible it is to have you back." And we shook hands . . . because . . . in our family it's against the rules for the boys to show emotion. . . .

Mostly Pregnant
BOOK FOUR

Book Four

The original art work was poorly reproduced. Technology has come a long way in 40 years. And working with original photographs is always much better.

CHAPTER 65

War Zones
And Goo

Our roaches had roaches.

They must have.

Our big black roaches crawled home in the morning only to find a horde of little brown ones scattering from their subterranean nests.

We never saw a big black roach stomp on a little brown one, but it must have happened.

⬤

Chattanooga roaches come in two distinct varieties. Big, ugly, brazen black roaches that crackle when stepped on and that are stuffed with yellow goo. These we called, rightly or wrongly, cockroaches.

Then there were the smaller brown ones that ranged in size from about one-half to one inch. The smaller brown ones could be stepped on without that obnoxious crunching sensation. And they were not nearly so filed with goo. These we called brown roaches.

At times, the big black cockroaches would dominate in our two-story mon- olith of a house. Other times they would be overwhelmed by sheer numbers of medium-sized brown ones.

And sometimes both species seemed to prosper, coexisting in peace.

And sometimes, we would coexist at peace. With all our roaches.

But over the years we carried out numerous police actions. Had prolonged search and destroy missions. And even routinely declared all-out war. The roaches, though, could not be defeated. They could be superficially eradicated. They could be pushed back to established parameters. They might temporarily go into hiding, retreating to their deepest and darkest crevices. But, always, the roaches would launch a new offensive.

We could have spent those years fighting Chinamen, as Amer- ican men in the Fifties were wont to say, and gained more ground than we did against those always encroaching roaches.

⦿

Ours was an old house. Finished in 1917. Its first floor built of jagged, reddish-brown stones ranging in size from basketballs at the bottom to softballs at the top.

Old houses in the South are notorious for their roaches — and ours was a credit to that reputation.

The roaches held themselves to one general area of the house — the mess hall. They stayed almost exclusively in the breakfast room, kitchen, and the small, roughly finished basement that ran below those two rooms. Occasionally one big black roach might find its way to the upstairs bathroom, or several of the brown roaches might  travel to that forbidden realm. But the elders tried hard to keep inexperienced youngsters from venturing upstairs because it was well understood in the dark depths of roachdom that Mrs. Erickson reacted to invasions of her bathroom by declaring another all-out war.

We occasionally eavesdropped from the kitchen as they held congress at their roach headquarters in the basement. Over time and successive generations, our roaches had evolved to speaking loud so they could be heard over the constant clamor we plagued them with from our part of the house. We would overhear the leadership, the elders, order its members, aptly called an "intrusion," time and again to *never* climb up to Mrs. Erickson's bathroom. Still, delinquent juveniles almost annually insisted on seeing what was up there — what made this territory so forbidden. What was up there was Mrs. Erickson's bare feet.

This was the one room in the whole house that she insisted on walking into without wearing her shoes or slippers. What was up there was the commander-in-chief of the relatively small — but only when compared to the number of enemies — Erickson Household Army. On its side, the Household Army had the advantage of technology. Our roaches had numbers. And evolution.

All our roaches had to do to survive the routine daily skirmishes was dash into hiding at the first sound of a foot, or dodge the shoe targeting it on an open floor. But when the ante was upped by a second-floor incursion, the Erickson Household Army launched Chemical Warfare.

Retaliation for an invasion of Mrs. Erickson's bare-footed space was prolonged and heavy. The roaches in the bathroom could easily be annihilated with only two nights of spraying. But there were punitive damages attached to that offense. Thousands of innocent roaches — if there could be such a thing — who had obeyed their leaders' warnings and stayed only in the breakfast room and kitchen would be driven from their feeding grounds by a ten-day series of nightly sprayings into the many crevices that made these rooms such cozy quarters for our prehistoric housemates.

Several times over the years, an enraged and wrathful Mrs. Erickson even enlisted the forces of an impressive ally — our next

door neighbor, Mr. Haddock. Mr. Haddock just happened to operate the city's Terminix Exterminating Company franchise. Convenient, but ultimately just one of life's sad ironies.

Mr. Haddock would move in with heavy artillery. Big, hand-held silver tanks with long spray hoses that dispersed chemicals so lethal average Chattanoogans were not allowed to spray them. And he upped the ante even higher: Biological Warfare. The time bombs he planted in strategic corners and trails attacked their reproductive cycles, causing considerable grief and disruption of both civic and family life within the roach communities.

Mr. Haddock took the war to the actual basement, an area that remained a demilitarized zone in our day-to-day, month-to-month skirmishes. Our conventional weapons were impotent in that dark subterranean nesting ground.

It was small in its functional area, barely large enough for the water heater and furnace, and not suitable for any significant storage other than small fire hazards of the oily rag variety that visiting firemen would annually instruct school children to look for around their houses. But extending from the basement's one open room — its rough, black stone walls and its dark, forbidding con-crete floor barely illuminated by a single hanging bulb — was a vast field of dirt underlying the entire rest of the house, about one foot beneath the floors above. This massive area could not be penetrated by anything human, but was a dark, dirty delight to our roaches.

Mr. Haddock's best efforts were awarded with high-tech lulls, but the roaches always returned in force.

⦾

Over the years, our roaches at least tried to cooperate. The brown ones and black ones fought between themselves for food supply and breeding space but both species seemed to strive for long periods to achieve unprovocative cohabitation with the Erickson family.

One rule they obeyed almost universally was they did not come out during the daytime. Or even at night while any of the less evolved residents of the house were still up.

During the summer and over Christmas holidays when the bipeds might stay up regularly until two or three in the morning drinking beer and telling each other what life is all about, the roaches had to make great sacrifices to adhere to their status of feigned non-existence.

The person stepping from the breakfast room to the refrigerator in the kitchen for another round of beers often reported hearing the roaches whining behind the nearby basement door. One shiny black beast overheard saying, "Aren't those loudmouths ever going to go to bed!?!" A young roach's high voice responding, hopefully, "I heard one of the older brothers say he would have just one last beer." An elder retorting cynically that he had known that "one-last-beer" routine to go on until just before dawn when the old man who lived in the house got up and started cooking his daybreak bacon. "Why did you have to go and mention bacon!?!" the first roach would moan. "I haven't eaten anything all week except for that awful tasting insulation they've got wrapped around the water heater. And my kids are now telling me that's junk food. No nutrients."

The roaches weren't any more excited about our coming home from college than was the laundry lady, Mrs. Erickson.

⦾

Mother roach tells baby how to dodge the bottom of shoes.

The mother roaches tried to teach their babies how to behave with people.

They taught them that if they ever got caught out in the open after light to run for the nearest wall and stay there until it was safe to get back behind the floorboards. "If you can't get under a floorboard, climb the wall."

The mother roaches knew it was permissible — sometimes mandatory — that roaches on the floor be stepped on, but that the mother of the bipeds did not allow smashing them into the walls.

"It's because we have yellow goo instead of blood," the mother roaches explained.

◫

Killing thousands of roaches with our impersonal sprays and other elements of chemical warfare was easy. But killing them one at a time with sheer, brute force was degrading. For both species.

Thoughtfully illustrating what might be the single advantage of human evolution, we found that the best way to kill roaches individually was to wait until an errant roach —spotted crossing the kitchen floor any time during the day or during our nightly beer-fueled therapy sessions — gets closer to someone else in the family than it is to you. Then, with feigned alarm, you point to the roach's existence and the person closest to it is obligated by family tradition to immediately cease that roach's existence. Unless, under the guise of making the kill, he can scare it closer to another sibling. "Quick! *You* kill it!"

Stepping on a roach — especially the black, crunchy variety — creates a horrible sensation that reverberates through the stepper's entire body, to say nothing of the roach's. However, taking off a shoe and smashing the roach by using the shoe as a flat, flexible paddle significantly depersonalizes the experience. At least for the human. Flip-flops make ideal roach bats.

Cleaning up the gooey mess is distasteful no matter how you kill a roach. So we mastered the art of killing roaches with blows just fatal enough to break down life functions, but not hard enough to knock the stuffing out of them. This battering takes more time since the light first blow often only stuns the roach and it might take two more touches to achieve the desired effect of absolute death.

Absolute death is the only acceptable kind of death when dealing with roaches since it is a known fact in the South that any roach with even one percent of its life remaining abuses that one percent by crawling into a crevice — maybe even out of a trash bin

and then into a crevice — where, with its last putrefying particle
of life, it will lay three million fresh roach eggs.

6 6

Summer Sundays
Our Rituals At The Lake

The Ericksons seldom gather in whole these days.

Family vacations to far off places — which always meant nowhere more nor less far than St. Joseph, Missouri — were as few and far between as our new station wagons.

St. Joseph, Missouri, was home of the Pony Express. Riders mounted horses from the corral, grabbed a mail pouch, and started galloping to Sacramento.

St. Joseph, Missouri, was also home of the clapboard house where Frank Ford shot Jesse James. And Mother's family.

We drove there in the new 1953 red Ford station wagon. And again in the new 1957 yellow Ford wagon. Daddy couldn't get away from work in the summer of 1962 when we had our new blue Chevrolet station wagon. The home of the Pony Express had to do without Ericksons that decade, and forever after.

But our summer vacations from school were filled with fun. Routine fun. "Routine" because everything we did was what we had done before.

Same ball games in nice weather. Same card games and board games in the rain.

And the same trips to Camp Columbus every Sunday after-noon. "Trips" because we didn't all fit in the station wagon, so the older ones, with a teenage driver, would make the 30 minute drive along narrow, twisty, country roads in Daddy's flower company's delivery van, with the younger of those elders perched, in the days

before seat belts, or even seats, on steel wheel wells in the back. Or as was of-ten tried with very poor re-sults, sitting (sliding) un-secured in the back of the van in the two fold-up lawn chairs the parents would later sit in when they got to the sandy lakeside beach.

Our vans were white, and clean, but often carried six "passengers."

The early Ford Econoline vans had only a front driver's seat and a passenger seat. The next best, and only relatively se-cure position, reserved for the third oldest in the van, was sitting on the black engine box between those two seats. Fourth best position was sitting on the back half of that same engine box, facing backward. The engine box got progressively hotter and hotter during the half-hour nonair conditioned drives. But it was still notably better than the rear wheel wells or our repeated failures to make lawn chairs hold up to accelerations when lights changed, braking, and the several 90-degree turns as the driver raced to the lake.

In later years, when John, always a take-charge kind of guy, helped Mother by sometimes grilling hamburgers and hot dogs for the evening picnic to replace her fried chicken, those perched on the sweaty steel wheel wells in the back had a grill on wheels to contend with as they bore the 30 minute drive in the hot box with no air circulating to the rear

Mrs. Erickson, her pregnancies behind her, with Louis (No. 10) to her right and Charles (No. 13), on her left.

Chickamauga Lake was formed within the Tennessee River when TVA built a series of dams to generate electricity. Chattanooga's electricity came from the Chickamauga Dam, whose crossing, the expansive lake on one side and the narrow river far below on the other, was the unofficial halfway mark of those weekly summer drives.

Camp Columbus was another 15 minutes down the road. It was owned by the Knights of Columbus, the Catholic Church's version of Shriners. Instead of clown cars, the Knights showed up at Sunday Mass a couple of times a year in full regalia: tuxedos, capes, chapeaus, white gloves, and, by far most important to any young knight-to-be, their glistening, silver swords.

281

It cost $50 per year for Knights from Chattanooga's three Catholic churches to get a key to the lakesite's front gate each

summer. But $150 for non-Knights. Daddy was a non-Knight, in both fact and spirit. But somehow, early in our bunny-like expansion, he had talked the Knights into letting him buy the annual key at the Knight price. Probably because the Knights also sponsored the Boy Scout troop, of which his growing number of boys were prominent fixtures.

After that first year of our establishing a routine of going to the lake every Sunday on Daddy's discounted key, the next routine was the one in which every May the pregnant Mrs. Erickson would tell her husband during supper that he needed to call about the key since summer Sundays were boring down on us. It always took that first mention, followed a few days later by a reminder, then a few days after that by an *order* for Daddy to make what was likely his most uncomfortable annual phone call.

He didn't like begging. But, even less, he wasn't about to part with $150 ($27 million or so in today's dollars) for something that could be had for a third of that price. So, every year, he would finally make the call explaining to each new King of the Knights that, for reasons he could never easily justify, his family has always been allowed to use the lake property at member prices. Every year, his phone calls secured a key, though there were a few in which the King Knight, an unknown man from another parish, might make him sweat and suffer by, instead of immediately agreeing, saying, "I'll have to look into this. Make a few calls."

But, every year, we got a key. And, every year, the Erickson family with its unshakable Sunday afternoon routine and its plethora of guppies, made almost as much use of Camp Columbus as all the benighted Catholic families combined. We were as much of a fixture as the damp bathhouse and the picnic tables.

Eileen pyramiding on the shoulders of Frank, right, and his high school friend.

After swimming for a couple of hours, instead of changing in the damp bathhouse near the roped-off swimming area, the Ericksons would pile into their station wagon and van and drive to the picnic area on the hill that only they seemed to know about. The one with a dry bathhouse whose men's and women's showers had hot water. And after those hot showers and a change into dry clothes, the Ericksons would gather at one or two of the otherwise never used tables and, every summer Sunday, eat the chicken pieces Mrs. Erickson had spent two hours frying Saturday night before stowing them into the refrigerator and then stuffing them into Daddy's two well-iced coolers filled in the early years with a lot of Coca-Colas, and a few beers. The Cokes were the "large" 10 oz. size, whose green, returnable bottles were stamped on the bottom with the names of various random, distant towns where they had been bottled. "Small" Cokes were in 6 oz bottles, but we always went "large." Well, at least this one time.

As younger ones kept getting older, the cooler was packed with a lot more bottles of Carling Black Label beer and not so many of those large bottles of Coke.

The legal drinking age in Tennessee was 21. Our "house rules" allowed drinking on your first visit home from college.

No one ever questioned whether one of the older ones shouldn't be driving a van full of unanchored younger kids home after having had two beers. The even younger kids were in the station wagon. No seat belts. A steel, unpadded dashboard that proved fatal in so many 1960s crashes.

We survived. And returned every empty bottle of Coke for the 3¢ deposits.

6 7

A Claim To Fame

Radios and telephones.

Gamblers and kids.

Football and higher education.

①

When I was in college, I worked full-time my sophomore year at the *Knoxville News-Sentinel*.

I was in the sports department. On football Saturdays, instead of writing, I kept a large scoreboard that carried the results of most of the college games played that day. My job was to answer our "community service Sportsline" and report the scores to any interested callers.

I did not know it at the time, but the reason 99% of callers wanted to know a college score was because they were playing football parlay cards: Cards on which you place bets on the Saturday college games after the oddsmakers have worked out a point spread.

As a budding sportswriter, I was so naive as to think men just loved scores. I was not enlightened to the reality that what those callers really loved was money until years later when, at age 30, I began helping my youngest sister fill out her football parlay card for her weekly office pool. We then sat around on Saturday afternoons paying inordinate attention to the scores shown during televised games.

I had to drive somewhere on one of those Saturday afternoons and dialed in a radio scores program to learn some additional results relevant to Carol's investment in football futures. That's when it occurred to me why football scores are in such demand.

♫ *"Give me money. That's what I want."* ♫

⊕

Every sizable city has a radio station that devotes Saturday afternoons to scores, and sells advertising to local merchants on the promise: "Trust me. Every gambler in town will be listening." Actually, what they promise is, "Every sports fan in town will be listening." But mixed with the mob of gamblers and the few scattered alumni hoping to hear how their distant team fared is a very small third group: People who like to call the radio station and ask for scores because they like making phone calls but don't have anyone to talk to.

These are the people who call in every Saturday and ask, "Could you tell me how Slippery Rock did today?" I know. I used to be one of those people. When I was ten years old. I was, in fact, the very first of those thousands of followers all across the country who called in to the local radio station to ask, "Could you tell me how Slippery Rock did today?"

⊕

Playing with the phone was great fun for kids. But it can get you in trouble. If you just punch (we, of course, could only *dial* back then) a series of numbers at random chances are incredibly high, based on my early research, you will hook up with one of its worst customers — a mean old woman who feels her life has been threatened by your call and promises to track you down and prosecute. Likely a church-going lady. Southern Baptist.

We were all hesitant about playing with the phone lest we be tracked down and shipped to the state penitentiary where the much-feared murderers and drug addicts lived.

So my brother Philip and I were pretty excited when we discovered there was a radio station in Chattanooga that we could call every Saturday afternoon without fear of prosecution. And we called it every Saturday afternoon. There was a catch, though. When the man at the station answered, he said, "Hold that line." Then he paused and we were supposed to ask about a football score we were interested in.

"Hold That Line" was the name of the radio program. It is a play on words that has been used in nearly every town with a scores program. It is an old cheer, much like "Block-that-kick!" that student bodies back in Herbert Hoover's playing days chanted when their team was on defense. "Hold that line!" implored the fans' defensive stalwarts to not give up another yard on the next play. On the radio program it also meant "hold the *telephone line,* while we look up the score you asked about." Cute.

⓪

Philip and I discovered this program in 1958. That was the year our oldest brother Harold went off to college. He went by train to Carnegie Tech. Carnegie Tech was, and still is, in Pittsburgh. Now Carnegie-Mellon, it is one of the country's premier science and engineering schools.

In our excitement about Harold going off to college, we looked up Carnegie Tech in the family's "new" ten-year-old set of *World Book Encyclopedia* a family friend donated to the house to help with homework assignments. The "C" encyclopedia affirmed that Carnegie Tech was an excellent school. In bold type at the bottom of the short narrative about the school, it conscientiously referred the reader — in this case us, to its only other reference to Carnegie Tech. It said, "See Football."

We clawed out the big, cream-colored "F" book and looked up football. Staring us in the face, figuratively jumping off the page, was a large black-and-white photograph of "footballers" armored with bulging pads and antique leather helmets while waging war on a muddy turf. One of the teams pictured was Carnegie Tech. I can't be sure of the other. Maybe Hofstra. Or Bucknell?

The caption said Carnegie Tech was a national power in football in the 1930s when the photograph was taken. That was news to us. Harold had never mentioned that Carnegie Tech was so renowned. We asked him about it when he returned home for his first Thanksgiving holiday. He seemed surprised to learn his school had a famous football team.

Feeling so much smarter than Harold, Philip and I assured him Carnegie Tech's real claim to fame had little to do with engineering and science. Its renown was for its role as a former football power: One of two schools in the explored universe whose team merited a picture in the encyclopedia.

This random bit of research in the *World Book* was the catalyst to our becoming engrossed with sports for years and years to come. Meaning whoever gave us those encyclopedias failed miserably in her efforts to encourage the Erickson brain trust. Sports fans are notoriously narrow-minded and ignorant. Indeed, as the younger half of the family became more and more interested in sports, the academic scholarships became less distinguished and farther between.

⦿

Carnegie Tech was no longer a powerhouse in football when Harold left for its distant smokestacks. Even we fledgling sports fans figured that out soon after our early infatuation.

But we had discovered in September 1958 that Carnegie Tech had a team. And that meant its name would appear every Sunday morning in *The Chattanooga Times* within the long column of small black type headlined "College Scores." That gave us something to look forward to — seeing that stupefying name so prominently displayed in the newspaper.

In our anticipation of the big day when the season finally began, we remembered there was a football scores call-in program one of the two men who worked for Daddy listened to every Saturday afternoon on the little radio in the back of the store. We didn't have to wait to see the name in the newspaper to find out how Carnegie Tech fared, though seeing it there would be akin to seeing an actual word from Jesus written red in the Bible. No, before Sunday's paper hit the porch, we could call the radio station the afternoon of the team's opening game to find out the Carnegie Tech score.

This would accomplish three monumental feats: (1) We, who had become overnight Carnegie Tech fans, would know the score soon after the game had ended; (2) We would actually hear the exalted name "Carnegie Tech" said over the radio (and a lot of other people would hear it as well); (3) It provided us with a legitimate reason to make a phone call, so it couldn't be classified as "playing with the phone." (Though any half-witted prosecutor could easily convince a jury of little old ladies that what we were doing was nothing short of a dubious cover for the crime of "playing with the phone.")

⦾

The big day came. The first Saturday of the season. The man on the radio gave his "Hold That Line" number repeatedly, but we found it impossible to get through. We dialed and dialed and dialed, but never got anything but the loud, annoying busy signal.

I say "we" dialed and dialed, though I am certain it was me who did the dialing, while my slightly older brother Philip supervised that work. It was also me who had to do the talking since I always had to do the dirty work.

When I finally lucked my way past the busy signal and got a ringing telephone the next Saturday as we repeated this exercise, it was I who had to ask the deep-voiced man on the other end of the line for the Carnegie Tech score. He said "Who?" and that frightening "Who?" boomed across our own radio at the back of the bedroom since he was talking into a microphone as well as into my phone's receiver. I stood my ground and squeaked, "Carnegie Tech."

His initial uncertainty led me to suspect he was not a regular reader of the encyclopedia.

To his credit, he understood my words and grumbled in his deep booming radio voice so that the whole city of Chattanooga could hear, "Carnegie Tech? Hold the line. I'll have to look that one up."

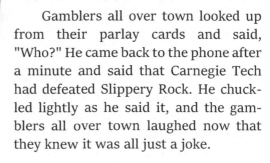

Gamblers all over town looked up from their parlay cards and said, "Who?" He came back to the phone after a minute and said that Carnegie Tech had defeated Slippery Rock. He chuckled lightly as he said it, and the gamblers all over town laughed now that they knew it was all just a joke.

Philip and I were ecstatic to hear our favorite former football power's name come booming across the big old floor console radio our grandfather had passed on to the house.

◎

The next Saturday afternoon we were back on the phone. Dialing and dialing. Sometimes I used the little pen that came with a pad that was kept on the upstairs phone table and has a little gold ball on the end that was supposed to make dialing easier. Usually I just used a rotation of my fingers since they worked better than the little gold ball on a stick.

At last I got through again. The man recognized the name of the school this time and probably recognized my high-pitched voice. He must also have known that I was really just a kid playing with the phone, but couldn't do anything about it. My tiny voice, fortunately, wasn't heard over the radio. Just his. I had asked a legitimate question, "Could you tell me how Carnegie Tech did this afternoon?"

As he repeated the name "Carnegie Tech" and said he would have to look it up, gamblers all over town, for the second week in a row, looked up from their potential gold mines and said, "Who?" Except for one gambler. One gambler knew what was going on. His name was Tommy. He worked for Daddy at the flower shop, and he knew Carnegie Tech was where Harold had gone off to college. He knew Philip and I were the ones making those calls.

He was proud to think Philip and I might grow up to be gamblers.

◍

On that second Saturday afternoon of the 1958 season, after getting the disappointing news that Carnegie Tech had lost, Philip and I decided to continue playing with the phone. We debated long and hard about what score to ask for. Being already circumstantially guilty of playing with the phone, we didn't want to be guilty of asking for a score we would already have heard. That eliminated Tennessee, the University of Chattanooga, Sewanee, Notre Dame, and every other school we were familiar with.

It finally dawned on us that we could ask about Slippery Rock. We were skeptical the previous week when the radio man said that was the team Carnegie Tech had defeated, but it was reported in black type the next morning in *The Chattanooga Times* so there was little doubt in our minds that Slippery Rock was as real as distant weather. We — which means I — dialed and dialed until the man finally answered again and I squeaked out a request for the Slippery Rock score. The radio man looked it up and informed us — and the city's gamblers — that Slippery Rock had settled for a tie that week.

The gamblers had no interest in Carnegie Tech or Slippery Rock since neither, unless you could go back to the days of leather helmets, would be among the 50 schools prominent enough to gain a line on a bettor's parlay card.

On our third Saturday of dialing and dialing and finally getting past the busy signal, Philip figured out a likely pattern. He realized on the two times each week I got through to the station it was always immediately after the radio man had finished giving out a score and had hung up on the previous caller. We concluded if I dialed all but the last half of the last number, held that last number at the little silver finger guard at the bottom right of the phone's dial, and then released just as the previous caller was hanging up, mine would be the next call coming in. There wasn't a queue. It was just a matter of whose call came in first after the single call-in line was free.

The system was sensational. It worked so easily that we could have placed every other call to the station but this would have required us finding new schools to ask about. We restrained ourselves to two easy calls per Saturday — one to check on Carnegie Tech and the other to ask about our new friend Slippery Rock. We could tell by his voice that the radio man actually enjoyed telling radioland how Slippery Rock had fared. He didn't enjoy looking it up on the long AP wire tape, but he always chuckled as he passed the score along.

Near the end of that first football season, Philip and I were listening to "Hold That Line," waiting until we felt pretty sure our two schools had time to finish their games so their scores would be available on the wire. But then the radio man surprised us by booming through our grandfather's old console, "Slippery Rock? I don't believe I have that score yet. Let me see. . . . No not in yet."

We were stunned. Mixed emotions. Pride and jealousy. Someone had stolen our school. The next season, there were a number of calls every Saturday afternoon from people wanting to know how Slippery Rock had done. People playing with their phones.

Word somehow spread from Chattanooga to neighboring cities, then neighboring states. These many years later, there is not a radio football scores program anywhere in the country that doesn't get asked every Saturday, "Do you have the Slippery Rock score?"

The University of Michigan began announcing the Slippery Rock score every Saturday at its games in the largest stadium in the country.

I wouldn't be surprised if following its narrative under "Slippery Rock University" in today's World Book Encyclopedia, there is some bold type referring readers to the "F" book where they will find another reference to Slippery Rock under "Football Scores Programs."

293

68

The First Of Those World Record Journeys To College
By Harold

It wasn't all that easy getting into college and deciding where to go but that's another story.

Finally I was going. Bought a footlocker at the Army surplus store, a suit at the then equivalent of a discount store, and was ready to go. Everything to the Greyhound station for the 20-hour trip. Big moment saying goodbye to Mother and Daddy, I don't know if anybody else was there. Then the long ride, farther than

I'd been since the trips to Missouri in the old days (I'd gotten out of the most recent ones).

I knew things would be different up North. Chattanooga still had drinking fountains marked White and Colored, and, of course,

OFFERED SENIOR

Ericson, Notre Dame, Not Decided on Carnegie Tech, Notre Dame U., Chicago

Harold P. Ericson, a senior at Notre Dame High School, has received large science scholarship offers from the University of Notre Dame, the University of Chicago and Carnegie Institute of Technology. He has not decided which offer to accept.

All three offers were made on the basis of his score on the College Board Examinations, his high school record, and personal recommendations.

Ericson, the son of Mr. and Mrs. A. L. Ericson of 168 Glenwood Dr., hopes to study physics in college. Upon graduation he plans to enter nuclear physics research.

Blacks didn't come into white restaurants and they sat in the back of the bus. Maybe a few exceptions, but integration still had a ways to go.

Having heard it would be different, I wasn't totally unprepared when we got to Ohio, stopped for breakfast and the Blacks on the bus came in the same restaurant. I wasn't even too shocked when a Black guy sat down in the very seat next to me. Even though it was one of those crowded counters with seats very close to each other. I knew that they had the right to sit anywhere, and up North they did. And I was, in theory, in favor of it. But I'll have to admit that I was a bit surprised and nervous when he tried to strike up a conversation. I don't remember what we talked about. But I think I manage to hold up my end of the conversation. Things have changed.

When I arrived in Pittsburgh my bags weren't there. They came in a few days later, but it

Bus ticket in pocket, Harold becomes the first of many to leave the house for college.

caused me serious concern. Greyhound doesn't send luggage out by taxi.

Also, I lost my Travelers Checks. I've always lost Travelers Checks because you're supposed to put them somewhere different from the record of the numbers, which I keep in my wallet. I've never lost that record nor any real money. So now I just take real money, which is fine if you're careful, and most people are with money.

I also remember that first week realizing that I didn't have any idea where I was. I was never very interested in geography. I could hardly believe that West Virginia bordered Pennsylvania so I had to get out a map. It does. I looked at all the states and cities we went through but it really wasn't that interesting. I finally memorized the route after maybe a dozen trips. Once I went on a plane, that was really great. Fast, comfortable, exciting, and you couldn't care less about the states under you.

— Harold

The Journeys:

Harold Erickson – Carnegie Tech (now Carnegie Mellon), Pittsburgh / Johns Hopkins (Ph.D.), Baltimore – Cambridge University, Cambridge, England

Frank Erickson – St. Bernard College, Cullman, Ala. / St. Mary's College, Baltimore (M.Ed) / University of Tennessee College of Law, Knoxville

Allen Erickson – Assumption College (now Windsor University) Windsor, Ontario / University of Tennessee College of Law

John Erickson – St. Bernard College / Catholic University, Washington D.C. (M.Ed)

David Erickson – University of Tennessee, Knoxville / University of Texas, Austin / Rochester University (M.Eng)

Philip Erickson – University of Tennessee, Knoxville

Michael Erickson – University of Tennessee / University of Hard Knocks (M.Pov)

Eileen Erickson – University of Tennessee

Douglas Erickson – University of Tennessee / Duke University, Durham / Vanderbilt University Medical School, Nashville (M.D)

Louis Erickson – University of Windsor / University of Tennessee College of Law

Cecilia Erickson – University of Tennessee / University of Chattanooga

Paul Erickson – University of Tennessee / University of Tennessee College of Law

Charles Erickson – Duke University / University of South Carolina School of Law

Carol Erickson – University of Tennessee

6 9

The Games Of Life

Dear Nieces and Nephews, and Valued Readers,

There are many games in life. The two most popular are the sex game and the money game. For many people, one or both of those is all there is to life. I play those two games about as well as I shoot pool. And I shoot pool about as well as I fly.

Pool, unlike virtually any other sports-like activity, is a game of engineering rather than creativity. Even the trick shots in pool are just feats of engineering. There is no allowance for spontaneity.

Winning at pool, women, and money are among the only games I haven't mastered. I can blame my failures with the cue on a natural knack for fouling anything more mechanical than shoe-laces. I blame my failures with women and money on the fact that the games in which they are the goals, like life itself, are not played by the rules. Rules call for a sense of "fairness."

The games of who gets the women or the money actually mock propriety. This created a particular hardship for me and others in the family. Everything we ever did as children was regulated by carefully arbitrated rules. That arbitration had only one goal: Fair play.

They say, "All is fair in love and war." What they mean is, "Money and sex have no morality." People will justify any imaginable action so long as it brings them money or sex. Pay attention, little innocents, and you'll see this for yourselves.

Relatively yours,
Uncle Rags

7 0

Games And More Games
Our Endless Cycle

"It must have been great growing up in your family. I never had anyone to play with."

I've heard that countless times. Yes, it was, in fact, great. Even if it didn't always seem so at the time.

It was and remains uniquely rewarding to have gotten to know so many fascinating individuals so intimately. And, undoubtedly, the greatest part of childhood was that it was virtually a non-stop play period.

We paused for school, for homework, for band practice, for licking Top Value Stamps, and for all those other little impositions. But when we weren't interrupted we were playing.

While classmates maybe never had that critical third person for their games of Monopoly, ours was the problem of having too

many. There are only so many cards in a deck, and so many pieces to a board game.

We passed innumerable referenda drafted to exclude players from participation. To be as fair as possible, we discriminated on the basis of age and sex. Sex was used only to keep the girls out of our football and basketball competition. Age was our way of dealing with variances in skill and intelligence — it being necessary to prevent an eggshell from botching a game of Scrabble among eggheads.

◎

There were always enough of us in the same age group to keep games fair — and enough vertical movement to give anyone an odds-on chance at his or her share of victories.

Eleven-year-old Louis could expect to finish last when playing spoons — a card game requiring silverware and quick eye-hand coordination — with a bunch of high schoolers. For competition, he could play with Eileen and Douglas at the older end and Cecilia and Paul on the younger side. If he couldn't win in that league but considered a victory necessary to his self-esteem, he could talk up a game with just the younger ones.

We never really played spoons as children — that game being introduced to our seemingly adult lives by my lovely ex-wife. What we played was "slapjack" — a game that thrives on the same balance of speed and violence. I will spare you the explanation — and my dissertation, "Zen and the Art of Slapjack."

◎

The younger ones spent their formative years getting crushed whenever they ventured into big-time competition. As any anthropologist could have predicted, they came into their own upon hit-

ting their early-20s and have consistently clobbered their wrinkling elders ever since in any contests that rely on physical finesse.

Louis, third brother from the bottom — the bottom, of course, being Charlie (sorry, Charlie) — claims that he went undefeated in slapjack for five years after finishing high school. No one has categorically disputed that outlandish claim. Which means there might be *some* thread of truth to it. Which means it is probably, incredible as it seems that Louis could contrive such an anomaly, a bold-faced fact.

Louis clearly dominates these years in golf, basketball, and tennis — with some of the other Little Kids not far behind.

⦿

We had one game virtually everyone played often, everyone at once. Square ball. It is a popular playground game more commonly known as "four square." Our ten-foot square playing area was chalked out on the grimy concrete floor of the garage.

Square ball, known also as "four square," was something we usually got involved in during the spring and summer rainy seasons. With the three big, sliding doors to this two-car part of the rambling old garage open, it was almost like playing outside. It was a lot more like playing outside whenever the ball got slammed through that wide open wall of air and began its steady roll in the puddling rain down the slope of our brick driveway toward the busy four-lane street. All debate about whose turn it was to retrieve the rolling ball had to be concluded in time for the retriever to overtake it before it and/or he got flattened in the street.

A square ball court can hold four players at a time. Nearly all games, from ping-pong to hearts and table hockey to Risk have limited positions. Usually two to six players. Those not in the game immediately called "winner's" — meaning they were allowed to play next against the person who wins the current match. There was often a second, third, or fourth person in line for that winner's position. In ping-pong, it might take the fourth person thirty minutes before he got his chance, so it was best to have a book to read, or some other way to pass the time. Whoever was rightfully next couldn't be skipped by those in the room even if he was elsewhere in the house, unless he or she didn't answer the third call to get to wherever the game was being played.

The winner's line in square ball can accommodate any number. Although the ultimate goal is to advance your way from the entry quadrant to the receive-serve quadrant to the next-king quadrant to the king or server's quadrant, the primary concern is to stay in any of the four courts and out of the tiresome waiting line.

But self-interest in this regard had to be constantly balanced against ethics and integrity. Ethics and integrity dictated that a player concentrate on ousting a brother or sister in the same or a higher competitive range, rather than taking the easy out by slamming a ball into the court of a weak little sister. Anyone deemed guilty of maliciously taking advantage of an inferior met quick justice at the hands of the others in the game as they would set each other with easy shots until the malefactor had been effectively slammed and temporarily banned to the winner's waiting line.

We never bothered making a rule in this game as to what constituted actual "winning." It was so popular among the horde that just being on the court instead of in the line was reward enough.

Ask anyone in the family, "Who was the all-time best at square ball," and there are only two possible answers: "I was." Or, from those who mince words, "Me."

The younger, more sports oriented and game oriented half of the family.

Square ball was played in the garage, but "the bricks," a large parking area between the house and the garage, was where we played badminton, basketball, wiffle ball, red light, and many other games. The Haddock's house is behind Carol, and behind that is the Glenwood Manor, which comes into play later for hosting its own kind of games.

7 1

Beating Ericksons — The Long Drought
By George

I'd like to take this opportunity to tell about the times I beat Michael in Chip-It Golf, Louie in ping-pong, Paul in basketball, and Charlie in an argument. But those things never happened.

I have chronically been embarrassed in my attempts to win during the Erickson Games. The final straw came when Michael, Philip, and Charlie soundly defeated Louis, Paul, and myself in touch football. We had greater talent and experienced youth. They had touchdowns. I still have nightmares of Charlie beating me deep and coasting into the end zone. The shame will shadow me to my grave.

One of the qualities that makes the Ericksons so unique is their willingness to sacrifice themselves for their fellow family members. Gaston Raoul and I were going out west in the summer of '74 and needed a third person to go along. Louie volunteered, explaining that someone had to look out for me in Celia's absence. One day we hiked to the bottom of the Grand Canyon and camped by the Colorado River. Gaston had worn his father's hiking books, which were two sizes too big, and severely blistered the bottoms of both his feet. His hike out the next day was very painful. I was far too small to carry the sadly overweight Raoul out of the Canyon, but Louie took it upon himself to assist Gaston to the rim. I will never forget the sight of Louis struggling to the top with Gaston across his shoulders. A humane beer buddy if ever there was one.

Eileen was also to make a major sacrifice for Celia and me. When she found out that our flight back from Acapulco after our honeymoon was on Eastern, she made arrangements to be a stewardess on that flight. The day we were to leave a major front moved in and our flight was delayed for eight hours. Not knowing that Eileen was being laid over for the same period of time in Atlanta, Celia and I spent our layover in the airport lounge getting loaded with the other more adaptable passengers. When the jet finally arrived, we were greeted by a slightly miffed Eileen. We thanked her for coming to see us, and promptly passed out for the long flight back to Atlanta.

My most embarrassing moment with the Ericksons came late one night after Celia had decided that I was unworthy of her love and drove up to Lookout Mountain to dump me. I wasn't going to accept this rejection, so I drove back down to Glenwood Drive to plead my case. By the time I reached that resolve and acted on it was around four in the morning, so I had to be careful about not waking the parents. I positioned myself below Celia's second-floor window, which was open that warm night, and began tossing rocks at the screen and telling her in a shouted whisper how sorry I was and how much I loved and needed her. After about ten minutes of this early morning confession, a dark figure appeared at the window to tell me in a deep voice that Celia was in Carol's room that night. Frank and Elaine were staying in Celia's room for the weekend.

— George

7 2

Beer

We were raised devout Catholics.

We converted to devout beer drinkers.

Beer is probably the richest tradition in the Erickson house. Mr. and Mrs. Erickson relaxed every night of their lives by drinking two or three beers apiece at the kitchen table. They were engaged in this ritual long before Harold, the oldest and family valedictorian, could even spell the word.

Mother, I don't think, has ever been intoxicated. Daddy only twice in our 40 years of chaperoning. Still, we were brewed in an embryonic soup religiously laced with suds.

⦿

Poor Mr. Erickson had no idea that his simple habit would be picked up and enlarged upon by his entire brood. Poor Mr. Erickson is filled with guilt for having raised 14 bottomless beer drinkers.

Everyone drinks beer on his or her own when away from home. It transmits a warm feeling of familial tightness. A few, aided strongly by the influence of wives, have introduced a touch of moderation to their personal drinking habits.

When gathered at the house, though, and especially when they are sitting down at night around the kitchen table, their husbandly habits are bottled up in formaldehyde like Cecilia's worm and they fall easy prey to the time-honored family drinking debauchery.

Louis

⦿

Louis has a tee shirt he might wear the morning after an important drinking occasion (e.g., any weeknight). It states on his behalf, "I don't have a drinking problem. I drink. I get drunk. I fall down. No problem." The family doesn't have a drinking problem, either. It drinks. It settles into a state of bliss ranging from loud (John and Frank) to rambunctious (Paul, Louis, and Cecilia). But it never falls down. Almost never.

Once Charles fell down — or at least, in. He was only a high schooler at the time and was illicitly experimenting with beer with friends at the lakefront cabin we had taken possession of. Charles was standing on the dock late at night discharging his foamy little bladder into the lake when he lost his balance, fell down, and in.

At the kitchen table, no one falls down. Or even gets obnoxiously drunk. Against the rules.

The rules are simple. Whenever two or more siblings are home at the same time, unless they're playing ping-pong, they sit at the table and drink casually with the parents from about eight at night until ten when the parents go to bed. Then they have to drink seriously with each other, garnishing their disagreements about solutions to real and imagined family and world problems with irrelevant personal attacks until at least two in the morning, maybe four.

Charles

There's one more rule. After a long night of this group therapy, the last ones to struggle to bed must clean off the kitchen table before fumbling — not stumbling, since getting that besotted isn't allowed — up the stairs in the dark.

Cleaning the kitchen table is easy enough to have been accomplished by residents under the influence of both alcohol and hallucinogens.

It consists of carrying all the brown, long-neck returnable Busch bottles from the table in the breakfast room to the far corner of the kitchen and slipping them neatly back into the cardboard cartons. Empty bags of potato chips, Fritos, and Cheetos must be discarded and their crumbly little remains swept off the table's surface. Glasses have to be rinsed, and any plates, skillets, and other utensils foreign to drinking but well suited for early morning sandwiches must be superficially washed.

⑩

Cleaning the kitchen table was a post-drinking ritual started long ago to spare Daddy the humiliation of knowing for sure that he had raised a bunch of intellectual swills. When his sons first began coming home from college — the permissible drinking age — they left his table under all the above-mentioned debris. I say "his table" because at six o'clock every morning Daddy came downstairs to cook his breakfast before going to work. He ate his breakfast alone at his table. You can see why he might become upset. Six in the morning is seldom fun. It's even less fun when your breakfast table looks and smells like it was just vacated by

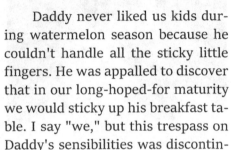

two dozen striking teamsters with a lot of time on their hands.

Daddy never liked us kids during watermelon season because he couldn't handle all the sticky little fingers. He was appalled to discover that in our long-hoped-for maturity we would sticky up his breakfast table. I say "we," but this trespass on Daddy's sensibilities was discontinued long before I joined the late night beer fests.

Respect for the father figure (and bar owner/inventory manager) was one reason we initiated the practice of cleaning the kitchen

Carol

after drinking, but there was another factor: The cleaner the kitchen, the less severe Daddy was in his inevitable interrogations. "How late did you kids stay up last night!?" "How much did you drink!?!" Daddy always asked how much did we drink.

His overwhelming guilt compelled him to ask. There was never any question in his mind about the volume consumed each night because he bought and inventoried the beer. He left only so much in the refrigerator before going to bed himself, hoping, forever hoping, that might limit our drinking. But he never failed to notice while loading the refrigerator the next evening that maybe two, maybe four extra six-packs had been consumed from the cases of returnable bottles still in the garage.

David

He would say, "I don't see how you kids can drink that much! It was just another of those things we were very good at.

Eight o'clock, and Daddy is still wearing his dress shirt and tie. But has traded his suit coat for a sweater.

73

Rarely Bored
We Had Board Games

Once it was started, square ball could go for days on end with breaks only for eating and sleeping. The same was true of all our games. Had it not been for changes in the weather, our play habits would have been much less broad — but hardly less intense.

With the rain came change.

It might be wiffle ball or kickball or badminton we were playing outside when the rain hit. Everyone would reluctantly retreat to the house and paste their long faces against the windows, wondering how life could be so drippingly cruel. Hours might pass.

Hours that raced with the speed of garden slugs. Until eventually someone might say, "Let's play Risk."

Everyone would chorus, "We don't want to play Risk. It's a dumb game. We want the rain to stop so we can go back out and play kickball!"

Lots of suggestions would be voted down in favor of our determination to look glumly out the windows feeling sorry for ourselves. None of us ever wanted to play whatever "stupid game" had been suggested. The promoter of the stupid game usually didn't have his heart in it either but had a vague recollection that we used to consider it fun. However, if he ever motivated himself to pull one of the board games from the shelf, or find a complete deck of cards, a pencil, and a score-pad — we were trapped.

Sometimes the promoter even took it upon himself to clean off the end of the dining room table used for playing board and card games. Before the cards could be dealt, there would be a fourth, fifth, or sixth clearing his or her space at the table. Of course, everyone at first pretended he or she was agreeing to play only for the benefit of the other contestants. This attitude changed as soon as there were more competitors than the game could handle.

"We don't need you, Louis! Go play something else!" "You said just a minute ago that you didn't want to play!" "Yeah, Louis!" "Yeah!"

Those disparaging comments were no more predictable, though, than Louie's rebuttal. He would claim he won the last game of whatever was getting ready to be played whenever it was last played. "If you play without the defending champion," he babbled futilely, "your game is meaningless."

Then he reluctantly joined two or three others in line for winner's, anxious to get into the game even if it meant looking at those playing instead of staring glumly out the window at the falling rain.

⓪

On and on. It never ceased. No matter what the game — Risk or rummy, Monopoly or hearts — the losers always demanded a replay so they could prove they were actually born to win.

We would still be sitting at the dining room table long after the sun had broken through and outside was drier than Mother's

round steak. We would grow there until she threatened, "If you kids don't get outside and out from under my feet, I'll . . . (loud sigh) . . .!" She was an idle threatener.

Eventually, we drifted back outside and thumbed our noses at various "stupid" suggestions until someone finally dug out the bats and balls, rackets, or chalk or whatever was needed to get things moving, at which point some undeserving sibling could be counted on to have the combination of luck and audacity to win whatever was being played, requiring an immediate and incessant string of rematches.

⓪

Jacks. Another game that could go for days once the little red ball started bouncing. Usually played on the hardwood entrance hall floor. Mrs. Erickson was a star at jacks i n high school and often got down on the floor to compete with us. John and Eileen were the best. Michael was probably third best over the years. Perfect rounds were common. Ones . . . twos . . . threes . . . foursies . . . all the way to grabbing all ten dropped close together.

⓪

Many of our games were mindless by nature, but we maintained mental agility by supplementing our play with the

317

rewriting of rules. We cleverly arbitrated new rules to virtually every game known to man and/or the Parker Brothers.

Our tampering was done not so much to exercise those future legal minds as to make the games more fair to younger players. Or more rational. And always less dependent on blind luck. This legislative process was slow, but responsible. Once adopted our rules rarely changed. The tampering was easy to justify since we were certain we had played considerably more rounds of every worthy game that came into the house than its middle-aged creators and original rules writers had ever thought possible.

Our tampering further exiled us, though, into our own little world — away from strangers. When we ventured to area playgrounds, the other kids had trouble understanding that our rule governing what constituted an illegal "overhand" hit in square ball was anything more than capricious.

Their world, the real world, functioned on the bully system. Always has. Always will. "Might makes right" was and is the universal extent of most people's ability to compromise. That was fine at the time because we didn't need them, anyway.

⦿

We had a number of unwritten rules as well. Ethics.

We moved around that gray-green Monopoly board so many thousands of times over the years that we developed an intrinsic understanding of the relative value of the different color groups, the railroads, those worthless utilities, and every color group's

timely relation to an acquisition-minded brother's development capital. We would not allow an older brother to con a younger one into a raw deal.

When playing Monopoly with outsiders, we are usually amazed at how little the run-of-the-mill player knows about fair trades. I suspect most of those greedy players grew up with younger brothers and sisters who didn't mind getting swindled, or grew up accepting raw deals from their elders.

All of our games had three major traits: competition, fairness, and lots of moans, squeals, shouts, and arguments. Though scrupulous in our ethics, we were unencumbered with the formalities of sportsmanship, so we were allowed to tell winners and losers alike exactly what we thought of them before, during, and after each repetitious contest.

The worst football photograph ever staged. A play that could never happen.

Christmas Day. New basketball. Very well dressed players as Douglas scores against Michael.

7 4

More Beer

The beer tradition was not planned. It just happened.

One after another, the older brothers came home from college and began sitting around the kitchen table at night talking with the parents — trying to tell them what life is really all about.

The college students all learned in their first semester of school that beer is an essential ingredient of brilliance, so they always drank as they talked. It would be the first time for each boy in turn returning from his initial trip to college that he was allowed to drink beer in the house.

Trying to tell someone many years your senior what life is really all about requires a lot of drinking. The parents would go to bed after their allotted three beers apiece without ever having learned what life was really all about.

As the number of college students grew, they stayed up later and later, downing more and more beers around the kitchen table, arguing over what life is all about. The younger kids stayed up with their older brothers, eating pizza and drinking Cokes, and paying close attention to what life is all about. The younger ones longed for the day when they, too, could go off to college so they could return home, drink beer as they stayed up late, and enjoy what life is really all about.

⑩

The late night/early morning table bull sessions took on a new direction once enough of us reached what we mistook for maturity. They became group therapy sessions. Often brutal. We began by tearing everyone who wasn't present to shreds. When there was nothing left of the absent people's characters to tarnish we would begin moving around the table, preying on those present. We strived to belittle one sibling after another for any personal defects, real or imagined, that could pass the easily-obtained majority vote. We callously lacerated unalterable but highly sensitive moral, physical, and mental traits.

More than once, we felt bad for a moment or two after driving Eileen from the room in tears. We could go back a long way. We could resurrect why David, the family engineer, was once called "Lame Brain" because he was the first Mother had to help with spelling assignments. We could penetrate the depths of what we saw as Allen's psychosis — keying on how he must have retreated to arctic New England because, while yet an infant, his even infanter but sickly brother John was given more Jell-O for dessert.

As with $50-an-hour group therapy, those present generally felt just as bad when their special cases were being ignored as they did when their special cases were being scalded. Before this Virginia Woolf game would get rolling, and sometimes during the game just to break the tension, the late-night kitchen table discussion might center around a priest and a high schooler ardently correcting the engineer's alleged misconceptions about the laws of physics, or an accountant teaming with an unemployed food stamp recipient to argue tort with an attorney. Inevitably, the tort alliance crumbled once the accountant and the beggar found a detail they could disagree on between themselves.

The breakfast room, which housed the kitchen table, was often filled to capacity as late as two or three in the morning. Friends, in-laws, and future-in-laws would vie with the Big Boys, the Little Kids, and we of the nameless, faceless masses for the six legitimate chairs. It was one of only two rooms in our twelve-room house that was air conditioned. The other was the parents' bedroom. The noise was as important as the cool air in helping them sleep. The big air conditioner in the breakfast room window had a ferocious roar, but was never heard once we started our own roaring.

A few chairs would be dragged in from the dining room and squeezed on the periphery of the table. There was room on the washing machine that sat against the breakfast room's outside wall for one or two people to sit, and an old green chest offered bleacher sitting.

The half-assed among us, and I was one of five, including all of the girls, could actually fit inside the high chair that had never been moved from its corner next to the dryer.

◎

The kitchen table conversations meandered like a raging river, flooding every little stream and swamp along the way.

Maybe they meandered more like spilt beer — full of foam and landing indiscriminately on someone's sensitive lap.

NEWS-FREE PRESS

City Edition

d News Service, AP Wirephoto and Telemats, Acme Pictures and NEA Telephoto Mats and Features

ESSEE, WEDNESDAY, OCTOBER 6, 1948.   Entered at the Postoffice at Chattanooga, Tenn., as Second-Class Mail Matter   FIVE CENTS

BLANKS INDIANS, 1-0

COUNCIL HALTS FOR POSSIBLE RUSSIAN REPLY

3 Nations Accuse Reds Of Illegal Force in Berlin Blockade

PARIS, Oct. 6 (UP)—The United Nations Security Council gave Russia another chance today to accept American, British and French proposals for ending the Berlin crisis.

The council heard representatives of the western powers open their case against the Soviet Union by charging it with "acts of aggression" in Berlin, vowing they would never surrender their hold on the western sectors of the German capital, and then calling an immediate big four foreign ministers' conference on German problems in return for lifting the "illegal" Soviet blockade.

Promptly then the council, in which Soviet Delegate Andrei Vishinsky sat silent, agreed to a suggestion by Chairman Juan Bramuglia of Argentina that an "intermediary waiting period" be taken in the case.

Bramuglia did not specify the length of the recess in the proceedings which amounted to a trial of Russia's Berlin actions before

BOYS, OH BOY!—During the past eight years, every blessed event in the household of Mr. and Mrs. Harold A. Erickson has been a boy. There are seven little Ericksons now—just two short of a baseball team. Mom and dad, who look after the "team's" training, claim the lively little guys "are no trouble at all." Left to right, standing, are John, 5; Allen, 6; Harold, 8; Frank, 7; David, 4. Mrs. Erickson holds 7-week-old Michael, while Philip, 2, sits by his dad. The Ericksons live at 2710 East 12th Street. He is wholesale manager at Joy's Flowers. Story on Page 5.—(Staff Photo by John Goforth.)

LLER
ED IN
ASSIC

s Singles
ross in
ning

| 000—0 | 4 | 0 |
| 01x—1 | 2 | 2 |

Sain and

or the first
Series: (Season's and pitchparentheses)I

BOSTON

or the
Series:

BOSTON
Dark, ss .227
Gordon, lb .211
Elliott, 3b .283
Rickert, lf .311
Salkeld, c .311
Masi, c .211

tanky, 2b .312
Salkeld (th-1b)
ewart (NL);
L); second,
rieve (AL);
Pinelli (NL)

Boston, Oct.
ried the first
ut since 1923
d Cleveland's
the Boston

75

Drinking's Double-Edged Sword

Dear Nieces and Nephews, and Valued Readers,

    Drinking beer was one of our most consuming pastimes. But not one of our best. Alcohol takes a heavy toll. I know.

⬭

    Webbed within the problems that realigned my nerves several years back was the reality that I had had too much to drink over too long a time.

I was seven years out of college and, with the exception of two nights, had consumed from four to 12 beers every day of those post-college years. On those two errant nights, I drank hard liquor. The fact that I had drunk every night for seven years, when it finally occurred to me, was startling. At the time, I was drinking a mini-

mum of one six pack a night, often close to two. But enjoying it. And enjoying the ads I created and magazine articles I wrote while working late into the night. I never became intoxicated.

A few months later, still bothered by that fact I wish I had never uncovered, I tried to quit drinking. And discovered that I couldn't. Over the next few months I discovered a number of other disturbing aspects of myself. A little knowledge can go too long, and too dark, a way.

The great shakedown was imminent. It happened. And in the rebuilding process one of the bricks I had to leave out of the new wall was beer.

When Paul said he and Louis once lamented the fact that I was too far gone to ever come back, it didn't surprise me. I remember those days well. I remember believing the same. I remember especially believing that I could never fit with the rest of the Ericksons again — because I could never again share in the foamy but unique spirit that dominated those late-night kitchen table sessions. They were intensely entertaining and stimulating, but they were over — for me. And I had elevated them to such high status that, while bouncing off the walls of my Florida apartment, the fear of "being-without-belonging" seemed so real and so final that I almost stopped being. I would have exited except I had no right to make the others contend over the years ahead with the empty chair my selfish act would have left at their table.

⦿

That was several years ago. Life has improved. Considerably. Its main drawback being that it is not nearly as much fun as it was when I was drinking. Fun, I must believe, is not the ultimate goal.

⦿

The root cause of alcoholism is one of its mysteries, but the best statistics suggest the disease engulfs one out of seven people who drink at least weekly. Statistically, we should have another in the family. Very likely, we do. But identifying him is tough — there being so many ideal candidates.

⦿

And, finally, little nieces and nephews, stay alert to the sinister but debilitating symptoms of this insidious disease. There is nothing kind about having to give up what has become the most important part of your life. But when it becomes that important, there is no choice but to give it up. Sadly, one or two of you might soon enough find yourselves harnessed to a wagon you thought you were driving.

Relatively yours,
Uncle Rags

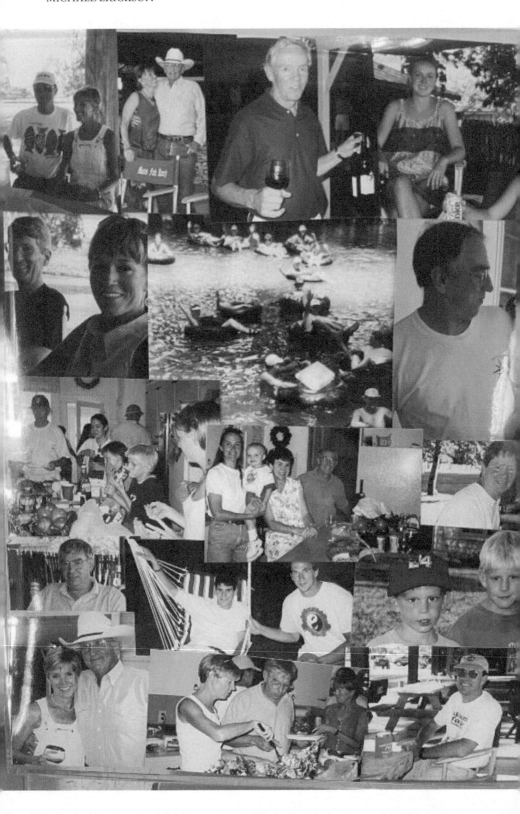

Mostly Pregnant
BOOK FIVE

Book
Five

CHAPTER 76

Staircases and Statues: Tragedy's Ugly Head

Instead of Santa or his elves, it was the Melpomene, the Greek muse of tragedy, and her comedic sidekick, Thalia, who visited our decorated home shortly before Christmas many trees ago, delivering their high and low.

⦾

The big entrance hall off the rarely used front door was the room always most carefully spruced up.

Our towering Christmas tree was annually planted in its green, metal holder —"Check daily for water to avoid fire!" —near the front window of the entrance hall, leaving lots of room for the

331

presents that would soon surround it, and the constant foot traffic that flowed past it in every direction until that slowly arriving day.

Daddy was a wholesale florist, and the Christmas trees were shipped to Chattanooga by one of Daddy's ferns and evergreen suppliers. To show their appreciation for his business, that firm cut each year's tree from their mountains in Oregon, selecting it for the symmetry of its foliage and making sure it would just barely miss scraping our ten-foot ceiling. It often arrived by train a month before Christmas and was kept in cold storage.

Our spruce or fir was as carefully chosen every year as the White House's own Christmas tree. It was deco-  rated every year with the same cheap red and green glass bulbs twisted by wire to the bottom branches where little babies could explore without being able to knock them off. But then with beautiful, hand-painted, fragile glass ornaments depicting marvels like churches, asteroids, Santas, and starbursts placed around the upper branches, out of the reach of clumsy grabs.

There were also strings of blinking and bubbling lights, streamers, bells, suckers, lots and lots of tinsel, and assorted odds and ends, but they are not important to this tragedy.

The blinking tree took up most of the wall to the left side of the entrance hall's massive front door. The right side held but

a small table on which the Christmas crib scene was displayed every year. The crib set was one of Mother's most prized treasures. Year after year, she warned us that its carefully molded and intricately painted porcelain statues had to be handled with extreme care because they came from Germany. I grew up revering the fact that the crib came from centuries-old Germany more than I revered the touching scene comprised of the Madonna and Child, flanked by Joseph, and wise men, and shepherd boys, a sampling of farm animals, and assorted angels kneeling in the straw or hanging from the rafters of the weathered wood shelter.

There were other decorations in the room. Evergreen streamers and such on the mantle over the fireplace, on the telephone table, and hanging from the broad walnut beams that crisscrossed that room's ornate ceiling. These scented and decorative ropes were nice, and we would never have had them had Daddy not dealt in floral products. But they are not important to this tragedy.

⦿

What is important is that one Christmas many trees ago, a few days before the big event, a couple of little kids (no names, but not necessarily any of the forever Little Kids) were playing ball in the entrance hall.

The best rubber balls for inside are about the size of soccer balls, but much lighter and squishier so they can be grabbed. And the best way to play ball in the entrance hall is to bounce that inflated rubber ball against the staircase that leads up from the entrance hall opposite the front door and near the telephone table. A ball tossed against the flat part of a stair will roll listlessly back down, bouncing just a little as it returns to its kid. Tossing and retrieving such balls is never the goal. Because a ball thrown perfectly against the front edge of the fifth, sixth, or seventh stair up arches beautifully back to its source, who can spear it cleanly out of the air with one triumphant hand. "Aiming for the edges" is the way to  play ball against a staircase. And the challenge is to catch it on the fly.

That's the way it was being done at our house one evening just a few days before Christmas by someone who will remain nameless, but who was probably Little Eileen now that I recon-struct the horror.

I know it was evening because Daddy was home.

I know Daddy was home because he stepped right into the middle of it. And was instrumental in ending it.

"It" began with a faint but easily recognizable crash. The kind of tinkling crash that could be made by only one thing — one of the hand-painted, cherished, delicate glass ornaments falling

from the tree and hitting the hardwood floor, disintegrating into hundreds of colorful, shiny splinters. The person who was "playing ball in the house" — an activity forbidden hundreds of times before — mishandled an exceptionally high bounce off the edge of the stairs and knocked the ball with his or her fingertips into the upper branches of the tree. Into one of the prized, irreplaceable ornaments. Everything in the downstairs of the house came to an immediate standstill as that faint but immediately recognizable crash penetrated our col-lective consciousness.

The ball mishandler picked up the ball and stood forlornly over the little mass of shattered glass, awaiting the righteous and vociferous indignation she would re-ceive from Mrs. Erickson, whose footfalls indicated she was rushing to the scene from the kitchen.

I know I was there, as were several others, because I remember all the big, quiet, guilty faces. We were all guilty of having played ball in the house since the last time such usually innocent in-solence had been banned. We were all relatively guilty and would be severely censured along with the one who happened to be most guilty at this si-lent moment.

It was much worse than we expected, or we might have swallowed our lingering guilt and run for cover in the farthest reaches of the house.

Mrs. Erickson didn't just reprimand. She ranted. And when she finished ranting, she raved. At the end of which she renewed her ranting.

Mother always walked a tight emotional line in those days just before Christmas. Though her shopping was mostly done during the previous year's after-Christmas sales, she was charged with wrapping two or three rooms full of presents. Plus dealing with the hundreds of special assignments —

The crib was always placed on a table to the right of the front door.

school Christmas parties, extra cooking, visits to Santa Claus, driving to see neighborhood Christmas lights, extra Church services, etc. — that plagued this "holiday." She was always at the breaking point as Christmas neared. And she was coming especially close this one evening while looking at the splinters of her prized glass ornament.

Daddy, who certainly didn't hear the delicate ornament disintegrate, couldn't help but hear the ensuing commotion in the entrance hall. There was no doubt that his wife was near the edge, so Daddy set down his evening paper, got up from the kitchen table, stalked sternly into the entrance hall, and, in full view of a roomful of children, broke her into splinters the size of those shards on the floor.

Surveying the damage, listening to the ranting and raving of his wife and the babble as his children tried to explain yet another "accident," and then seeing the rubber ball, he put it together very quickly. "Give me that damned ball!!" he hissed between his most volatile combination of clenched teeth and pursed lips. He grabbed the ball with the authority of the ages from its crying little holder and began to hiss again, "You kids are just—" That was as far as he got. We kids never learned what we just were because Daddy wasn't such a great ball handler himself. It slipped from his hands at the height of his grab, caromed off one of the ceiling beams and bounced hard into the crib on its table under the window, taking one of the beloved, hand-painted, staggeringly irreplaceable, porcelain shepherds with it.

A blow up of the crib, from the earlier photograph.

Mother was no more nor less stunned than everyone in the room.

Everyone except Daddy who was quick enough to realize by now that the problem wasn't the kids at all. It was all balls.

So he grabbed the inflated tool of destruction off the floor, began hissing some epithet about "BALLS in the HOUSE!!!" and threw it with great frustration toward the open living room. The colorful ball never made it. It bounded off one thing, and then another, and then another, before finally finding its way back behind him — *to the table with the crib.*

This trip it nailed a rare old wise man who had been peacefully standing there, oblivious to the uproar, just trying to give some myrrh to the Baby Jesus. It took the wise man to the floor where his pieces mingled with the shepherd boy's.

As her life passed before her, Mother came to the recent part about the treasured ornament, reeled on to the first broken irreplaceable crib statue, looked down at the second broken statue, and came, understandably, unglued.

She ran upstairs to cry — something she had been needing to do for several days.

Daddy took a last mean look at the rubber ball which was now resting quietly by the door, between the Christmas tree and the remnants of a crib, took a mean look all around at all of us, then trudged despondently upstairs to go through the futile motions of comforting his wife.

We aimed our big round eyes at the ball, and then at each other. The room, in fact the whole house, was very quiet as we tried to figure out how we could get that vicious, treacherous, murderous rubber ball out of the entrance hall and back to its home in the corner of the closet without anyone having to touch it.

77

"I'm Not Actually Touching You."
By Paul

Too young to torture?

It is my firm belief that as a young child I was being punished for some act I must have committed in a prior life or I was being punished for some dastardly deed I had not yet committed.

While I admit it was difficult for me to live under the unrelenting rule of Queen Cecilia and Queen Carol (Queen Eileen was ruling over my other brothers), it must have been entirely too much for Charlie. It started sometime during the year MCMLXIV and continued for several years thereafter.

Maybe life became too difficult for me also, and it was simply "the forces" that led Charlie and me to take out our frustrations on each other. For, that is exactly what we did.

We vented our frustration through torturing each other. The madness to our methodologies was quite different. Reflecting on it today, I realize Charlie was much more cerebral in his approach than I was. He was probably making preparations for his college education, practicing how to outwit his professors. Or perhaps he just knew that someday he would find himself in a smelly bar, backed into a corner by some stupid redneck who was about to pound his head in and he was practicing for his escape.

You see, when I determined that Charlie had gone too far, had bothered me too long, I simply laid a few punches on him until he left me alone, generally in tears and hurrying to tell on me. It was detrimental to both of our reputations around the Erickson household for us to have behaved the way we did but that did not stop our behavior.

One of Charlie's favorite tortures was to come up to me while I was sitting comfortably in a chair and proceed to almost touch me. For some reason, Charlie thought that if all he did was put his index finger very close to my face (maybe one-quarter of an inch removed), but did not actually *touch* me, then I had no right to hit him.

Sometimes I just hit him anyway because he was bothering me. Most of the time I waited patiently wait for his hand to slip and touch my face. He would flee for his life and I was hot on his heels planning to teach him that he should not do that type of thing. When I caught him, which I almost always did, I would lay a few punches on him. Now when I refer to "punching," "beating," or "hitting" Charlie, you must understand that around our house, even when fighting, you were not allowed to hit anyone in the face. That was one of our rules for boxing also, which resulted in many an Erickson boy getting punched in the head when boxing with his friends who had never heard of such a rule. Anyway, after I hit Charlie, he would run and tell Mom or one of our older brothers that I beat him up and all he did to me was barely touch me with one finger on the face. That characterization generally made me appear to be the big bad bully. Even after I presented my defense to the charge, it was still believed that I was a big bad

bully, and when it came to Charlie, maybe I was.

Of course, Charlie pulled these same stunts with his other siblings on occasion, so he didn't always get a whole lot of sympathy from the members of the household. It just made us both look bad, and I don't think it made either of us feel good.

Paul, left, and Charles.

Now to answer the question of the title, we were neither too young to torture (the act of torturing another) nor too young to torture (being the recipient of the torturing).

— Paul

7 8

If He Can Make A Saxophone, Surely I Can Make A Guppy

We were as rich with tradition as the South is with kudzu.

Some, like the tradition of always backing the car into parking spaces so that the next driver — possibly less experienced — would not have to back out, were good.

Some, like getting screamed at for letting the screen doors bang closed, were indifferent.

Some, like competing in the annual school science fairs, were discriminatory, iniquitous, and just simply unfair.

This particular tradition was unfair because it was started by Harold, the oldest. He enjoyed great successes in the school science fairs, so everyone in line was encouraged to take advantage of this seemingly easy opportunity to display our supposedly innate intelligence.

Of course, the parents — being new at the game as Harold was developing — had no idea at the time that this first-born would, in fact, become a scientist of some note while many of the others laboring with their annual exhibits were destined to be ignorant CPAs and attorneys.

Harold always won first prize. The winners of the school competition qualified for city and state fairs, and Harold did as well in these expanded fields as he did on the smaller parochial front. Frank and Allen, the next two in line, also earned sizable stacks of colorful ribbons at the science fairs, if you consider blue to be colorful.

John was too busy running the high school to be bothered with such modest pursuits. He admitted in recent years that he always made a point, even as a child, of never participating in anything where he could not be certain of victory.

David, who was to stay on the fringe of the science field by making a career in engineering, was a very good exhibitor.

I was awful. I have no inclination for mathematics or science.

Terrible as I was, I still picked up ribbons with exhibits on magnets and mutated guppies. But even with the detailed display posters Mrs. Erickson drew in front of my dull eyes, I found that magnets were impossible to understand. Nonetheless, they were great fun to play with. A local magnet manufacturer gave me some powerful industrial samples for Mother's display that entertained me for years after. As for guppies, I accidentally mutated mine by keeping too many from the same bloodline for too long in too small of a tank. I guess Mother's gold-lettered posters implied I had intended for all of my formerly beautiful rainbow-tailed guppies to evolve into ugly little brown embarrassments.

⬭

The two most dramatic family exhibits came from Harold and David.

Harold invented an electronic saxophone. Perhaps the first in the history of the world. He played saxophone in the school band, but hardly ever played this one of his own making. In the year he worked on it, the gadget probably made only two hours of music. I don't think it was in working order as it swept the school, then the city and the state science fairs, but the elaborate charts that accompanied the instrument probably so confused the judges they convinced themselves it worked. The stem was made of round wood, like a heavy mop handle cut in half. This brown mop handle accumulated a growth of small, round, white keys amidst colorful wires.

I'm sure the instrument would have worked well if Harold had a reasonable budget. But he probably put it together from the parts of a couple of old radios, a burned out sandwich toaster, a worn out but still buzzing electric hair clipper, and a couple of discarded irons. This electronic saxophone was a product of the Fifties — an era when electric guitars had just barely shattered the airwaves, and the pop synthesizer was 20 years in the future.

Frank turned an old refrigerator into a "window air conditioner." Impressive. I can still easily see those brass coils frosting over as it roared to life. I hoped we could use it when summer came, but none of our windows were the size of refrigerators. Nor was it particularly safe, with so many toddlers racing and crawling around, to put refrigerators in windows.

David's most memorable achievement was a pair of radar controlled automobiles. The vehicles were made of aluminum and shaped like Brinks money trucks. They were the size of baby armadillos. They had electric eyes that made either of them stop if the other pulled into its path. I was impressed because I could never have made the little battery-powered aluminum animals run in the first place, much less have them stop on signal. There was a signal, too. A traffic light. When green, the approaching vehicle could keep going. When red, the approaching vehicle didn't stand a chance — no matter how grave the driver's hurry. The future looked so safe back then.

The saxophone and the cars of the future are preserved in a box in a dark little corner of the second floor of our garage. The servant's quarters. Most of the other exhibits — which largely consisted of electric wires and lights — have long since been turned back into radios.

Some of my mutated guppies live on in a little tank, shrinking and discoloring themselves still further with each new generation. And two of my magnets have been in service for 20 years holding the door closed on a tall, narrow metal cabinet that fills a small corner of our breakfast room and whose latch was faulty. Before I changed the world by discovering the power of magnets, we took turns holding that cabinet door closed. We were cheaper than hardware.

79

Back When Bombs Were Child's Play
By Harold

There were some dull experiments where you mixed a couple of solutions and "observe the brown precipitate." What good is a precipitate. Hydrogen sulfide does stink but is overrated. Things that burned, like thermite mixture, were fun.

The real treasure in the set was potassium nitrate, the magic ingredient for making gunpowder. For some reason I never made any really good gunpowder. Lots of nice colored flames and a few fizzles, but nothing explosive. I think maybe I never got it dry enough. I never had the courage to put it in the oven. Later in high school Tom Ainsworth and I came on the real treasure, a large quantity of real, genuine, factory-made gunpowder in the Notre Dame chemistry lab. Our class had been banned from doing experiments after a few minor accidents, but Tom and I got permission to come in on Saturday to work in the lab.

We did a lot of experiments right out of the book, but we also modified a few. For example, when we came to making chlorine we decided not to waste it just bubbling it through water to make acid or salt. We scaled it up several fold and got some dry

ice to liquefy it. In a couple of hours we had collected a nice bottle of green liquid, certainly enough to kill everyone in a closed room. Maybe everyone in Ridgedale for all I knew. Maybe nobody, we didn't really know. After we made it we realized that it wasn't going to last forever, and pretty soon the green liquid would evaporate and turn to poison gas, World War I variety. So I took the bottle and remaining dry ice home, to the house on Twelfth Street, and thought about how to get rid of it. I finally went outside and threw the bottle as far as I could to the corner of the back yard. A small cloud of green gas floated across the back alley and disappeared. The Erickson family and Ridgedale had escaped. All's well that ends well.

Back to the gunpowder. This was good stuff and we experimented a bit with making small and then larger firecrackers. What we really needed was something to pack it in. We didn't know about pipe bombs. The ideal container, safer than a pipe, was right at home — Lip IVO tubes. The predecessor to ChapStick. About one-and-a-half inches long and 3/8 inch in diameter. Punch a small hole in the metal side for the fuse, pack it carefully with gunpowder, and put the cap on. These homemade firecrackers made cherry bombs look tame. Great explosion, then the little bits of shrapnel from the IVO tube falling to ground.

I had several books from the library and knew by heart how to make nitroglycerin. Pour glycerin slowly and gently into a mix of concentrated sulfuric and nitric acid. Don't let it overheat. I still haven't tried it.

— Harold

Duke SCHOLARS@DUKE

Home   > People   Schools / Institutes   Research   About

Harold Paul Erickson

James B. Duke Distinguished Professor of Cell Biology

Cytoskeleton: It is now clear that the actin and microtubule cytoskeleton originated in bacteria. Our major research is on FtsZ, the bacterial tubulin homolog, which assembles into a contractile ring that divides the bacterium. We have studied FtsZ assembly in vitro, and found that it assembles into thin protofilaments (pfs). Dozens of these pfs are further clustered to form the contractile Z-ring in vivo. Some important discoveries in the last ten years include:

- Reconstitution of Z rin (... more)

Harold P. Erickson, Ph.D. (Johns Hopkins University)

James B. Duke Professor of Cell Biology
Professor of Biochemistry

Programs: Cell and Molecular Biology, Structural Biology and Biophysics

E-mail: harold.erickson@duke.edu

412 Nanaline Duke Bldg   ↑↑↑ 3709

Durham, NC 27710

8 o

Even Our Quiet
Could Be Contested

Off and on through the years and years we played two games that were as alike in nature as women are to cats, but as much a contrast in their physical makeup as the sun is to the moon.

They were not board games, nor card games, nor even ball games. They were people games. We had a lot of people, so they were easy to play.

One was called "Gotcha last!" It will be touched on later. The other — a game Mother probably liked better than every other activity we ever devoted our little selves to — was called "See-Who-Can-Be-Quiet-The-Longest."

See-Who-Can-Be-Quiet-The-Longest was played only at the table, usually at lunch on Saturdays during the school year or on appropriate days during the summer. An appropriate day was any of those routine noontime lunches when Paul and Charles or Douglas and Louis or Carol and God or any other of the volatile combinations might bring their ongoing feuds to the table.

Asking any of these battling factions to drop their dispute was like wanting vegetables to be Fritos. We had loads of rules against hitting under any and all circumstances, but no rule against arguing at any time, especially at the lunch table.

The only escape from a particularly relentless spat was to suck the combatants into playing See-Who-Can-Be-Quiet-The-Longest. At the first suggestion of playing this game, the crankier of the babies at the table always declared emphatically he not only didn't want to play but wouldn't even consider it. Were we ever disheartened by such adamant little spirits of uncooperativeness? Never. This was a very imposing and deafeningly quiet game that, by its invidious psychological nature, everyone *had* to play once it was started.

⓪

To get it started, some brother who had not done anything noticeably disreputable in recent memory and who therefore held the temporary respect of the fickle masses would follow the initial suggestion of playing the game by stating with great authority, "Okay. Everyone get ready and we'll start on three! One . . . Two . . . Three!" At that moment the table would become absolutely silent. But only for that moment. Douglas, or Charles, or whoever the cranky baby was who prompted the playing of the game in the first place, would immediately and typically break the silence by declaring, "I'm not going to play this stupid game!" Such a declaration constituted immediate disqualification from the game since the object is to be the *last* person in the room to speak, and certainly not the *first*. The first speaker is the first loser.

The crux of all of those bothersome lunchtime spats was that one baby was claiming his or her rights had been trespassed

352

by another baby. The baby who had done the trespassing and gained something not rightfully his, as is still the case with all grownups, was always in favor of letting the matter drop. The trespassed, however, was never game for anything short of arguing his case until we all agreed that he was quite the victim. Most such arguments were settled by a vote of peers or superiors but there were always some not worth either settling or hearing about. These were the ones most often sidetracked by See-Who-Can-Be-Quiet-The-Longest.

Let's assume Charles has been whining for five minutes about some minor atrocity Paul inflicted on him while they were playing Bop The Beetle upstairs shortly before the rest of us were called in from the outside basketball court for lunch. Paul, of course, is anxious to see the game of being quiet get underway.

Paul, Charles, and Cecilia with Bop The Beetle

Charles, of course, breaks that first moment of silence by reaffirming his earlier position and declaring, "I'm not going to play this stupid game!" The rest of us at the table look silently at Charles, our lips firmly pursed or a hand held tight over our mouth to show how seriously silent we are being, and point at him to convey in no uncertain terms that he has just lost and is out of the game.

At which point the cranky baby, Charles, expounds, *"I know I've already lost the game. But I wasn't playing. And you all aren't really playing the game either. . . . Are you? . . . [Long silence, lips still pursed.] . . . You're just playing this because you want me to forget that Paul cheated me out of my bat in Beetle! . .*

. [Silence answers again, though Paul vigorously shakes his head in denial of Charlie's accusation.] . . . *Well, I'm not going to forget that. And I'm going to sit here and talk all through lunch.* . . . [Long silence continues as everyone stares back at the whiner, a couple with hands still over mouths.] . . . *You babies can just go ahead and play your ba-by game.* . . . *And I'm, going to sit here and talk.* . . . *Talk.* . . . *Talk.* . . . *And talk.* . . ."

But one child talking to an unresponsive table could never go on for more than 30 seconds on his own. Even if he starts to sing.

⑩

We would let another long, quiet minute pass, by which time the cranky child has settled into a visible hurt by his growing awareness that everyone else is playing a game that he has already lost by virtue of not wanting to play in the first place. Then the voice of authority who succeeded in starting the game raises both hands, palms out to signal an official timeout, and, becoming the voice of compassion as well, says, "To be fair to ba-by Charles, we'll start the game over. Beginning on three. One-two-three!!" The count is made fast so that no one else can get any words out of their systems during the timeout. And the game resumes again, usually with the cranky one getting ready to disqualify himself in a last gasp effort to save face by stubbornly insisting again that he is not playing.

We acknowledge his desire to protest, but stifle him by gravely pursing those lips even tighter, aggressively shaking our heads and pointing at him, one or two holding his hands in the universal traffic "stop" signal, as if to say, "We know you're not happy about whatever it was, but this is your last chance — so don't you dare speak." The game finally settles into earnest com-petition. Everyone, even the crybaby, concentrating on just one thing: Keeping quiet.

⑩

Laughing and giggling were allowed, so long as the source kept his or her teeth closed and kept the utterance as closed-mouth as possible. Actually, laughing and giggling — even in the form of muffled snorts — were violations, but the rules concerning nonspoken mouth noises were unenforceable since it was impossible to argue them once the game was underway.

I was always terrible at this particular game. I never had anything that really needed to be said, but had a low threshold for silence. I might not be the first to talk, but in all the years this game was played I doubt I ever won. There is never any reason to be the first person to speak and take yourself out of this game. Cecilia, it seems, was often the first to simply forget the game was being played after we had moved beyond the active lip pursing phase and had settled into silence. She might just look up and say something. Everyone else would point, and, embarrassed, she would acknowledge she had just lost.

Once you talk and are out of the game a second phase begins. Misery loves company, so the first loser, and each of the subsequent ones, begin asking the rest of the players questions. Easy questions never cut it. They had to be along the line of, "Douglas, if you want me to serve 6:30 Mass for you tomorrow I can probably do it because I've got to go in early anyway. But you'll have to let me know now." Or, "Instead of finishing our hockey game after lunch, Philip, I think I'll just practice my drums. Is that okay?" Hell no, that wasn't okay. Not only was Philip leading 4-2 in a game to six, and not only was it against the rules for anyone to even consider quitting a game in which he was behind, but practicing the drums was something Philip couldn't do with me so he would have to find something else to do and someone else to do it with.

Sure, he knew the question was a set-up. But he also knew there was a slight chance I would follow through with the threat — especially if the game at the table drug on until well past lunch. He was left with a judgment call as to whether he should keep silent — or stand up for his rights.

Personal questions were also ideal for luring an active player into the losers' circle. You could ask Louis if his new fifth grade girlfriend was as ugly as you had heard — subjecting him to the intense pressure of having to follow custom by adamantly denying that he had a girlfriend and/or defending the beauty of someone he might have a crush on. You might tell Eileen she had a phone call just before lunch but you couldn't find her so you took a message. The message — which everyone, including Eileen, knew had only a microscopic chance of existing — would not be conveyed unless Eileen broke her silence to ask for it. "It was a boy," you might add after a pretentiously casual pause. "Something about going waterskiing, or something . . ."

One after another the contestants would Fail. Cecilia, as noted, always gave out early and would proceed to babble incessantly about how hard it had been to keep so quiet for so long — maybe three minutes— and how glad she was to be out of the game and able to finally talk again. Paul, Eileen, and Philip could outlast most of us but Douglas nearly always won. A loner and a stoic, Douglas was born to be the quietest, the longest.

8 1

Clothes Make The Man
And Whites Make The Angels

We were good little Catholics.

Great little Catholics.

We kept a lot of white clothes around the house. Little white Catholic clothes. Sizes five and six and seven. Little white pants and little white coats and little white dresses.

These little white garments got passed down the ranks as each of us grew into various Catholic ceremonies. Like First Communion. A very big day in the life of a budding little Catholic — receiving his or her First Communion. It is described by the Baltimore Catechism (the official Catholic handbook) as the biggest day in our lives. Holy Communion, per the manual, "contains the body and blood, soul and divinity, of our Lord Jesus Christ under the appearances of bread and wine." Receiving it that first time, without benefit of wine, is a formality teeming with holy trauma. All this pressure on a second grader, no less.

You can start receiving Communion after reaching the "Age of Reason" — the ability to tell right from wrong. The Church, in her wisdom, decided that fast learners and slow learners alike reach the Age of Reason in the second grade. The reason was often tempered with wonder. "Is it a sin to touch the sacred host with your teeth while trying to swallow it, Sister?" "Will I like the way God tastes?"

You have to wear white to receive your First Communion. To show you are pure. Ericksons were generally more pure than their hand-me-down white pants and little white coats and lacy white dresses.

⊚

Ericksons were pure because, like all Catholics, we had individual Guardian Angels looking over our shoulders to aid in our struggles with temptation. And, unlike most of our Catholic classmates, we also had loads of older brothers watching our every move.

Until the time of that First Communion, the older ones kept their inferiors in line by threatening to tell Santa Claus about anything they found offensive, even just bothersome. Once the younger ones reached the Age of Reason, discipline was maintained by threatening them with God. "That's a sin!" we routinely noted, with the clear implication that it was also noted in a ledger in Heaven. Not getting something for Christmas was a reasonable deterrent to offending older brothers but pales in the face of eternal char-broiling.

For blossoming, little Catholics, First Communion is a double-edged sword. Any child old enough for the unleavened bread line is also old enough to sin. So the Church schedules the little sinner's First Confession the Saturday before its white *Allen, third oldest, with Carol, the youngest, in her First Communion whites.* pants and white coat Sunday First Communion.

⦿

Ericksons knew a lot about their religion. Enough to put the nuns and priests on the spot pretty regularly during the daily religion classes that were a fixture of our parochial school education. Innocently interjecting the idea of predestination into one of those classroom discussions was a sure way to lose favor with that year's teacher. Catholic dogma steadfastly folds against that one. It states that predestination does not exist, while at the same time contending that God knows everything. It can't handle the obvious question, "If God knows everything, then doesn't He know before we are even born whether we will end up going to Heaven or Hell?" Dogma tries to answer with, "God gave man a free will." It doesn't want to hear the follow-up, "Yes, Sister. But even though we have a free will wouldn't God, if He looked ahead, still know if we are going to Hell? And why would He even create someone just to doom him to centuries of burning in Hell after just 60 years of sinning on Earth?"

We budding theologians always wanted to add, showing off to our classmates, "That's plain cruel," but didn't want to push the nuns and priests too far.

The nuns and priests didn't like having the many unquestioning kids in class subjected to such queries. "If God can do anything," we might ask on a slow day, "can He make a rock so big He can't lift it?"

Indeed, we knew a lot about our religion. We were forced to learn the technicalities because older and even younger brothers constantly accused one another of sinning whenever that pilgrim's progress was inconvenienced. We had to know all of the Church's centuries-old amalgamation of sins in order to justify our sanctity. "You're crazy, Eileen. It is not a sin for us to switch channels to the football game in the middle of your stupid movie — it's just majority rule. And majority rule is not a sin unless there is physical, mental, or spiritual harm. And there is no such harm to your not seeing the end of a Shirley Temple movie you've watched too many times already. So quit your bitching and go play with your paper dolls." (Collective gasp from agape little mouths.)

"Philip said a dirty word!"

"What did I say that was 'dirty'?"

"I can't say because it's a sin."

"Well, you're probably referring to the word 'bitch,' which, if you look in the dictionary, you'll find it is a female dog. So quit your female dogging and go play with your dolls."

"Yeah, Eileen. Quit your female dogging."

8 2

A Saint
Not A Sinner

Dear Nieces and Nephews, and Holy Readers,

First Communion is preceded by a child's First Confession so the soul can receive God for that first time in a pure state.

After that, weekly Communions are often preceded by weekly confessions. You go into the spooky "confessional" which is usually on the side of the church, close the curtain or narrow wooden door, kneel on the padded kneeler, slide a head-high little panel open exposing a priest whose own head is faintly outlined behind the tinted or opaque glass and then tell your sins to that priest — "God's representative on Earth."

The priest, who is supposed to be anonymous but recognizes all the kids, tells you not to sin like that anymore. Then he gives you a penance — punishment — which more often than not consists of saying three Hail Marys and three Our Fathers to symbolically make amends for the symbolic little tap your sins inflicted on Christ's crown of thorns.

Since we began every school day with eight o'clock Mass, we generally went to confession and Communion once a week — every Friday — to keep our souls cleansed and our spirits high. The weekly confession was justifiable for some students, the bad ones, because they did enough sinning in a week to need two confessions. The way life works, though, one could safely bet a few hundred years of indulgences these bad students tended to hit the confessional only about once a month — and failed to mention most of their more interesting offenses.

But I was a saint, not a sinner.

Once a week, I humbly stepped into that closet, knelt down, and recited, "Bless me, Father, for I have sinned. I disobeyed my mother three times. I disobeyed my father two times. And I lied twice." Every week the priest would tell me not to do that anymore and sentenced me to three Hail Marys and three Our Fathers. Week after week, year after year. But I was a good boy. I never disobeyed my mother or my father. Wouldn't have considered it.

The only remotely sinful act I might have committed during a 15-year stretch was lying.

And the only time I ever lied was once a week when I went to confession.

The Baltimore Catechism, the manual for good Catholics, never instructed us how to walk in once a week and say, "Bless me, Father. I have been perfect."

362

*I still don't lie — except maybe sometimes when I'm sup-
posed to confess something. And that's just a bad habit I picked up
at church.*

Relatively yours,
Uncle Rags

*Illustrations of the horrors of sin and how to live better lives from
the Catholic child's trusty handbook: The Baltimore Catechism.*

A CATHOLIC FAMILY STUDYING RELIGION

Father: "No daughter of mine will ever enter a convent."

Daughter: "Then I will have to wait until I am old enough and go anyway, since our parish priest and the Sisters tell me I have a religious vocation."

THIS IS GOOD

THIS IS BETTER

"I want to marry the person of my choice."

"I choose Christ as my spouse." (See 1 Corinthians 7, 32-34).

8 3

Spitty-Up Pans
And Other Gags

Back a long time ago — when most of us were just far-away glints in Daddy's black-haired eyes — Mrs. Erickson, who was pregnant just the same, bought a set of three light-weight aluminum pots. They were cheap. I know that because this particular kind of pot still shows up at flea markets, and they're still cheap.

The pots came in two sizes. One was the petite one-quart saucepan, the other two were of the larger two-quart capacity.

The pots were too cheap for cooking anything better than boiled potatoes, but they had other uses. The two larger ones were ideal for soaking shirts, socks, and other apparel too dirty or bloody to immediately wash.

And they were perfect for throwing up in.

◍

Those two pots became known as our "spitty-up pans." Whenever one or more of us was bedridden with intestinal ail-ments, the spitty-up pan was kept on the floor right next to our bed. It was our duty and responsibility to locate that pan on the floor should the spitty-up urge strike. No matter how bad we might feel, we were going to feel worse if we didn't get to our pan before erupting.

To be fair, we were allowed to throw up once down our chins or on the floor at the onset of an illness, if it could be reasonably proved that we had no way of knowing stomach disorders were settling in. But after that initial "accident," neither we nor anyone catching what we had could throw up in anything but the slightly dented and roughed up two-quart aluminum pans.

The spitty-up pans were used by so many for so long they took on an aura of their own. Though they were supposedly scoured clean after each illness so they could be used again for soaking laundry and boiling potatoes we could induce gagging in younger siblings by merely fishing one of the spitty-up pans out from the cabinet in the kitchen and holding it in front of their face for a second. We used to take special advantage of Cecilia by convincing her to close her eyes to receive a surprise and then have her open them only to be looking into the bottom of the spitty-up pan. The gullible girl would gag and turn pale.

Mrs. Erickson used those pans for boiling potatoes because she learned that the sight of them to us kids was so horrifying that it scared us out of the kitchen, and out from under her pregnant feet.

⦾

Intestinal disorders, much more so than headaches, tend to be contagious.

Sometimes two spitty-up pans weren't enough to go around. Rather than lose another pan to that nauseous mystique — who wants to see their canned Chef Boy-Ar-Dee spaghetti and meatballs warmed in a known spitty-up pan? — we had to share the two. One pan would be placed on the floor between the beds of two intestinal invalids. During larger plagues, one pan would have to serve an entire room.

Unfortunately, having someone else throw up in your spitty-up pan, induces more than just cosmetic gagging.

⦾

We had fewer than our share of physical injuries growing up, but made up for it with routine illnesses.

John had a rare anemic baby disease that was probably the most frightening of our long series of maladies. He recovered, but it left him with red hair, freckles, and a Napoleonic spirit.

Harold had an obscure disorder that kept his right leg from growing for more than a year while he was a child. The doctors couldn't do anything about it, so Mrs. Erickson, wearing her uniform maternity dress, applied Lourdes water (a special Catholic miracle drug) and the recalcitrant leg began a speedy growth that slowed only after both legs were once again the same length.

⦾

Lourdes water comes from a fountain springing from a cave in France where the Blessed Mother appeared several times in the mid-1800s. Thousands of believers have been cured and have left their wheelchairs and crutches hanging about the walls of that

367

cave. The water is packaged in little two-ounce bottles, some in the shape of the Blessed Mother herself, and distributed by nuns and priests for use by Catholics who cannot get to France or whose illnesses are not serious enough to warrant the trip. This miracle drug works especially well on warts and poison ivy. It is useless for the treatment of boils.

⓪

I rose dizzy, shaking, and otherwise deathly ill the morning after my second grade class had received its first dose of the remarkable new Salk Vaccine. I can still see the sudden flash of horror on my mother's face when I got down the stairs still in my pajamas instead of my school uniform, turned the corner into the kitchen and said, "Mommy, I don't feel very good." Apparently, I didn't look very good, either.

I was rushed to the hospital and immediately poured over by teams of doctors who feared that I had contracted polio from the vaccination — which meant they could anticipate a bunch of polio cases coming from second graders all over town who had been vaccinated the previous day. This had happened in five other cities. Our mother was aware of this possible complication, feared for her child, and alerted our family doctor, who alerted the hospital staff.

When it was finally determined to everyone's literal satisfaction that I was merely dying from a critical case of double pneumonia, the doctors congratulated one another on their fine work and headed straight to the golf course to celebrate.

8 4

The Little Drummer Boy's Polio Scare
By Mother

Call this "Life's Scary Moments" or "How One Thing Leads To Another."

Jonas Salk developed a vaccine that would provide immunity against the dreaded disease poliomyelitis, and the government decided to immunize all the first graders in the country.

About two weeks into the program, a few cases showed up where the kids actually developed polio from the vaccine, but the benefits were considered to outweigh the risks, so the program went on. After a real polio scare when Harold and Frank were small children, the idea of a vaccine seemed wonderful to me. At any rate, Michael got his shot along with hundreds of other grade schoolers at the Chattanooga field house, and he was fine that day and the next, when we took off for Parents Night and did not get home until after the younger ones were in bed.

The following morning he came down for breakfast still in his pajamas, instead of dressed in his school clothes. He complained of a headache, and feeling dizzy. I checked him, and yes, he did have a fever, so back to bed and no school.

First thing on the list was to get everyone else fed, properly dressed in their school uniforms, and into the car so they would make it in time for the eight o'clock Mass that opened every school day.

Well, Michael kept complaining, and I kept telling him that he would be all right. Finally, with more important things taken care of, I got out the thermometer and took his temperature, "Oh, my God!" "104!"

And then I thought of the polio shot.

When I got Dr. Starr on the phone, he was as alarmed as I was and told us to take Michael to the hospital immediately. So Daddy came and got Michael while I stayed home with the little ones, waiting near the phone for any news.

The two things being seriously considered were polio and spinal meningitis, both highly contagious, meaning all his many brothers would have been exposed.

Finally at about two that afternoon, the verdict was in. Dr. Starr said it was the first time in his career he had been glad to tell parents their child had a severe case of upper lobular pneumonia, also known as "double pneumonia." But, as bad as that was, it was much less disastrous than the other possibilities because it was not contagious.

It was still a very bad forty-eight hours. In spite of medications, his temperature continued to shoot up, and they finally packed his body in ice to fight the fever. This type of pneumonia was frequently fatal in young children, but thanks to the polio scare we had caught it at a fairly early stage, and the doctors, though struggling, were able to get it under a semblance of control in those first crucial hours.

And now to "how one thing leads to another." It was Wednesday when we took Michael to the hospital, and the rhythm band recital was going to be on Friday. Every time he became reasonably conscious, he would ask if he would be well by Friday, so he could play his drum in the recital. Oh, boy. In the rhythm band you only got to play the drum one year, and Michael's year was up. I finally went to Sister Barbara and asked her if she would break the rule and let me tell him he could play the drum the next year. She promised and that was reassuring to Michael as he was lying in his hospital bed. So he drummed for two years, and thus started his love affair with the drum.

Over the years I had endured clarinets and French horns, trumpets, saxophones, and a trombone, stoutly maintaining that I could stand anything except a drum. Well, when Michael was in  the fourth grade, he persuaded Mr. Baker to let him play the drums in the high school band. The former drummer graduated from high school the spring before and the long-time band director actually let this fourth grader try out to take his place. That still wasn't too bad, because the drums belonged to the school and he did all his practicing and playing down there. But then the band fell apart, and the drums got locked up in the storage room, and our little drummer boy was most unhappy. So I actually broke down, ran an ad in the paper, and bought him a secondhand snare drum for a Christmas present. The snare drum really wasn't that bad, and what the heck, if he wanted it that bad, I could stand it,

And the final episode in "how one thing leads to another" is definitely louder. When he was in high school, he bought Brian Cordon's drum kit and set it up in his downstairs bedroom (the room that later became the TV room). And every evening when I was cooking dinner, he would turn the hi-fi up so loud you could hear it on McCallie Avenue and drum away at a frantic level. Winters weren't too bad, but in the summer (pre-air conditioning) he might as well have been sitting right outside the kitchen door.

And while I am going on about how one thing leads to another, we did get Michael through his bout with pneumonia. When the worst was over, he refused to eat what they served at the hospital. He still needed injections of antibiotics several times a day but he wasn't making much headway when he wouldn't eat. Finally, Dr, Starr decided he would be better off at home if we could make some arrangement for him to get his shots. I had never met the little nurse who lived with someone in the duplex that Mrs. Koontz rented out next to our house, but Mamas will really try anything to take care of their kids, so I went next door, explained our predicament to this young nurse, and persuaded her to come over and give Michael his shots so we could get him out of the hospital.

Eventually, he got better, but after three trips to the hospital in one year, the first two for hernia surgeries, he developed a terrible case of stuttering.

Somehow, I always seemed to have to spend too much time worrying about Michael.

He came into the world several weeks ahead of schedule under rather bad circumstances, and while he weighed six pounds two ounces, he was 22 inches long and very skinny. Even though he was four months old at Christmas time, he was still on a three-hour schedule and had to have his bottle in the middle of the night.

When I came home from midnight Mass that Christmas and fed him at 2 a.m. I was quite unhappy when he started crying to be fed again at 5:30. By the time I got him fed and back to bed, the others got up ready to see what Santa had brought, so I spent that Christmas trying to survive with seven kids on three hours sleep.

Of course, at some point Michael did give up his bottles, but the next thing was the time he fell out of the high chair and suffered a minor fracture of the skull and a concussion. We were building on to the back of the house, and I had lugged that kid up and down stairs every time I had to go out to oversee some of the work being done, and then he fell out of the high chair when I walked ten feet away to put something on the chest of drawers in the bedroom.

The fall wasn't all that bad, though his father got mad at me for being so careless, but about a year later Michael started having spells where he would grab his head and start screaming. I forgot to mention he was almost three years old and did not talk. Not a word. Not "Mommy" or "Dada," or "Drink." Nothing. He understood us, because he went along with what was said. So we took him to Vanderbilt for a thorough check and were told that there was no physical reason, and he would probably get around to talking eventually, which he did, but we did not quite know how to handle a three-year-old who couldn't figure out how to talk. He made sounds, but not words, and communicated by pointing. We eventually got him toilet trained when he figured out that if he made a trip to the bathroom he could avoid the unpleasant sensation that occurred when he let nature take its course.

Finally, he came out with a few words, and progressed rapidly from words to sentences. He stuttered a bit at first, but we were so relieved that he had finally decided to talk that we didn't mind the occasional stutters. Still, he was an awfully quiet child, and while he liked stories, he had no desire to learn to print his name or learn any of the letters of the alphabet.

When I registered him for the first grade, I told the teacher that I seriously doubted if he was ready for school, but I knew that he could distinguish symbols, because he could play cards, even if he could not print his name.

There were problems. Michael could not figure out why he should make a whole page of ones or twos or threes. He would make a few, and then quit. I don't think he ever finished a paper.

And then in January, he had to go back to the hospital for a second hernia operation. He had had one operation the summer before he started going to school, but it had not been successful, so, he had a second one involving a more complicated bit of surgery.

And now after two operations, and viral pneumonia, he was stuttering so much he couldn't get words out most of the time. He was back to pointing. He would still try to talk to Philip, and sometimes to me. When school started, I explained what had happened over the summer and told the poor nun she was going to have to try to teach him without expecting him to read out loud with the rest of the class. Bless her, she really worked at it, and he made it, but he acquired the habit of daydreaming through many class activities.

It took a couple of years of planned neglect and our Michael finally did overcome his stuttering, but by then he had learned that no one bothered him if he sat quietly at his desk and withdrew into his own little world, so in the fourth grade, the teacher had to figure out how to get him to take part in class activities, without bringing on another round of stuttering.

C'est la vie.

That is how one thing leads to another.

— Mother

8 5

Smelly Permanents
And Those TV Boils
By John

Mother's virtue of thrift was, of course, the cornerstone of survival during what seems now to have been our fleeting youth.

One bi-weekly endurance of this virtue was the Saturday morning haircut. Her technique — one hand firmly on the top of the head while her other swiftly wielded the clippers — would probably not have qualified her for licensed practice, but the results were acceptable enough, in the greased-down days of Fitch Hair Oil, on to the days of burrs and flattops, and up to the amorphous forms that finally removed the measurable sense of accomplishment and caused her to retire from cosmetology.

Her skills also included engaging the girls in those smelly permanents that would empty the house for an entire day several times a year.

A last memorable exercise of thrift usually occurred at times of the major family diseases. Once the currently playing plague had attacked its fourth or fifth victim, the scale of economy justified taking the most stricken victim to the doctor and then purchasing the long-needed antidote with volume discounts at Smith Bros. Pharmacy in Ridgedale.

Most of us remember the great plague of "TV Boils." After the seventh victim fell prey to these nasty little sores, the doctor identified the likely cause as some unhygienic source shared by all the victims. With that description we considered burning the

house, or at least the downstairs bathroom, but Mother ardently rejected such practical measures. Since the only alternative was to wait them out, we decided that this disease should at least carry some moral implications. There was a growing addiction at that time to awful television shows such as *My Three Sons* and *Combat* and worse. Like the Biblical plagues against Egypt and the Philistines, we were quickly able to conclude that those who watched the greatest amount of television were without a doubt the most severely stricken by our boils. It was never accurately determined whether it was cutting back on TV watching or boiling the downstairs shower soap dish that ultimately killed the plague.

We were fortunate that, unlike our childhood bouts with chicken pox and measles, and the continual swapping of colds, the TV Boils never returned.

— John

The girls not only got permanents. They notoriously also got a lot more gifts than the boys at Christmas.

8 6

Childhood
Licks

Kroger's, the local supermarket Mrs. Erickson emptied every Thursday morning, gave out Top Value Stamps at the cash register. The gifts the resulting books of stamps were later traded for introduced us to middle-class America.

They first brought us a collapsible, aluminum, back yard picnic table. It seemed like a good idea at the time but was probably the least used of the *luxuries* that arrived from Top Value.

The stamps also introduced us to home movies. One year they brought us an eight-millimeter movie camera. The next year they brought us a set of indoor movie camera lights so we could make better use of the Brownie, use it to record Christmas instead of just Easter egg hunts and ensuing summer traditions. And the next year they brought us a movie projector so we could view the roll of film we had so frivolously shot up during the preceding two years. I shouldn't make light of the movie camera. It documented nearly a decade of Little Eileen's magnetic charm.

Each roll of film captured the hoard of ever enlarging but always ecstatic kids stampeding down the stairs on a Christmas morning aimed in the general direction of the Christmas Tree. I say "general direction" because what presents couldn't make it under the tree were spread in piles on chairs and along the floor in two or three adjacent rooms. After the yearly charge of the little brigade, there would be several minutes of film showing Little Eileen opening some of her  presents. It always took the girls longer than the rest of us. Actually, just long seconds that seemed like minutes when compared to everyone else's exposure.

The girls and Mother insisted their more focused attention, so obvious when a roll of film was finally fully shot, developed, and then shown on the Top Value projector, was because the girls took their time. We knew it was a matter of volume. Of presents. It was not beneath us to count.

There was always enough film left over from Christmas to show a posse of little kids stumbling around outside the house looking for eggs on mostly sunny but sometimes chilly Easter mornings. Then a few minutes of Eileen charming the viewing audience in her new Easter outfit. Christmas and Easter — even when the other two girls began getting a fair share of footage — were never quite enough to use up a whole year's roll of film. So on every six-minute roll there is a sequence of skinny boys horsing around at the lake on a summer Sunday, maybe building a human pyramid in the water and then several seconds of a one-year-older-now Little Eileen swimming gracefully. The roll had to be used up in August so a new roll of 8 mm Kodak film could be inserted into the camera to capture the Christmas stampede down the stairs.

Our years were simple. Christmas, Easter, swimming. It's a good thing we never went on vacations because we couldn't afford two rolls in one year.

◎

Licking the Top Value Stamps that were redeemed for camera equipment, the folding table, a waffle iron, and even one of those new, luxury toaster ovens, was one of our decidedly unpleasant growing pains.

Top Value and Green Stamps hadn't yet realized they could provide large denominations. So everything was counted out to the grocery buyer in sheets and partial sheets of single stamps which then had to be pasted individually onto the pages of the redemption books.

The books took 50 stamps per page and had 25 pages per book. We seldom sat down to licking with fewer than 30 books to fill. That's 37,500 licks. Five thousand tongue licks apiece, give or take, depending on the size of the tongue, if there were seven of us who couldn't get out of it. And this was much harder to get out of than the family Rosary.

Fortunately, there were occasional strips of five stamps across that could be handled easily enough with one long lick.

We experimented with all manner of sponges and wet wash rags, and longed for the day when Top Value would offer a licking machine in its catalog for about 1-1/2 books. We wasted a lot of time experimenting with leisure devices and dreaming about how great life would be, "When . . . "

We were always better at wagging our tongues than applying them to some useful purpose.

Licking took the greater part of a Saturday afternoon. The foreboding knowledge that licking was scheduled effectively ruined Saturday mornings. Forty thousand licks calls for an awful lot of tongue, so we made sure no one got out of this torture — no one younger, that is. Older brothers managed, at a certain undefined age to come up with more important things to do. "My science project is due Monday and I've got to solder this wiring!" But they could never get away with that unless the next older one had likewise found something of justifiable importance to disqualify him from the task.

It was just a matter of time before Philip and I discovered what all the older ones had — that licking is for little kids. The five- and six-year-olds could actually be talked into enjoying licking stamps if a respected, world-wise older brother made this new responsibility seem mature enough. Philip and I finally succeeded in getting out of the licking one year and Eileen managed to be doing something old and important the next, though, by all rights, it should have been two years before this queen of the realm got free.

Cecilia, Paul, Charles, and Carol — never had any littler ones to pawn these onerous duties off on.

They eventually returned most basic little kid tasks to Mother, who had promulgated such toilsome cycles back in the days of giants.

The Top Value Stamp catalog, where
2 ½ books could make you modern.

87

"Being Spoiled Is Wonderful." But . . .
By Eileen

My entire life, needless to say, had been a somewhat unusual experience. While the Nazi Youth Corps might have gone out of business, I can assure you that the brothers of the Clan Erickson amply filled their place, even if the mission had changed.

I realize my arrival on the scene was somewhat of an imposition on the seven boys already securely settled in their places. Thank goodness my gender bestowed many privileges on me — and I will be the first to admit that being spoiled is wonderful.

This process included such important events as being allowed into the sanctuary after Mass, a place most girls never saw. . . . Road trips with Daddy. . . . Sitting in the middle of the front seat instead of in the back with my white dress on. . . . Dancing lessons. . . . And being able to attend a party up on the mountain at the Caldwells before Michael and Philip.

Of course, this exalted position put me in line for much abuse. The grapefruit episode is a good example. When I was not served my grapefruit first, I burst into tears and ran up the stairs and threw myself on the bed as Scarlett O'Hara would have done. This instance resulted in everyone running around for months saying, "Don't disturb Eileen. You might upset her."

When I refused to play football one day, upsetting the numbers on the teams, they were simply reorganized, and I was never allowed to play again. (This decision on their part to block me from further physical activity obviously stunted the development of my breasts, for which I will never forgive them.)

Mom's down-to-earth and matter-of-fact attitude of "what you put in is what you get out" was often puzzling to me as a child. Looking back, I realize it was right on target. I will always remember, upon receiving a "U" (for unsatisfactory) in Conduct on my report card, Mom said, "That U will be there forever. And if that's what you want to see on your report card, it's up to you." Nothing more was said or done, but the point was made and the lesson learned.

I think, in retrospect, we all now realize that being part of a family of 16 has been more help than hindrance. I, for one, know that being part of this group has resulted in my life being much more enjoyable than it otherwise would have been, and I have appreciated every experience it offered me. For these experiences, we will all be eternally grateful to Mom and Dad.

— Eileen

8 8

To The Beat
Of A Disappearing Drummer

I could hold the same little regard for the band that I do for the Boy Scouts and the altar boys, but I don't.

If Scouting was a dead-end street, the altar boys was a vast, neglected pothole. A knowledge of Latin liturgy has proved about as useful as being able to tell time by observing which side of a tree the moss grows on. The band, at least, introduced us to the breadth and depth of music. That was the idea Mr. and Mrs. Erickson had in mind when they enrolled the Big Boys in the band many, many years ago.

⦿

All of us played in the band over the years — that is, until the year I finally quit while in high school and unintentionally but single-handedly disbanded this archaic school institution.

Harold played the saxophone, Frank the clarinet, Allen the clarinet and other reed instruments, John the trumpet, David the French horn, Philip a mean trombone, and I was a percussionist — which is a two-dollar way of saying I played the drums. Eileen played the clarinet, and Douglas the trumpet. Maybe it stopped there, or maybe Louis and Cecilia both learned instruments as well since I seem to recall little Cecilia struggling with a squeaky clarinet. As each of us in turn was added to the band, the house temporarily filled with the sounds of something only distantly related to music. The sounds of practice. The practice of scales: *dummmm, dummm, dum, drawk, dun, dennn, den, drringgk, drawk!* . . .

Most of us were good musicians. The only one whose talent was suspect was David with his French horn. His finesse with that brass instrument seemed limited to opening its bottom valve between songs at band practice and blowing spit out. The older ones used to say, "David, your lips are just too big for the French horn. Why don't you play the baritone or tuba?" Because there was a kid in his class with repulsively large lips, David couldn't get comfortable with the idea of sharing such an unseemly trait. He would pretend his lips were small and just try harder. In his determination, David became quite proficient — at blowing spit out of the valve between songs.

⦿

John was exceptionally talented on his trumpet. Perhaps he was no more talented than the older ones with their reed instruments, but they weren't able to show off so readily since a clarinet blasting into a solo of the *Notre Dame Victory March* isn't nearly as impressive as a trumpet preening its staccato notes.

⦿

It was a high school band, but there weren't enough talented students in the high school to make it work so grade schoolers — housed in the same red brick building downtown — were occasionally allowed to play.

I was the youngest member the band ever had. I played a little tin drum in the rhythm band during the first and second grades, took a year off to give my many fans a break from the frenzy of it all, then joined the real band in the fourth grade. I was about half the size of the bass drum I was charged with taming.

⊙

Several years after the band disbanded and it was obvious it could never be revived without a major expenditure, one of the nuns was cleaning out the old band room. She knew the Ericksons had been the mainstay of the band. In its glory years there were seven of us holding down various chairs. So she asked Mrs. Erickson if any of us would like to have some of the old instruments. They looked worthless to the nun, but Mother knew they would respond brightly to a little polish. She cleaned up.

Harold got his old saxophone back, Frank his clarinet. John and Philip can entertain visitors to either coast of Florida with trumpet or trombone solos. She did not return my bass drum — though filled with water it could make a comfortable back yard kiddie pool.

I think she didn't get me a drum because I'm still being punished for quitting the band. She also had problems finding David's old French horn. Hmm.

Above: Two Eileens. Below, Daddy, Michael, and Frank.

8 9

The Year
Of The Elk

We didn't just eat dry round steak, mashed potatoes with gravy, and applesauce day in and day out.

We also ate elk.

One year, we ate a whole lot of elk.

The Year Of The Elk.

⑩

One of Daddy's brothers — it's hard to say which one because they are all so distant and unknown — was tromping through some far corner of the Earth called "Alaska." Alaska was closer to Russia than it was to statehood the year this distant uncle from Washington state came upon an even more distant elk. Our elk. He shot it, which is just one of three imaginative things people can do with an elk. The other  imaginative things people can do with an elk are let it live, or eat it.

This elk was about the size of Mount Rainier. It was far too large for Daddy's brother to stomach on his own, so he kindly and proudly sent half of his elk to a noise called the Ericksons in a place called Chattanooga.

⑩

Rumors of the elk preceded the actual arrival of the elk by several weeks. Mrs. Erickson, of course, did not like it. She had a difficult enough time liking the things she was accustomed to, and she had neither the time nor the disposition to be adjusting to anything new.

She found a lot of faults with this half of an elk rumored to be on its way. "We don't have room for half an elk!" she grumbled. "I can't possibly carve an elk!" she grieved. "I don't even know how to cook an elk," she beefed. There were lots of problems rumored to be on their way from this cold frontier called Alaska.

⑩

Daddy solved as many of the problems as he could. He solved the biggest problem — where to put half an elk — by clearing out space in the freezer bin he leased from a cold storage company in Chattanooga to keep his floral greens preserved. He laid out half an elk among the funeral ferns.

The next biggest problem — how to carve an elk solved itself when the meat arrived neatly butchered into serving-sized portions of shoulder steaks, leg steaks, saddles, ribs, blades, osso buco, and several modestly sized packages of ground elkburger meat. Individually wrapped in heavy white butcher's paper and marked according to the cut, these portions were easily stored in the bin where the temperatures hovered around zero.

The elk, coming from Alaska, probably found Chattanooga's cold storage bin uncomfortably warm. Mrs. Erickson, not one to be any more easily placated than the elk itself, said, "It must have cost him a fortune to have this stupid thing cut up like that. Why didn't he just send us the money."

⦿

We ate the elk.

We ate it for the whole next year.

Our elk eating was occasionally supplemented by formerly routine repasts like round steak with mashed potatoes and applesauce, but the elk clearly dominated that year's digestive tracting.

Mother really had no trouble fixing the elk. You cook it just like beef. You can fry it, broil it, charcoal it, stew it, or convert it into chipped elk on toast. It can be seared just as dry as the next mammal.

The only problem Mother had was with the elk steaks. Some were thick — one to two inches. Prime cuts. It had been decades since she had done anything with thick prime cuts of steak other than look down her nose at them at the meat counter in the Kroger supermarket. Now she had to de-juice them for the first time in her adult life.

Daddy, of course, aggravated whatever problems she could come up with. He stopped by the cold storage bin about once a week to load up on white packages of elk meat. His main offense was bringing home the wrong packages. He had practiced this art of allegedly bringing home the wrong things over the years by regularly bringing home the wrong number of loaves of bread. We used hundreds of loaves of bread

every year in the nightly ritual of preparing school lunches. Daddy bought them every other afternoon at the market down the street from his store so to assure Mother was serving us only the tastiest, freshest white bread, often baked that very morning.

But Daddy, in the empirical judgment of Mother, nearly always brought home the wrong number. If he bought three, she complained, loudly, she needed *"four!"* If he brought four, she exclaimed, *"Three!"*

Daddy, if one trusted Mrs. Erickson's loud judgment on this, and there was really no option for him or others, had a surprisingly strong affinity for bringing the wrong thing home. Even when he was hunting elk at the local cold storage company.

⦿

That big old half-an-elk was shot during one of Alaska's short summers. As Chattanooga's next long summer came to visit, we were thawing out chopped elk meat and charcoaling elkburgers in the back yard. We were growing weary of elk. We were even growing tired of elk steaks, though it would be years before any of us would be far enough from home to cut into another steak even close to the size and quality that half an elk gave up for us.

⦿

Elk has an unmistakable taste.

It is a game animal — venison. We used to remind each other of that because it made us feel vicariously rugged. Sometimes visitors, especially local priests, would be invited to join us for prime elk steaks and they would note it reminded them of deer. We didn't know because we had never tasted deer. I still haven't. I haven't tasted quail either. Or guppies. I am not what you would call an exotic eater. After years in Florida, I have yet to attempt a slippery oyster on a half shell. I have yet to eat my first tomato. True. I'm not adventurous. White bread and meat get the job done.

⦿

Consistent with the taste of elk is its smell.

When turkey is being baked in the oven, its aroma fills the house. When elkburgers were being sizzled in the skillet, that distinctive bouquet also permeated the house. It was common to enter by the carport door after playing outside with a group of brothers and sisters and hear one of them whine, "Gawww! Not elk again tonight!"

Few people can claim "Not-elk-again-tonight" as a common childhood complaint. Not many ever will.

Most of the half an elks left in Alaska are hiding out in protected areas. Happy to keep their unmistakable smells to themselves.

Above: Paul and Cecilia. Daddy with first three (Harold, Frank, and Allen). Then first five. Below: Frank and Eileen.

9 0

Hello George
By Charles

George meets Momma.

As usual, the green Cougar was parked out front. Not in the front driveway or in the front yard, but in the street in front of the house. The Blacks now living throughout much of our neighborhood must have liked seeing that fancy Cougar parked out front. The stereo in the living room was likely playing some kind of rock and roll music, probably the Rolling Stones' *Hot Rocks* album that I managed to buy from George for $2.50. Brand new album. Only problem was one cut, *19th Nervous Breakdown,* had a slight scratch. Still one of the best deals I ever got on an album.

Mom came into the room. George was disquietly sitting on the couch next to his girlfriend, my sister, Cecilia. He hadn't yet bargained for meeting the parents and he was a little nervous.

Mrs. Erickson (as she enters the room): Hello George!

George (his head buried beneath the cushions of the couch): Hello Mrs. Erickson.

Mrs. Erickson: Well, I just wanted to see if everything was okay.

George (voice muffled): Everything's fine.

Mrs. Erickson: Well, it's always nice to see you George.

George (head still buried in the cushions of the couch): It's always nice to see you, too, Mrs. Erickson.

Sometime after this meeting George managed to show his face. Sooner or later, the cops made him quit parking his car on the front street. For a while, he parked the car on Oak Street, along the side of the house, but somewhere along the way he got bold enough to park in the spacious driveway and actually walk through the kitchen door.

— Charles

9 1

When Last
Is Far From Final

Mother loved it when we played Let's-See-Who-Can-Be-Quiet-The-Longest. She gladly interpreted our hand signals as answers to her lunchtime questions about what kind of soup or sandwich we wanted. She bent over backward to accommodate our playing that game. She thought it was the greatest thing since God had given her girls. But, much as she relished the peaceful lunches it inspired, she would have traded them all to be spared just one game of "Gotcha-last!"

(0)

Gotcha-last! had simple rules. To play, you just touch a brother or sister, announce "Gotcha-last!," and dash madly out of that person's reach before he or she can touch back. It was that rare game in which participation was required by the mere act of living. The games of sex and money come also to mind.

No matter how many times Douglas might declare that he wasn't playing, his better judgment might fail as he passed Louis sitting in the TV room watching a football game while he, Douglas, was on his way to the downstairs bathroom to take a shower. He knew Louis was extremely proud of having gotten nearly everyone last and was posted in the big green chair watching carefully for any past victims who might attempt to run in, touch him, and get away without being touched back. He could tell by Louie's casualness that this would-be champion was finally convinced Douglas was truly not playing since he hadn't bothered getting anyone back for several days. So, before starting his shower, Douglas opens the bathroom door, making sure it can be easily re-entered and locked, tiptoes across the bare carpet until he is just in reach of Louie's head, lightly brushes the back of that head, and claims "Gotcha-last!" while sprinting into the bathroom and locking the door.

Louis would have to wait outside the door until Douglas finished his shower if he hoped to remedy the situation. Douglas, of course, would announce through the door, "I'm-going-to-wash-my-hair!!" Which was just another way of saying that he might be in there until football season was over.

⑩

An older brother — Allen — might walk through the breakfast room after scraping his dinner plate into the trash can and touch the whole line of babies at the kitchen table on his way out, whispering to each one, "Gotcha-last!"

The game's only rule was that this expression had to be made to each individual at the time of the touch.

The babies would be trapped when the older brother swept in like that because recklessly spilling milk while playing the forbidden game of Gotcha-last! at the kitchen table was our all-time most unforgivable offense. We were supposedly not allowed to play Gotcha-last! in the house. Especially at the table. But it had long been determined that it was not a sin when we violated those

unjustifiable strictures. We did not ask, we reasoned, to be born into either the house or this forbidden game.

Free will was not in play when it came to Gotcha-last!

⦾

Another rule for this game, which was really a rule for the family in general covering all games, activities, and fights, was that you couldn't hit anyone hard.

"Hard," however, is subjective. The touching inherent to Gotcha-last! created considerable crying as babies brought their cases to Mrs. Erickson, claiming to have been hit hard. That is what Mother didn't like about the game. That and the constant running, diving, and jumping as kids tried to escape after having touched someone else — or as they avoided each other for days on end careful to keep chairs, tables, or even Mrs. Erickson between them.

Mother's dislike of the game was monumental. Because of this well known feature, one of the safest places to hide once you had gotten too many people last and were on everyone's hit list was under her feet. She might be in the kitchen drying out that night's round steak and have two or three children dodging around her, playing their cat-and-mouse game of brazen Gotcha-last! Only the smaller children could really hide between her legs, and when she was pregnant even the babies had trouble finding sanctuary there. But every few months she was faced with kids using her for cover. They could never say what they were doing there, because we were technically not allowed to play Gotcha-last! in the house. Still, they were there and there was no doubt what was going on.

"What are all of you doing in the kitchen!" she would demand.

"Oh, nothing," everyone would admit with ill-concealed guilt.

"Well, then do it somewhere else!" she would command.

"Come on, Paul. Mommy said you have to get out of the kitchen," Charles would nag from his vantage point in the breakfast room doorway where he had been camped for 30 minutes waiting to get Paul last.

⦾

The games lasted a minimum of two days, and a maximum of two weeks.

They were especially prevalent during periods of rain outside, since that was the only place the game was technically allowed to be played. And there was never just one game. It was more like 10 to 14 individual franchises playing out a triple elimination round robin tournament.

When these games were in season, nothing could stop them. One might sneak out of bed at night, creep into another age group's room, and tag a bunch of toes while whispering a bunch of "Gotcha-last!"s

Long suffering.

The worst thing we could have done, and never avoided doing, was play the game in the car. On the way to church on Sundays and on the way home, if the game was in progress, there would be considerable reaching out and touching one another, and a lot of whispered declarations. Concealing a forbidden game of Gotcha-last! in the car is about as easy as hiding gas in a bathtub. Mother would insist, demand, then command, from the front passenger seat of the tumultuous station wagon that the game be stopped! Over! Ended!

We always appreciated her position, but these commands were impossible to obey.

One of our most inflexible rules was that no one could quit a game while he was losing.

By every measure, Gotcha-last! was loaded with losers.

A small subset of the antagonists.

92

Hairy
Saturdays

Dualism: As good as Saturdays were, they were equally bad.

It was the day we licked Top Value Stamps.

The day we folded paper.

Saturday nights meant shining shoes for Sunday Mass.

Saturdays were also haircut day. An every other week plague.

One way to show the world your kids were decent — if you couldn't dress them that way — was to keep their ears scrubbed and their hair cut.

A family that couldn't afford doctors certainly had no room in the budget for barbers, so Mrs. Erickson opened shop. Five thousand haircuts. That would hardly faze a professional barber. It hardly fazed this pregnant lady, either.

⫟

Even when crew cuts and flattops were the rage most of us preferred keeping our hair trimmed just a little on the long side. We liked having a little wisp up front to bother with whenever the day became boring.

We spent a lot of time trying to "train" our hair, our euphemism for trying to get that little wisp of a bang to lay down just like we wanted so all the little girls would melt when we ignored them. We passed around a lot of secrets garnered from the Big Boys about how to train hair. Their secrets were worthless. Those whose hair was naturally straight and floppy were credited with being able to control their mops. Those cursed with unruly curly hair were ridiculed and encouraged to throw our mops away. It was often suggested we might want to change handles as well.

⫟

Dealing with our hair between haircuts was but a minor matter of psychological duress. The haircut itself was physical duress.

We were called in order because that was always most efficient. The parents didn't lose track. Kids knew who was next. Haircuts, baths, medicine for communal diseases — we were called up by age to ensure no one escaped.

Haircuts interrupted play. If it wasn't you being called to the stool, it was whoever you were playing with.

Our barber chair was a weak, wobbly, aluminum stool. There were a few random spots of red left, but everything around the seat and support bars across the bottom had been worn down to the gray aluminum by an endless series of feet and rumps as we and the wobbly stool submitted to those five thousand shearings.

⑩

The worst part of haircuts was the way we were wrapped.

Shortly after the invention of polyethylene, Mrs. Erickson discovered that if you wrap moppets in the thin plastic bags that protect suits picked up at the dry cleaners, the black silk snippets of hair roll off, onto the floor, saving her from having to slow down the assembly line by walking to the back door to shake out the sheet. She was quite pleased with how well this worked. Indeed, it worked well enough — for her.

But wrap yourself in Saran Wrap and sit for ten minutes indoors in the 90 degree heat of August. You'll notice it makes you sweat. February can be just as sultry, wrapped in plastic.

The reusable plastic sheet Mother pinned around our pencil necks was a hair or two thicker than the dry cleaner's bag, but made you sweat just the same. And fans didn't help. Air can't penetrate plastic.

Being first in line for haircuts wasn't something anyone ever volunteered for, but that position had its merits. You didn't have to step over a half-foot-deep circle of black hair to get to the stool. And the plastic sheet was at least dry on the inside.

We always took our shirts off so hair didn't get down our backs. We never quite got all the little bits of loose hair out of our cropped heads before putting our shirts back on, so, while the early part of every other Saturday was spent dreading a haircut, the latter part was spent itching and scratching.

I routinely suggested that we could save a lot of scratching if we could use the vacuum sweeper to suck the loose ends out of our scalps before they crawled down into our shirts. Mother, supported by her older and supposedly wiser children, insisted it would never work. It never did, but only because it was never tried. I employed this technique many times later in life. Works fine.

I should have cleverly cloaked my oft-rejected proposal vacuum under the guise of a science fair project.

But I think Mother's main objection was she didn't want to waste the air.

◍

Harold and the older ones used to talk about how they would listen to the radio on Saturdays and how they tried to get haircuts done during *Buck Rodgers* or *The Shadow* or some of those other famous oldies. I can't speak for their memories because if I was there at all I was busy dirtying diapers, but I know one of the main complaints from the first television generation was that the electric hair clippers Mother used in our time dramatically interfered with TV reception, causing the picture to wiggle or start rotating and making the sound crackle. I guess Harold and Frank remember life as being better than it really was — or maybe they listened to their radio programs before the days of electricity.

There wasn't anything productive to do while wilting under the plastic. No multi-tasking. Mother wouldn't let anyone else come in and talk to you for fear he would get hair on him and track it through the house. I wanted to spend the time reading magazines like Ozzie Nelson did on television while getting his hair cut, but Mother insisted that would get in the way. She was right about that. Ozzie was putting us on.

Mrs. Erickson stayed on top of any new developments in the barber industry. Hers was one of the first shops in town to experiment with and prove the convenience of electric clippers. She wore out a number of those compact, hand-held devices. Electric clippers are fine until they develop a nick on one of their many cutting blades. Nothing could repair a nick on one of the blades, or  otherwise make it go away. And nothing could stop those little nicks from heartlessly attacking our little necks.

Mother always felt bad when one of her clippers slipped from her rapidly moving hand and hit the floor or stool hard enough to get nicked. She couldn't afford to replace it until it had at least three or four such blood-sucking imperfections.

It's bad enough knowing you're going to have to interrupt play in a few minutes to sweat through a haircut. It's much worse when an older brother who has already been through the treatment and has shaken his loose ends down into his shirt comes out to ostensibly warn you, "The clippers are really nicking this afternoon."

That's like being in line for your typhoid shot, which is one of the worst lines to ever be in, and having an older brother assure you, "The shot won't hurt too much. . . . But I remember that nurse from last year. She breaks needles."

*Not all haircuts are created equal. It's
likely this one was dictated by the times.*

93

The Day The House Went Quiet

Dear Nieces and Nephews, and Holy Readers,

I never quite finished that story about how we were such good little Catholics with our little white Catholic clothes.

I wouldn't bother finishing it except there is a point to the story. The point will come later.

First we have to go back to the little white pants and suit coats and dresses. There were some bigger white togs as well because two or three times a year the nuns insisted on lining all the school children up and proceeding them around the church. These proceedings were called processions.

On certain religious holidays — Holy Thursday of Easter Week being one, something called Forty Hours Devotion being another, and, for lack of being able to accurately identify a third I'll just say Shirley Temple's birthday is also one — but anyway, on certain religious holidays we had processions in conjunction with special evening Masses at the church.

At a prearranged point in these special Masses, the student bodies of both Notre Dame elementary and high schools, which were housed in the same building a block up the street, stood from

their honored seating positions in the first 30 or so pews and stepped row-by-row, into the aisles. For the next 15 minutes, the students paraded up and down every aisle in the church.

The nuns thought it fitting for everyone to wear white for these processions — at least white pants and white shirts. There were hundreds of students involved, and as this long white worm snaked its way through the church it sang a monotonous Latin hymn. "Pange Lingua" was the most popular procession march. When part of the long white worm paraded out of the main hall of the church to make a turn in the vestibule, it usually came back singing either a few measures fast or slow. The worm constantly meandered in and out of the three doorways leading from the nave to the vestibule so it didn't take long for the chant to become totally fragmented with each group of 40 students working on different lines. When a group came back into the church singing its own new *stanza the procession was over and everyone returned to their pews.*

∞ — ∞

Our nuns derived great pleasure from processions.

It was their way of showing off how big their school was getting since their little white toys, testaments of the national post-war baby boom, took up more and more aisle space every year.

∞ — ∞

We were separated for processions according to grades and sex, and then paired according to size.

I was always one of the two smallest boys in my class, so I was always stuck in the front.

It was tough enough being small without having to parade your shortcomings in front of God and the rest of the world.

I finally started growing in my junior year of high school —

A 1950s Catholic procession.

our first year in the new school now miles distant from the downtown church and our first year of no high school participation in the processions. I would have been near the back of my class once there was no longer an opportunity for such esteem. Poor little big me.

∞ — ∞

If there was anything redeeming about processions it was that practicing for them took up a lot of class time.

It's dubious, though, if practicing that tedious slow walk day after day was any better than sitting through geography class and learning about Catholic countries. But the nuns never asked what I thought. Unless they could tell by the way I was squirming that I didn't have the answer.

∞ — ∞

Smiling in church wasn't allowed, so we had to keep a straight face whenever we might look across the aisle we were practicing proceeding down and see a younger brother or sister proceeding up the next one. Hands folded, eyes straight ahead. You could see by their expressions that the really young ones — the first- and second-graders — were trying so hard to get it right.

∞ — ∞

I said at the beginning there would be a point.

One Easter I was home from college and noticed everyone in the house was running around screaming at each other as they came closer and closer to not leaving on time to make it to the downtown church for the annual Holy Thursday five o'clock procession.

The grade schoolers were all dressed in white because they had to participate. The high schoolers were required to attend because they were still subservient to the whims of God and Mrs. Erickson. I didn't have to go because I was in college and was permitted to make my own bad decisions.

Finally, after about an hour of the mania that typically takes place whenever four or five people are trying to get into the same necktie, the big carport door slammed and I could hear all the screaming and shouting coasting down the driveway and out into the traffic where it belonged.

So I walked into the kitchen, popped a nice cold beer, sat at the kitchen table, and looked blankly at the evening paper while trying to come up with something to do.

The house was quiet. Clamoring with quiet.

The house was so quiet it was distracting. Which I guess is why it was several minutes before I understood why I was feeling so uncomfortable. At age 19, this was the first time I had ever been in that big old house alone.

Relatively yours,
Uncle Rags

Michael. First year home from college. First time in an empty house.

94

Waging War
On The Home Front

As much as we were all opposed to war the way it turned out to be played in the real world, it was one of our favorite escapes as kids. Playing war was an easy — maybe a natural successor to our toying around with cowboys. Coinciding with the rash of World War II movies that began appearing on television in the Fifties, we hung up our six-guns and holsters, and brandished machine guns.

The machine guns usually made authentic popping sounds, until the popper broke — about two days after Christmas, at which time we little troopers were reduced to making gunfire sounds with our little mouths.

During our cowboy days, which preceded the built-in poppers, six-guns could be loaded with rolls of exploding caps. But at ten cents for 10,000 the caps were prohibitively expensive. Our action was defined by the shooter's oral gymnastics, which could indicate whether those few non-lethal bullets fired as much from his throat as from his gun were ricocheting off rocks or echoing ominously among land masses. We often backed Germans  into the same Western canyons we had previously cleared of savage Indians and gangs of outlaws.

Michael stands over his latest victim, Philip.

While playing army outside we were usually all on the same side with the war being waged against imaginary Germans. Never, for some reason, Japanese. The Germans holed up in the abandoned, servant's quarters above the garage. Two of the Little Kids were dispatched to return fire from the side window since they were not allowed to enter this slightly hazardous structure. The older ones rushed the narrow wooden door at the bottom of the stairs — dodging enemy fire as we darted from the bushes and gallantly zigzagged across that treacherous, barren terrain otherwise known as "the badminton court."

We waited at the foot of the stairs just long enough for the hapless Germans to forget we were at their door, then stalked quietly up, careful to avoid those steps that always creak in the movies when bad guys are trying to sneak up on good guys. Once up the stairs, we wiped out the nest of surprised Nazis, who always had their backs turned as they leaned out the side window trying to kill Paul and Charles down in the back yard.

We always hollered "Drop it!" — a courtesy we had learned as cowboys — before firing on them. This gave the Germans, who never paid any attention to our warnings, a chance to turn and fire first. Even

Paul and Charles are ready to defend their sisters.

in war, it's unethical for good guys to shoot bad guys without warning, especially in the back.

Back down the stairs, we collected the decoys we had left in the back yard, the Little Kids, walked around the house, sharing the pleasant camaraderie of a crisp Fall afternoon, perhaps trading war stories, only to come upon a new two-story garage loaded with a new band of scurrilous, soon-to-be-defeated Germans.

Mother's family was only a couple of generations removed from Germany. But that wasn't talked about much in the Fifties.

When playing war inside the house we usually divided into teams — one group sieging the upstairs, the other defending. When divided like that we faced the problem of who would be the Americans — the good guys. We never solved that one. We just killed those on the other side — which is pretty much the historic essence of war.

9 5

War
And Peace

Dear Nieces and Nephews, and Valued Readers,

Everyone in the family participated at times in our ongoing war games.

We were all proud of our individually cunning ways.

That cunning came in handy years later when the Vietnam War bombed its way into the life of this country.

We all proved adept at standing legally clear of that war's smoke and fire. Pride is probably not what we're supposed to feel for the fact that not one of 11 able-bodied brothers, which includes the two exempted for having flat feet, ever spent a day in the Army.

Had the war been different, our participation might have been different. I don't know. I hope I never have to find out.

And I hope, little nieces and nephews, that you never have to find out either.

Relatively yours,
Uncle Rags

9 6

Knocking John Out — Redux
By Harold

We fought a lot but weren't really a violent family.

Punching in the shoulder was allowed but hitting in the stomach was not. And hitting in the face was never thought of. So it's surprising to remember that I actually knocked John out cold, twice. I think I dropped a bucket of bricks on Frank's head once but that was a long time ago. I never liked John much. We mostly wanted the "little kids" to just leave us alone. But John was inquisitive and uppity.

The first time I knocked him out was when he touched my model airplane. It was one of those things made from little balsa wood sticks and covered with tissue paper. I doubt that kids ever make them nowadays, prefab plastic parts are much faster. Anyway, I had put a lot of work into this plane and it was beautiful. I think John knew how nice it was but do you think I wanted to show it to my little brother? I just wanted him to go away. He kept hanging around so I told him not to dare touch it. I guess he couldn't turn down a dare because he went up with one finger out and touched it, ever so lightly. I was mad, too mad to just punch him in the shoulder. So I pushed him against the wall as hard as I could (away from the plane). He banged his head on the wall and Zonk. OUT COLD. He was out for a minute or so and the parents were pretty mad but I felt justified. I had told him not to touch it and he deliberately did it.

The second time was more in fun. We had a big box and were taking turns inside being rolled down the hill on the side yard. We got a little vigorous with John inside the box, really bounced him down the hill as fast as we could. I don't really remember what happened, maybe he hit the metal clothesline pole at the bottom of the hill. Anyway, once again OUT COLD. And even though it was probably mostly an accident we got a lot of grief, because everybody knew that we older ones really didn't like the "little kids." – Harold

A few years before the big knockout, Harold, Frank, and Allen, the original Big Boys, were already marking their ground against an unforeseeable string of newcomers.

9 7

Sex.

A book, like life, would be incomplete without sex.

Sex was an especially touchy subject around our house. Good Catholics that we were, we pretended it didn't exist.

For many years it was neither talked, about nor alluded to.

When older brothers first headed off to college and began coming home for Thanksgiving, Christmas, and spring holidays to start the tradition of sitting up late at night drinking beer and explaining to everyone what life is all about, they managed to dwell effectively and expertly on every topic except one: Sex.

It's possible, especially considering two of the oldest four were seminarians, and another was a nerdy scientist, none of them was either effective or expert in the realm of sex. Perhaps that is why this subject — even after the parents had gone to bed for the night — was always changed as quickly as it might unintentionally raise its troubling head during those kitchen table free-for-alls. There was something wrong here. Something amiss. I'm certain most of those same older brothers whiled away hour after hour at college talking about sex with their roommates and fellow students, because I know sex is the most popular subject at any university.

There was no other topic in the entire spectrum of humanity's knowledge and ignorance that could not be expertly debated at our kitchen table. We argued about the effect of inconsonant proton disruptions aberrant in the vacuous static of an electromagnetic gravity field as easily as we differed over whether a too-familiar Rod Stewart melody was pilfered more from Fats Domino or Rossini. Religion, politics, and even the weather were fecund material for our differences of opinion. We, milking our majority status, might occasionally veer to the mystery of the female psyche. But the frightening physical properties of the human female animal, her most glaring and sometimes redeeming quality in a man's world, was a treacherous ground seldom probed.

And when the subject of sex occasionally stole into the late-night kitchen table conversations, it, unlike any other calamity, including rare beer spills and even rarer audible flatulence, stilled the thunder. The body of universal experts quickly averted its collective vision uncomfortably toward each theoretician's brown, long-necked, returnable beer bottle. The more nervous among us were joined by the less nervous in the wholesale peeling of labels off those long-necked security blankets.

An older one would finally recover and quietly suggest the subject be changed because of the presence of younger ones. The younger ones would sputter for the record that they could handle it, but would be as pleased as the others to get out from under the pale or the flush once a quick wit could launch a suitable new topic. Southeastern Conference football, the season ahead or be-hind, was always a reliable jumping-off point capable of re-ignit-ing the early morning roar.

⓪

For many years we never even addressed, publicly or pri-vately, the most obvious questions in our world: What was Mother and Daddy's sex life like? What's the story behind their uncom-monly long line of progeny?

That Mother and Daddy had sex was obvious even to us non-scientists in the crowd. That they had it often was equally ev-ident. That they might have enjoyed it was never considered. The most the parents have ever said about sex has stemmed from Dad-dy's frequent poke at his harried wife, "Well, you shouldn't have had so many children." To which she responded each and every time: "I didn't have them alone, Buster!" At which point Daddy, alarmed at the prospect that this touchy subject might leap beyond the bounds of taste, returned his nose to his evening paper.

⓪

When the younger ones, the Little Kids, male and female alike, finally came of age, they broke the long-standing ban and began talking openly about sex. The once hushed subject began making, sometimes dominating, the late-night agenda at our bar away from bars.

Like most everyone in the world, the younger ones did not begin by talking about sex — they began by faintly bragging about it. The males, that is. And that, I believe, is one of the key reasons the topic was taboo during those earlier years. The older ones had nothing to brag about.

Harold, the oldest, seemed to be limiting his involvement with women to a clinical probing of their cellular structure. Now, Allen did have an eye for pretty girls. He once flew to Buenos Aires just to see his college sweetheart — a girl rumored to be the reigning Miss Argentina. Perhaps Allen had something to say — which is to say "brag" — about sex, but kept quiet out of deference to the environmental innocence of those two seminarians.

⑩

The first real change cropped in once Allen and David got together at the university in Knoxville. They did not speak their minds about sex at the kitchen table, but by the time I joined them on campus, "going out whoring" was an activity often planned and talked about — though seldom, if ever, executed.

A few years before I joined Allen and David and their grand plans in Knoxville, David had further broken the ice once and shaken my Notre Dame High School morality to its core. He was home from college for a few days his sophomore year and the two of us were driving somewhere in the truck.

We were pulling out of the driveway when David, four years older, making me a much lower form of high school sophomore, came right out and said, "I'm horny as hell." I knew where hell was because the nuns taught us that in geography and most of our other classes. I could tell by the inflection that "horny" was probably on the highway to hell. I realized years later that only a few weeks before David came home and humiliated me with that shockingly vulgar admission he might finally have passed the non-credited university course that justifies why God made girls. The lab sessions in that course were hotly anticipated.

⑩

Philip never spoke of sex. And still doesn't. He dated only a few girls before settling down with a beautiful underclass coed he met in college. They married as soon as he graduated, and the two of them have lived happily ever after. Nauseating.

⦾

I was fortunate enough not to find out about the sordid details of this women/girls mess until one of those early college courses. By not finding out about them until then, I had at least avoided finding out what I was missing. Having found out, I have missed it with alarming, compulsive, soul-wrenching, heart-breaking, mind-numbing consistency almost ever since. Poor, poor me.

⦾

I can't say anything about the younger ones because it might be fact instead of speculation. I will say, though, that Paul and Charles began bragging about sex instead of blushing about it at an early age — early by our ludicrous standards. And I know Louis was a late talker but has fairly babbled ever since, and has fewer scruples than most of us.

⦾

Until such time as the numbers thinned out our household environment was not conducive to developing a suitable rapport with those girl people. With enough kids at hand to play any game, we rarely bothered becoming acquainted with strangers. And women, through no fault of their own, are certainly among the strangest of people.

The younger brothers not only had the benefit of a depopulated house once they fell prey to puberty, but had the added advantage of growing up with sisters. We older ones had only Eileen. And she was so special in every way that we couldn't help but infer all girls were special.

Respecting women, as Faulkner realized, is the surest way to assure an inability to relate to them. "Because women have no respect for each other or themselves," he wrote once — and probably meant it.

While most of us grew up surrounded by Eileen and thought girls were special, Paul and Charles grew up surrounded by Cecilia and Carol, and knew better.

It was perfectly acceptable and even expected that Eileen would have a lot of boyfriends — but, from the time we were six until we left for college, the slightest hint of interest in a girl from one of the boys brought on a sing-song chant from younger and older brothers alike. The chant would go, "Mi-chael has a gur-ul-friend . . . Mi-chael has a gur-ul-friend . . . Mi-i-chael has . . ." The only responsible answer to that sing-song chant was, "I-DO-NOT!" An admission would open yourself to exactly what those adolescent feelings actually were . . . how deep . . . how jumbled . . . what you were hoping . . . etc. . . . . Things one boy would never talk about to another, much less to an entire room of critics.

To be seen talking to a member of the cartwheel sex after school was considered sufficient evidence for the girlfriend accusation. To be caught talking quietly on the upstairs phone was only circumstantial evidence — but we hung many a guilty party on circumstantial evidence. If the accused ever insisted on there being a *corpus delicti*, a body, that was easy. Listening in from downstairs to one of those secretive upstairs phone conversations was not allowed, so a sizeable jury would merely confront the party suspected of being human and roll off a list of likely candidates until one of the names succeeded in colorfully raising the denier's facial temperature. When you're enthralled with the most perfect specimen of femininity to ever walk the face of the earth, even if she likely has no clue as to your infatuation, you will be incensed to hear her precious name spill from the boorish mouths of older brothers. That, coupled with just the reminder of her ambrosial perfection, will make you blush.

⦶

Philip was a freshman in college and I was a junior in high school when Daddy decided it was necessary to tell us about "things" — about the facts of life — because Eileen's best friend had just had to quit high school during their freshman year to have a baby. That didn't happen often among the girls who wore their navy blue jumpers, white blouses, and black shoes every day to Notre Dame, although the head cheerleader in my class disappeared the next year because of that same sort of female trouble. I had danced with that very pretty girl only a few weeks before her disappearance. It stunned me for a long time to think that I had been close-dancing . . . with . . . with . . . a . . . *pregnant woman*! I mean, Gosh! Could I have gotten pregnant myself!?! (No, I wasn't quite that naïve, but I was close.)

Anyway, a year earlier, Daddy waited until the kitchen was empty of everyone but Philip and me. He held his newspaper spread out before him as a prop and, glancing up, said, "That's a real shame about Cindy." He pursed his lips and shook his head to show the sincerity of his feelings. We agreed it was a real shame, which it was. Cindy was a very pretty and delightful girl. Her visits to Eileen were enjoyed by all of us. But, so it appeared, not to the same degree that someone else's older brother was enjoying them. Daddy was especially fond of Cindy. Yes, it was a real shame. Not so much that she was pregnant, but that such a seemingly nice girl could do something so unspeakably and bottomlessly bad. At least, I imagine she was bottomless at the time.

There was a pause, then Daddy looked up again from his paper, managed to glance us both in the eyes at the same time and mustered all of his courage to mutter, "You two know about these things, don't you?" Philip nodded his head affirmatively, and I stammered a, "Ye-es."

Daddy looked greatly relieved and ended this frank talk about the facts of life by summarizing with pursed lips about how, "It's just a real shame," then quickly found his way back into the newspaper. There was an uncomfortable silence before I could think of some plausible reason for Philip and me to leave the room. As soon as we were away, I said to Philip, still very nervous about the whole sordid and demeaning experience, "Boy that was close.

I couldn't tell if he believed us about knowing about those things or not. I'm glad you lied or he might have started telling us, and I'm sure," hoping to cover my exceeding nervousness, "one of the Little Kids would have walked in." I remember Philip claiming that he hadn't lied. I questioned if what he was saying was that he actually understood about sex. He mumbled something about academic knowledge. I didn't really believe him, but I couldn't press the issue because we didn't talk about sex around the house.

That is, not until Little Paul learned how to spell it.

Mostly Pregnant
BOOK SIX

CHAPTER 9 8

Jim Jones
Was A Simple Man

Jim Jones was no more a part of the family than was the family truck.

The family truck belonged to Daddy's business. Jim belonged to the truck. He was Daddy's truck driver.

Jim Jones worked for the wholesale flower shop for as long as Daddy ran the place. Maybe 40 years. He started as a young man and took it from there. He left only when Daddy left and the Chattanooga operation, owned by a family in Nashville, folded. For all those years, Jim made only a few cents an hour above minimum wage. He made pretty good money, though, because he worked the same ten hours a day that Daddy put in himself six days a week. He made his living off time-and-a-half overtime.

Jim took care of getting boxes of flowers to the downtown Greyhound and Trailways bus stations as orders came in from florists in nearby towns. He also delivered flowers to the local shops. And picked up incoming flowers from growers in Denver and California at the suburban airport. That was his main job. Jim's secondary job all those years was chauffeur and handyman. Jim drove the Erickson kids home from school every afternoon.

The school was just two blocks from Daddy's store. Both were at the fringe of downtown Chattanooga. After school we gathered at Daddy's store and got in the way until everyone finally made it down the hill from the combination grade school and high school. All accounted for, we piled into either the station wagon or the truck — both belonged to Daddy's wholesale flower shop — and Jim drove us home.

Once the older ones became licensed they drove everyone to school in the morning in the station wagon and took us home in the afternoon, keeping the wagon at home the rest of the day. Daddy felt guilty about the company car spending so much time parked in the driveway of his house. Some years it would rarely smell a flower. The people in Nashville who owned the company knew what was going on, but they understood Daddy's kids were important — right up there with the few million long-stemmed roses he sold for them.

⬤

Whenever anyone forgot a lunch or book at home, Jim trucked the six-mile round trip to the house to pick it up. He dropped the forgotten lunch or box off with a nun in the office who sent it to the forgetter's classroom. Jim didn't like talking to the scary nuns. He was a Southern Baptist. Baptists like nuns even less than Catholic schoolchildren do.

Many of us tried to convert Jim over the years. The nuns insisted that good Catholics have a duty to convert everyone they know to Catholicism. Jim was about the only non-Catholic we knew. We regularly tried converting him on our way home from school.

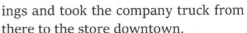

Jim Jones never quit while he worked with Daddy. He never even talked about quitting. There was another man who worked there for most of those forty years, the gambling man, who used to quit all the time and then come back a year later after quitting his next job. Daddy always hired him back because this man, Tommy, knew the business. Plus, he could read and write. Whenever Tommy wasn't already quit, though, he was talking about quitting. Not Jim.

Jim Jones had found the secret to life. The secret to life is working enough to pay for a truck of your own and painting a horse head on the truck's cab door. That's what Jim did. I hit a baseball into his colorful horse's head when the pickup truck was still new. It took a lot of courage to tell Jim it was me who dented his secret to life. Jim parked his truck at our house a lot of mornings and took the company truck from there to the store downtown.

After the dent, he started parking in a narrow little, but safe, area alongside the garage. We were offended at first because this narrow little area, when not serving as our muddy horseshoe pit, was our graveyard for a number of pets like turtles, fish, a kitten or two, and a few misshapen reptiles who had not survived science club projects.

Jim assured us it wouldn't hurt the buried pets for a pickup truck to be parked over them. We believed Jim about most things he told us over the years. He could whittle. We believed him about the truck not troubling our pet skeletons because this man with a horse's head on his door was also a good coon hunter and raised coon dogs and knew a lot more about pets than we were ever going to learn with our goldfish and turtles.

⟪Ⓞ⟫

Jim Jones was a stocky man. About five-foot-eight and heavy. Jim became our handyman as well as our chauffeur. He built a basketball backboard out of some wood and hung it to the second floor of the servant's quarters over the brick driveway-turned-badminton court. He had to make one adjustment during the basketball goal's first year, but after that the old wooden backboard hosted thousands of hours of action before Jim was asked to come back 15 years later and take it down.

⟪Ⓞ⟫

Jim also fixed tricycles and repaired wagons and did minor electrical and plumbing jobs around the house and worked on the washers and dryers and refrigerators and was pretty much there all the time doing whatever he could to help.

I felt bad about not being able to convert Jim Jones to Catholicism because we were instructed that anyone who wasn't Catholic could not go to heaven. I worried about that. It seemed Jim was plenty good enough to go to Heaven. I finally asked Mother about this and she told me not to worry about what the priests and nuns said about that one technicality because God would make allowances for big-hearted coon hunters, though she didn't say it exactly like that.

⟪Ⓞ⟫

My favorite thing of all about Jim Jones is that his name was not really Jim Jones. It was Joe Jones. But everyone called him Jim, and that's what he always said his name was except when he was dealing with something legal.

Jim Jones had two sons. He was understandably proud of them and named them after himself. He named his first son *Joe* Jones, Jr. He named his second son *Jim* Jones, Jr.

99

Trucking Those New Babies Home

Dear Nieces and Nephews, and Valued Readers,

> *To understand the extent to which Jim Jones became a fix-*
> *ture in our family, I should note that as Mother's propensity for*
> *producing a new Erickson on an annual basis became more routine*
> *than romantic, Daddy actually started sending Jim out to the house*
> *to drive Mother to the hospital. That is, whenever she was consid-*
> *erate enough to go into labor during the workday.*

> *Mother was not pleased with this arrangement. She made*
> *Daddy promise to at least drive her and the new baby home from*

the hospital — a promise Daddy kept whenever the dubious circum-stances of his duties at the flower shop allowed. Which means Jim often drove her home as well.

Ever the thoughtful one, though, Daddy tried to see that Jim could make those pick-ups and deliveries in the station wagon ra-ther than the truck.

Relatively yours,
Uncle Rags

1 0 0

Everybody Has To Come From Somewhere

Dear Nieces and Nephews, and Far-Flung Readers,

Everybody has to come from somewhere. And we came from Chattanooga.

If only because everybody has to come from somewhere.

∞ — ∞

No one lives in Chattanooga anymore — except for the parents, and they will probably join the exodus to Florida before too long. Cecilia is the only one who married a Chattanoogan. Frank is the only other one who didn't have to reach out of state for a spouse who would have him.

∞ — ∞

We were from Chattanooga.

But there was always this very strong sense that we did not belong there.

I'm not sure where we did belong. Possibly in some over-populated Catholic country. Near the equator. But the Tennessee-Georgia border was not a natural habitat.

We had an unwritten rule that everyone had to move away from home. Out of state was preferable. Out of the country was acceptable.

Over the years, various members of the family have resided in Paris and Cambridge, in Atlanta (two or three of us), Washington D.C. (several), Canada (two), Boston (three), Puerto Rico, Knoxville (loads), New Jersey, Rochester, Austin, Houston, Durham (three), Macon, Clearwater, South Carolina, Alabama, Athens, Baltimore, Pittsburgh, Wilmington, Foxboro, both coasts of Florida, Nashville (several), Tullahoma, San Francisco (several), Alameda, Sacramento, and Chattanooga (one).

∞ — ∞

I don't think Daddy ever felt settled in Chattanooga. He seldom talked about moving elsewhere, except maybe to get Mother going on otherwise slow nights. But he always projected a sense of being alien and temporary.

He landed in Chattanooga during the Depression. I believe he was trying to impress his new bride when he answered an ad in a national trade magazine placed by a Nashville firm seeking a manager for its wholesale florist shop in a city on the Georgia border. He was given the job, so he headed south from St. Joseph, Missouri, home of the Pony Express. After getting settled, this young man — 25 to 30 years old at the time — sent for his young bride. Before he could find life's next great opportunity in some Northern city, the Depression had faded into a world war, and his little house in this little place called Chattanooga was rapidly filling up with little kids.

Forty years later, the year after his youngest child graduated from Notre Dame High School, Daddy retired as manager of that wholesale flower shop — still vague as to what he was doing in Chattanooga.

Relatively yours,
Uncle Rags

Daddy had an entrepreneurial spirit. He launched a business embossing stationary. Stamping business and personal letterhead with "raised printing." He calculated his many growing sons could stamp several hundred sheets of paper each in their spare time. It didn't work out. But we had a closet full of embossers in the old house that he finally got rid of when moving to the "new house." Like many men of his generation, he was handy with tools. Had something called an "iron table" in the garage for working on tough projects. It was stunningly heavy. Made of iron. He invented a weighted pulley system to close the heavy doors of large refrigerators like those at his wholesale flower shop. Again, no takers, but that invention kept his own shop's doors easy to open and close for two decades.

444

1 0 1

The Road To Chattanooga
By Mother

Neither family was exactly happy when Harold and I told them we were going to get married.

No one on either my Mother's or Dad's side of the family had ever married a non-Catholic, and the Lutheran Ericksons had certainly never expected to be mixed up with a bunch of Papists.

It was 1935 and we both had jobs — a major accomplishment at that time — and we were both contributing to the family budget. Harold quit his job, borrowed on his insurance, and took off for Fort Dodge to start his own florist business. Both families thought that was insane, which it was. Nevertheless, we got married on a cold rainy day in October. I had to buy the marriage

445

license, since he was not going to get into town until Saturday at noon, when the bureau was closed.

We got married in the rectory in a shabby room with the paint peeling off the walls. Harold's sister refused to come to the wedding, so after the ceremony Harold's mother came back to the house with the family for cake and goodies, and then we left late that afternoon for Fort Dodge. On the train heading for Fort Dodge, my new husband explained that we really did not have the apartment he had written me about because Mrs. Hicks, who ran the apartments above the business complex where his store was located, wouldn't rent him one. So, he explained, we would have to go to a hotel that night and get out the next day and find a place to live. Of course, it wasn't all bad because this way I could help him decide where we would land. Translated, that meant I could find out for myself just how bad it was to rent an apartment with very little money.

We ended up with a family who had turned a couple of rooms in their house into an apartment of sorts in order to survive the Depression. The walls in the bedroom/sitting room (a bed, two chairs, and a table) were brown with little pale pink and green sponge marks that looked as though a puppy had been turned loose to run around with wet paint on its paws. There was no running water in the kitchen. I had to carry it from the bathroom. And we shared the bathroom with the family. They were kind and friendly, but their apartment was so cold in the winter that one night my grapefruit froze sitting on the kitchen table. In the summer it was so hot that I spent half the summer sleeping on the porch swing.

I managed to get a job in a department store, and we bought a little furniture on time and moved into an unfurnished apartment. It was definitely better than our first one, but had one main drawback — no hot water. The only way to take a bath was to heat a teakettle full of water on the stove, pour it in the bottom of a huge tub, and do a quick sponge. My ingenious husband solved the problem by grabbing a quick shower at the Biltmore complex, but I spent a year sponging and then washing my hair in cold water.

Business just did not get better in that small town in northwest Iowa. In the summer of 1937 I lost my job, and it was all too obvious that the Erickson Floral Co. wasn't going to make it. My paycheck had been covering the rent and most of the groceries, so it was a pretty grim summer.

Harold made various efforts to figure out where he could manage to get a job in the florist business. In one of his efforts, he wrote to a man named Tom Joy whom he had met at a florist convention that he had attended with Doc Murphy in Denver. It turned out that Tom Joy had died, but the members of his family who were now managing the Nashville business wrote back that they were looking for a manager for a new wholesale florist operation they had started up in Chattanooga. Harold went to Nashville for an interview, and they offered him the job. At that stage of our life, I think we would have gone to the worst spot on earth if we could get enough money to live on, so Chattanooga sounded like a great idea.

As far as I am concerned looking back now on all those years, Chattanooga was a great idea.

Those decades in Chattanooga included receiving lots of gifts from her children. Some she liked. Some she faked liking. We never knew. It's possible she didn't either.

1 0 2

Where The Sun Rises In The West
By Daddy

I never liked living in Chattanooga, it was an entirely different world.

The sun came up in the West and after a long day of work it always set in the East. The frigid winds came up from the South in the winter and the warm spring breeze came down from the North. I was completely turned around in the directions. However, I only had to drive out of the city limits toward Nashville, Huntsville, and Atlanta and the world straightened out for me all by itself. But not Knoxville. I would always drive the 110 miles West, facing the rising sun. But I've been away from the mountains of Tennessee and Georgia for the past two years in exchange for six months of Florida's hot summer suns. Even though they get up and set on the right ends of the world, those mountains keep tempting me to return again to my turned around world.

Ah, yes! Kids. We did have quite a few kids and now that they are all grown up and settled in their many different careers, I wouldn't wish my life achievements to have been any other way. I love every one of you from the very bottom of my heart and with the greatest of pride.

— Daddy

"Daddy with his "Little Eileen" and a bigger Eileen.

103

The Civil War
In Our Back Yard

Averaging maybe two inches a year, we Chattanoogans had more snow than sunsets.

The city is surrounded by Missionary Ridge, which our house backed up to, and three mountains. Lookout Mountain, where the really rich old-money families lived. Signal Mountain, where a lot of newly prosperous doctors, lawyers, and business-men lived. And undeveloped Raccoon Mountain, where raccoons lived.

A number of factories prospered in our valley. Their smokestacks pumped fumes into what the EPA determined, after most of us had left, to be perhaps the largest bowl of trapped and heavily polluted air in the country.

The sun would have risen over Missionary Ridge, and set over those three mountains. But, because of the long shadows, we never saw sunrises nor sunsets. Those mounds were always in the way. Of course, if you've never seen sunrises and sunsets, you don't think about what you're missing. They just weren't part of our lives. Until we got to places like California and Florida, where they're part of the fabric.

Cecilia shows off a new Easter outfit with nearby Missionary Ridge in the background.

Missionary Ridge, though, was definitely part of our lives.

Our back yard was at its foot. We hiked up its steep slope as an afternoon diversion several times a year. Enjoying fall's colors. Winter's barrenness. Summer's heat. Teenagers, pre-teens, six- and seven-year-olds, with the occasional toddler in hand. A horde of Erickson kids. There were no houses on the side of the ridge. Just trees.

The first part of the walk was up the steep road coming down from the ridge that flattened on the north side of our house. When Oak Street curved left 100 yards up the ridge, we continued straight, into the woods, and trudged up the side from tree to tree until we got to its crest.

At the top, taking the straight shot from our back yard, there was a Civil War monument honoring the success of a regiment from Ohio. Thinking in the 1950s we were supposed to be proud Southerners, we always regretted having to see Yankees from Ohio celebrated in stone at the peak of our climb. But the park at the top also offered two cannons whose barrels we enjoyed straddling. And which we often pretended to be firing — at those damn Ohio Yankees.

Used by permission. National Park Planner. NatopnalParkPlan.com

Our parents were Yankees. Daddy was from Iowa, and Mother was from Missouri. They never talked about the Civil War. It was irrelevant to Midwesterners. But we kids were ostensibly products of the South. We liked the many TV shows like *The Rebel* and *The Gray Ghost* (about Mosby's Raiders) that celebrated Confederate exploits. But we, unlike so many in Tennessee, didn't have any great-grandfathers or great-uncles who were killed in that unseemly mess.

Our fellow Chattanoogans rarely talked about the Battles of Missionary Ridge and Lookout Mountain. They were embarrassments. They happened on consecutive days in 1863 — November 24th (Lookout Mountain) and, November 25th (Missionary Ridge). The Southern Armies were strategically entrenched on the top of both of those seemingly easy to hold precipices. But dishonorably retreated almost as soon as the Yankees started climbing and shooting. Maybe even Yankee yelling.

What we didn't know, because our fellow Chattanoogans never talked about those retreats, was that the Yankees, Sherman's Army of Ohio, launched their assault right through our back yard and right up the same part of the ridge we hiked up and down several times a year.

We never saw any belt buckles or hats or any other now valuable souvenirs. But we never even considered looking as we scrabbled through the trees and

Eileen, left, and Michael, right, in 1958 with a visiting Yankee cousin.

brush. We thought the battle had happened a mile or so away. That the 80-foot-tall obelisk built by Ohioans who came back to smirk in 1905 was raised directly above us should have been a great clue. But we missed it. Real Southerners, real Chattanoogans, which didn't include us, never talked about that embarrassing retreat from the top of the ridge. And ignored that monument.

It turns out, our ignorance bordered on bliss.

We children were probably better off not knowing that many of the thousand men killed a hundred years earlier likely died on the very ground we hiked across. And we especially wouldn't have wanted to know that, as I discovered much later in life, some of the hundreds of Confederate bodies were likely buried, at least temporarily, perhaps permanently, in our own back yard once the decaying dead were pulled down from the ridge by those victorious guys from Ohio and thrown into ditches dug in the first level areas at the foot of the ridge. Our level playing field made for a prime burial ground.

I'm glad we never considered we were enjoying back yard badminton, kickball, football, red light, and, yes, even playing war, over the bones of men and boys who weren't fortunate enough to join that embarrassing retreat from the crest of Missionary Ridge.

Talk about shadows, and life's sunsets . . . there are some you're better off missing . . .

"The Bricks," our expansive back driveway and parking area got a lot of play as our badminton and basketball courts. The bricks were bordered on the right by the "outfield" when we batted wiffle balls from the left, and by our grass football field as the seasons changed.

104

See Who Can Be
The Richest

It was inevitable. As competitive as we all were, am, and forever will be, it was inevitable that we would have a contest to see who could make the most money.

"See-Who-Can-Become-The-Richest" is another of those games in which participation is mandated by virtue of living. It came with our navels.

It is an undeclared contest — but it's there just the same. And has been ever since pre-teenagers used to threaten older brothers by warning, "You might be bigger than me, but when I grow up *I'll buy you!*"

The game is unfair, almost tragically so, because life is hard enough without the pressure of having to make money simply to impress others. But our Race For The Gold is there just the same.

The most ludicrous aspect of this race is that — never knowing when a sudden windfall might change the standings — the race won't be officially over until such time as we have a winner of the even more ominous game of See-Who-Can-Live-The-Longest.

⦿

We did not concoct either of those games. They were just there.

Like mosquitoes in the summer. Memories in a weary mind.

⦿

Without further apology, I'll pass along the mid-1980s standings in the contest to see who can become the richest:

Harold, the oldest, gave up the advantage of starting in the post position by consciously gearing himself for a career that keeps him at the monetary mercy of the government and education industry — two notoriously modest but comfortably steady compensators. Dr. Harold used to be troubled by younger brothers raking in hordes of money in their early free enterprising. But the professor has come to grips with the realization that money and comfort don't necessarily equate. You can have lots of one without requiring mounds of the other. Besides, Harold is still the leader in the See-Who-Can-Be-The-Smartest, and gladly sustains his perennial lead in See-Who-Can-Live-The-Longest.

Frank is a strong runner in the Race For The Gold. He got off to a late start because of the vow of semi-poverty that accompanied his stint in the priesthood, but has since bolstered himself with a law degree. His Knoxville firm has been doing exceptionally well. Frank is not so sold on materialism, but loves to work hard.

At his rates, he is going to be swamped with money. Frank will finish high.

Allen has been a lawyer longer than any of the others, but his fascination with the futility of life keeps getting in the way of his practice. Allen is maybe too intelligent for the real world, and should have stuck with teaching or some other byproduct of the system. The system — especially the legal one — likes life to be cut and dried, black and white. Allen sees too much of the gray. I know how he feels. But being a lawyer, he always has the potential of getting into the middle of a massive exchange of money.

Captain John, second from the left, welcomes siblings and spouses aboard his little dinghy on Harold's 60th birthday.

John was favored to win this race from the time he was five years old, and has not let the fortune tellers down. Almost since the day he left the seminary, he has held a commanding lead. John's houses have all had swimming pools. His latest has a guard gate out front. His cars and boats have grown bigger as the cost of gas increased. To go with his other toys, he now has an eight-story office building overlooking the Atlantic Ocean, and a college overlooking Baltimore that he is turning into a retirement community. John keeps saying he is slowing down. He might be taking fewer strides, but each step seems to be covering more and more ground. John will win the race — as we always knew he would.

David, like Harold, withdrew to the sidelines early by going with government instead of industry. David discovered at an even earlier age than Harold that you don't need all the money in the world to buy contentment. Wherever David finishes, he has earned my respect.

Philip has run a surprisingly strong race. A dark horse from the beginning and hardly considered competition, he stormed out of the pack in the early-70s and has run second behind John ever since. We didn't even know what accountants were until Philip became one. Seeing how lucrative it could be, two of his youngers joined his profession. By lucrative, let me explain that Philip retired to Florida in his mid-20s and has made a fortune working ten-hour weeks. If he ever decides to really work for a living, he'll have to buy Republican politicians just for the tax write-offs.

⦿

I am in sole possession of last place. It wasn't supposed to be this way, but . . . My only hope is that the race will go on for a while and that history doesn't really repeat itself. I always have a million-dollar idea or two up my sleeve. It's just that my sleeves are usually worn pretty thin around the elbows and those million-dollar ideas keep falling through before I can get them to the bank. Maybe it would help if I got a job . . . But I've tried that before and it always offers only temporary relief.

Eileen disqualified herself by marrying a millionaire. Before she did that, though, she embarrassed me for years by making more money serving coffee and tea on Delta's flying buses than I ever did — even when I was employed.

Douglas is probably going to finish third. He's a doctor, and the national statistics certify to everyone's immense dissatisfaction that doctors make more money than anyone — attorneys and accountants included. Douglas could care less about the money. But his wife favors nice things. She'll find a good investment counselor and Douglas will finish about third. Third because one of those lawyer- or accountant-types is going to defy medical tradition and nose out the good doctor.

Louis is destined for glut. Not just because he's an attorney, but because he can be mean when it comes to money. Just a few years out of law school, he's already making so much that he can go out to eat without suffering the trauma that such surfeit produces among even the wealthiest of Ericksons. He takes more vacations than anyone in the family. Flying from Florida to fish in Alaska and Maine. Yeah, I'm jealous.

Cecilia disqualified herself by marrying a multi-millionaire. She would never have made that much money teaching.

Paul looks good for second or third. In fact, though having just finished law school as I write this, he is already in second or third place. Not bad for one of the Little Kids, considering the head start they gave the rest of the field. Paul kind of cheated though. He won $200,000 from his roommate's insurance company after coming back from the dead. But Paul would finish rich regardless. He's miserly when it comes to money, already has his CPA license, and will work just as hard at law as he does at everything. His first goal is probably to buy Philip, a former employer.

Charles was making a ton of money as a computer programmer, but it wasn't enough. Already in a high income bracket just two years out of college, climbing Dupont's corporate ladder, that would have been enough for anyone but an Erickson. An Erickson mired in the morass of competing to be the richest. After a few comfortable years, Charles yanked his smooth running machine off the road and pulled into pit row. Time for a lube job — that all-purpose law degree. He'll do very well, but, like so many of the players, might never be entirely comfortable. Considering "comfort" isn't objectively measured as having the things you need for yourself. In this game, "comfort" is subjectively re-defined as having the things you need to show off for others.

Carol is the only girl in the race. She is already doing very well in her early career as a CPA, and will probably launch her own firm. She is pushy and scrappy enough to offer formidable competition, but, being a woman, she has to face that awesome threat of losing ground while taking on the weight handicap of motherhood. I can't guess where Carol will finish. She has enough Mother in her to wipe out the field.

⦿

There it is. Pretty frightening, for a pauper.

I'm going to stop now and take a long stroll down the beach.

Yes, poor as I am, I'm the only one who lives on the beach.

And I've got a new million-dollar idea I need to work on before the tide rolls out.

Uncle Rags

Future competitors. Unwittingly born into the game.
Two of the three girls didn't play exactly fair.
But money always has its own rules.

105

You Can't Take It With You
If You Can't Prove It's Yours

All the money in the world is of little use, if none of it belongs to you.

Poor as we were there was never a shortage of money in the Erickson house.

Anonymous money.

The tarnished pewter money cup was the only communal source. But close by, in a cluttered corner of the kitchen counter one might find a couple of dollars of loose change. The money belonged to someone; we just never knew who. It tended to stay

467

there and accumulate more of the same over the years. Even Mother could not account for whose it was or how it got there.

Because of its ownerless nature that money could not be used to pay the paperboy, buy hole punchers, badminton birdies, or meet any other small emergencies. The same can almost be said for the assorted bits of paper money that lived on the dining room furniture.

Five dollar bills — back in the days of 20-cent gas and 50-cent pounds of hamburger — were a common sight lying among the clutter of letters and papers on the edge of the buffet. When asked who the various one and five and ten dollar bills in the dining room belonged to, Mrs. Erickson always had an answer.

"The ten is a present from Grandma to Allen for graduation and I meant to give it to him when he was home from college. The five dollars was for Eileen's ballet lessons, but the teacher cancelled the class." That was a killer. The budget made no allowance for money coming back. The acute pain of spending was felt that moment money was handed to a child, from whom it would be sucked into the world's vacuum. If some paper dollars came back, they were stashed in the top drawer of the dining room buffet, or maybe left for months on its top right edge. But they had no future. No place to go. They couldn't be budgeted again. But, unlike the Money Cup in the kitchen, they didn't procreate. Those bills were celibate.

◎

Upstairs in Mother's bedroom, lying on her dresser, is a final stash of money that shares our poverty.

Another little silver mine. Another unstaked claim.

This is nickel-dime-and-quarter money.

It has trickled over the years from the pockets of pants going through the wash. It is saved on the dresser to be returned to the rightful owner. But none of us ever made a convincing enough story that any particular dime or quarter was "specifically," which is on a higher level than "rightfully," ours.

If we ever mentioned a missing quarter Mother suspected we were trying to trick her out of some of her washing machine money. She would say "How much do you think you lost?" And we might guess, "About 35 cents." She would ask, "When do you think you lost it?" And we might venture, "Probably last Tuesday or Wednesday. I think it might have been in my pants pocket when I threw them in the wash." Mother would win by concluding, "No. I didn't find that much money then."

No one really wanted this laundered money, but it would have been a memorable moment for someone to have beaten her out of some just once. She never spent this money. Accumulating it was her reward for never mentioning any of the other things that might have shown up in her sons' pants pockets over the years.

⓪

The best way for a poor person to get along comfortably in life is to be independently wealthy. Our family was poor. But the slew of children were fortunate enough to be independently wealthy.

From Philip and me on down — which is more than half — we all started college with a minimum of $3,000 in the bank. As I started my freshman year, I had enough money to stay in Chattanooga, pay $4,000 cash for a new Corvette, and live like a rock star. Most of the younger ones had enough to buy a Corvette, *and* gas. But we all played the long game, using that windfall for books, tuition, and meals.

We started earning our individual fortunes at about age seven and, with the exception of myself, never changed trajectories. I just can't seem to become worth as much as I was before getting educated.

⓪

We were aided in constructing the foundations of our financial empires by our poor father.

Whenever he needed outside services at the wholesale flower shop he managed, he took a good look inside the house. From truck driving to bookkeeping, there were a number of jobs we filled for him, but the first and the simplest was one called "folding paper."

Daddy spent part of every day packing big, long, cardboard boxes with carnations, mums, and ferns to send off on a bus to one of many tiny Tennessee or North Georgia towns where the cut flowers were arranged by that community's straight or, even in rural Tennessee, sometimes gay florist into pleasant smelling hearts and other sprays for some dead person's going away party.

He had to add a thin covering of ice over the top of the flowers to keep them fresh during the journey. To keep the ice from melting during the long ride on warm days he insulated the boxes — bottom, sides, and top — with sheets of old newspapers. For efficiency, he used newspaper sheets that were completely unfolded to their maximum height and width.

Daddy kept up to a five-foot stack of neatly unfolded papers at the end of the long work counter at his store. When it got below a foot, he ordered more from his subcontractors. Us. The little Ericksons.

To unfold a newspaper, you take a day's worth of their news, sports, comics, Ann Landers, and advertisements and unfold them section by section so that they reach their maximum size, which was about 2 ½' x 3' in that era — or half the height of a nine-year-old. Pull out all the single cut sheets and stack them in a separate half-sized pile with the tabloid sections. Stack all your neatly unfolded sections one on top of another. Routinely press your mounting stack down nice and neat so the ink will wear off and make your little hands look shiny and black and so your nose will itch and you can leave a little black smudge when you scratch it. And that's basically how you unfold papers.

What we called "folding papers."

"Folding papers" was the first job each of us ever did to earn money.

Daddy, through his store, paid us two cents a pound, which was the going rate established by outside suppliers.

He had a big scale at the store that he used for weighing his boxes of flowers before sending them off on the bus. That same scale weighed our stacks of paper, which were rolled neatly into bundles and tied with twine. A medium sized bundle might weigh 20 pounds and earn 44 cents for two hours of Saturday work. Daddy never put his elbow on the scale or did anything to give us more than we earned. He was an impeccably scrupulous slave driver.

Seven was a good age to begin one's career folding papers. There was a substantial difference between the final size of the stack of a seven-year-old when compared with those of the eleven- and twelve-year-olds. We usually felt so sorry for the struggling beginner that we would chip in a few worthless half-ounces. Charity begins at home.

⑩

The money we earned from folding paper never went anywhere. We might build character by carrying two quarters around for a few days without spending them, but what didn't get confiscated by the washer ended up in our miniature tin Coca-Cola machine piggy banks alongside the dollar bills we got from Grandma every year on our birthdays.

Each year's seven-year-old, like every seven-year-old Erickson before him, was advised how imperative it was to save for college. Most kids would have spent their money as it came in. But Mother convinced us — without ever painting herself into a corner by formally stating it — that spending money was one of the Catholic Church's less publicized but more grievous sins.

We were pretty good at staying sinless. And acting poor.

To lighten our load, Daddy assured us that we poor people would be loaded in Heaven. He quoted from his Bible (which often differed from others), "The poor on earth shall be rich in heaven."

Mother always told him, "Poppycock!"

1 0 6

The Whore House
On The Corner

Perhaps the most surprising aspect of our so rarely talking about sex when growing up was our unusual proximity to it.

No, I'm not talking about the upstairs bedroom where the parents "slept." I'm talking about the whorehouse two doors away.

Not too long after moving into our "new house" on Glenwood Drive, we became aware of the Glenwood Manor, a small motel at the intersection of our busy crosstown street and an even busier one, McCallie Avenue, which was the main thoroughfare to downtown.

The Glenwood Manor was Chattanooga's, and possibly all of Tennessee's, most notorious whorehouse.

Our near neighbor was built in the 1940s. Just another large house until it was converted in the 1950s to a motor court and raised a neon sign to catch Yankee tourists drawn by the ubiquitous "See Rock City" signs painted on barns and stamped on birdhouses throughout the North and Midwest. A brilliant advertising strategy that brought an endless number of Northerners to Chattanooga, where many of them also forked over money to ride the elevator 150 feet into Lookout Mountain to "See Ruby Falls." What many families saw first, though, was the Glenwood Manor. It was the first tourist court weary drivers met once they came through the Missionary Ridge tunnel and entered the city of Chattanooga. A good place to pull over and rest up for the big day ahead.

The new Holiday Inn and Howard Johnson motel chains quickly made Mom and Pop tourist courts obsolete. Some found a way to repurpose those empty bedrooms.

We didn't learn what the Glenwood Manor had turned into until the Haddocks, a Catholic family, though not nearly as Catholic as we were, moved in next door. They had a son in Eileen's grade school class and a daughter in Cecilia's. We had never spoken to the previous neighbors.

The Haddocks quickly noticed there were an awful lot of men pulling into the driveway of the busy little motel next door to them. Staying only an hour or two instead of overnight. Most with local license plates that started with the number 4.

Chattanooga was in Hamilton County, Tennessee's fourth largest, so all of its plates began with a 4. Drivers out of Memphis, the state's largest city, had plates that began with 1. Nashville was 2. Knoxville/Knox County was 3. Chattanoogans felt bad about being from only the fourth largest city, but cars from nearby counties had much worse numbers. 37. 63. All the way down to 95. The Haddocks were suspicious about all of those sedans whose license plates began with a 4 pulling into the house whose sign offered rooms for the night.

The Glenwood Manor, officially defined in occasional court documents as a "bawdy house," was run by a frumpy woman in her 40s, Naomi Roden, who spent most of the day in a loose-fitting cotton house dress that she wore when she stepped outside to check her mail or collect garbage cans from the curb.

The police weren't very interested when the Haddocks called them to investigate. They already knew about it. Everyone knew about it. This whorehouse was as protected as the city's many bars that illegally served liquor long after the statutory 1 a.m. closing. But one officer the Haddocks implored finally suggested they write down license plate numbers. Some of those numbers turned out to belong to judges, local politicians, and even high ranking police officials. Which explained why she was able to operate so long and so openly. Favors given; favors returned.

Under steady pressure from the Haddocks, Naomi was busted every three to five years. Paid a small fine. And resumed her courtly business.

This was going on right under the nose of a family with 11 boys. But, like everything else related to sex, while it might come up during the day when Mother was speaking in hushed tones with Mrs. Haddock, it was never spoken of during those kitchen table sessions at night. Indeed, even when it became general knowledge in our household that the Glenwood Manor was a whorehouse, that meant little to the vast majority of the 11 boys who were ignorant as to what whores did. But we were pretty sure it was a sin.

The church steeple poking up from bottom right is a nice touch.

Naomi must have dressed up, or maybe just undressed, at night because court documents said she was one of the two or three women who went with one of the undercover detectives into one of her rented rooms to provide services. She was fined $50. Maybe even spanked, depending on whether the judge was a consort.

The madam sometimes had live-in whores. The only reason we know this is because of the one-armed boy.

The one-armed boy showed up one summer afternoon when we were playing wiffle ball, batting from the opening in the hedge that led to the Haddocks' back yard. You bat from the opening in the hedge across the bricks that constituted our basketball court, badminton court, and parking area into our grassy back yard. He stared at us for a bit from two houses away before bravely walking across the Haddocks' yard to ask if he could play.

We didn't like strangers. But we knew it would be a sin to turn our backs on a kid. Especially one with just one arm. So we let him play. He batted one-handed. He was maybe 11 years old. The same age as one of us. Older and younger than others of us.

He started coming over every day. We didn't like him. Never asked about his arm. Never really talked to him about anything. We even let him go to the park down the street with us one time, because we were going, he had shown up, and there wasn't any way around it.

We didn't know his mother was a whore. If we had, we could probably have refused to let him play with us, trading one sin for another. Our catechisms didn't really cover that situation. Nor did the nuns. But, overall, we knew we were doing the right thing in tolerating, if not exactly "taking in," this disadvantaged stranger.

I'm sure Mom and Mrs. Haddock were as uncomfortable about this kid being in our midst as we were. After two weeks, to everyone's great relief, he was gone. Disappeared.

But what a great story we brushed up against: A one-armed kid raised by an itinerant prostitute. What did he know about his mother? When did he learn? What became of him?

Naomi stayed in business for years and years. It was rumored she had girls from the public high school three blocks away working for her at one time. The judges, councilmen, and police commissioners would have loved that.

We loved being two houses away from Chattanooga's most popular whorehouse. Instead of right next door.

The Haddock's house is behind Carol as she stands on our badmin-
ton court/parking area. And Naomi's bawdy house is behind it.
Innocence is bliss.

107

Home Grown Nobility
An Evil Weed Story

Back before a number of us were even born, Allen discovered a distressing feature of our shared physiology. We were to be, and are now, grotesquely allergic to poison ivy.

Where poison ivy creates itchy red patches on the arms of most people who come in contact with it, Ericksons typically suffer foul splotches of running, red, puffy, volcanic sores that creep up and down their arms until it lays undeniable claim to their little chests and brittle backs. From there, it slides to their foreheads and slips down between their toes.

Fighting poison ivy on one of our bodies with lotion was like a ranger trying to blow out a forest fire after eating crackers. Our poison ivy feasted on the watery, pink calamine juice.

⫿

Allen was in grade school when he was nearly consumed by this evilest of weeds. It became an annual exercise of his to catch poison ivy on spring camping trips with the Boy Scouts or at the annual altar boy picnic and then miss the next week of school, confined to bed, wrapped like a mummy in cotton gauze soaked  with calamine lotion, which, for him, was little more than pink poison ivy food. He was the first in a long line of victims of the vine.

I had to stay home a few days from my job as a summer intern at the newspaper because the infamous urushiol had spread to the top of my ears where it formed a crust that cracked open and gooed the black receiver every time I had to do a phone interview.

⫿

When someone's poison ivy got entirely out of hand, Mother resorted to the only known cure for the Erickson version of consumption: The dreaded poison ivy shot. Poison ivy shots had no after effects — other than causing a complete cure within 48 hours. But being a shot was cause enough for us to put off taking the cure until we had fought a losing battle with the crusty, bubbling masses for two or three miserable weeks.

Because he was finally declared by Dr. Mrs. Erickson to be extremely allergic to poison ivy, Allen was required to suffer a poison ivy shot every spring before its supposedly distinctive "leaves of three" ever crawled out from under their logs. This kept him immunized. The rest of us only had to have shots if we were dumb enough to find the plants. We were pretty dumb when it came to poison ivy.

Charles was smart when it came to poison ivy. He claimed to be another who was extremely allergic. Not quite allergic enough to require an annual immunization, he argued, but far too allergic to comfortably cut our ball-eating hedge every other week during the summer. Or help with any other outside yard work.

⊚

No one in the family was actually dumb enough to burn poison ivy leaves in a campfire and breathe the smoke. A lot of people tell stories about friends who have done that. It causes poison ivy to begin bubbling and crusting inside the nose, throat, and lungs.

Actually, some of us were dumb enough to do that but lucky enough for it not to happen. Besides, smoke follows beauty — and, excluding myself, most of those other Erickson boys were safe on that account.

Maybe none of us were dumb enough to burn poison ivy as incense, but Louis and Paul did something almost as dumb. Noble, in its own way — but painfully dumb.

It was 1970. Louis was a junior in high school. Paul was a freshman. Douglas, who was a freshman in college, had brought some marijuana seeds home with him. Remember now that it was 1970, which was a few years before marijuana had rooted itself into the country's high school culture. It was 1970, when grade schoolers were still drinking chocolate milk rather than rolling joints with chocolate-flavored papers.

So, in the spring of 1970, Douglas brought some seeds home from college. Louis had already smoked a few times. Paul hadn't smoked at all. There weren't even any rules established in the house covering this novel activity.

Douglas left the seeds with Louis and Paul and also left a little paperback manual on how to cultivate marijuana. Louis and Paul studied the manual, then decided they could grow this illuminating beast. They soaked their seeds between wet paper towels until the kernels germinated. Then took their little seedlings to a place on Missionary Ridge where we often played. Known for years as "the place where the abandoned house is," this little section on the side of the ridge had not been visited by anyone other than Ericksons in the past 15 years. Though it was right off the main road which came down from the ridge (our house was at the end of this road) and just a stone's throw from an apartment complex, the place was so abandoned that Louis and I once saw our first and only bobcat stalking near the abandoned place's abandoned house.

The house wasn't just abandoned — it was in complete ruin. It had no roof and only a semblance of walls. It is doubtful that it was ever completed. And, if it was completed, a truck must have fallen off the road winding down from the ridge and landed on it one day, rendering it abandoned.

So Louis and Paul, very nervous about transporting their illegal germinated seeds, hiked up the ridge under cover of night to the place where the abandoned house is. They cleared a little patch of land — just like the manual suggested — and planted their seeds. What the manual didn't suggest was that would-be harvesters carefully check the patch of land to make sure they weren't clearing poison ivy.

Louis and Paul claim to this day that since they planted their felonious contraband at night, wisely taking advantage of a full moon for light, they couldn't have been expected to identify the botany they were uprooting. With the land cleared and the seeds planted, they returned home to wait for spring rains.

Spring and summer rains are a pain to water skiers, tennis players, softballers, and others of us outdoor types. But rain is a blessing to gardeners — those growers of green and yellow table mush — and to marijuana growers.

Louis and Paul had hardly enjoyed their first rain before their bodies began bubbling over with sores. They came down with likely the worst cases of poison ivy in the family's long blistery history. Discounting Allen's life-and-death struggles back in the days of giants, the earlier worst case belonged to Philip whose poison ivy dripped to his feet one spring requiring Dr. Mrs. Erickson, who was pregnant at the time, to call St. Joseph, Missouri, for a pair of Grandpa's size-13 shoes which Philip was required to wedge his cankerous feet in to so he didn't miss school.

Louis and Paul had it much worse than that. They missed school. A whole week each. For a whole week they were sentenced to bed with the rule that they couldn't touch their itching bodies.

Since marijuana was still more mystique than mania among high schoolers, they both received considerable prestige among classmates as word of how they had destroyed their bodies leaked from their disapproving sisters. His reputation as a dope grower certainlydidn't hurt Paul's successful bid for student body president two years later.

While the poison ivy was beautifully rooting itself to Paul and Louie's bodies, their marijuana was just as beautifully rooting itself to the sunny side of the ridge. It soaked in the spring rains. It stretched in the summer sun. And after they carefully harvested it in August, they cured it to perfection in the warm oven one night after the parents had gone to bed.

It was excellent marijuana. Tennessee home-grown is always outstanding, but this was superb.

A baggie of their rich harvest was couriered to John, Eileen, and me, who were in San Francisco that summer. It was distinctively better than the high quality Mexican weed we were accustomed to. But that's not what makes this incident noble.

What makes this incident noble is that Paul smoked some of his marijuana after curing it. It was the first time he had ever smoked.

And Paul is probably the only one of this nation's 80 million past or present marijuana smokers whose first experience was with grass he had personally germinated, planted, grown, and then cured to perfection.

Noble.

By Mother: "Paul was a pistol. Just one year younger, he often horrified Cecilia by not following the rules. And when they had to share a classroom when they were in the first and second grades, the poor teacher could not punish Paul when he frequently misbehaved because his poor sweet little sister suffered more than he did."

108

Pushing Boundaries — The Sixties
By Louis

There were many jokes and pranks as we grew up.

Paul once almost "scared his mother to death" when he yelled "boo" while hiding behind the laundry room closet door.

Paul was playing around with matches in the garage when he nearly burned the garage and the old wooden servant's quarters to the ground. Paul was probably the one who also tried to burn the boys' bedroom down.

My pranks usually got me into more trouble than those Paul and Douglas were guilty of. Try wearing Michael's hand-me-down plastic leather dress pants to a Sports Banquet. Dumb enough under normal circumstances, close to criminal negligence when your mother is a hostess and you are picked to receive the tennis team's award. It is also wise to wear anything but jeans to semi-formal pre-rehearsal wedding dinners.

There were occasional harmless pranks. David and Janet indirectly helped with one. While they were getting married in New Jersey, Cecilia, Paul, myself, and maybe Douglas, were left behind to continue with school. I've heard the wedding was fun. We who were left at home just had to make do. The house became a hangout for many of Notre Dame's elite (I know the Big Boys won't believe it). Many events took place there during the week we were on our own. As usual, there was more pot smoking than drinking. At one pot party, Paul publicly declared that he might resign from the student council presidency if he won the upcoming election. History shows that this radical statement almost cost him the vote, but proved true to his promise.

As the parents were scheduled to return, we unwanted and left behind ones decided to let them know how well we behaved. Someone in the house had a cat that year and even a bag of catnip. The catnip was placed in a baggy and put in a conspicuous place where Dad would be certain to discover it soon after getting home. He found it, and thought he had caught us red-handed. We explained to him that he had found nothing but some cleverly packaged catnip. He decided to put Mom through the same experience, so he presented her with our baggy. She also concluded it was an illegal substance, and she, too, became upset.

For brief moments there was much unwarranted concern about our behavior while left behind for weddings. But the house is still standing, and we are still behaving, more or less.

— Louis

Louis introduces Michael's Irish Setter puppy to the dock at "Don's Cabin" on Chickamauga Lake which the younger half appropriated as their own rustic hangout.

John, always resourceful, introduced us to Don's Cabin through his "adopted parents." He routinely pushed boundaries himself, with notable success.

1 0 9

The Cheese Pizza Diet
By Carol

I always got hand-me-down clothes. If they weren't from Eileen or Celia, they were some of the Saks Fifth Avenue dresses that Uncle Paul sent down from Detroit as his girls outgrew them.

Mother's going to say I'm wrong, and she'll be right, but I distinctly remember that the first dress Mother bought just for me was a red corduroy jumper with a zipper down the front. I loved it. I got my picture taken in it, and Mother still has the color photograph. She even let me wear her little crown pin for the picture. I was probably in the second grade.

Things picked up when I was in the seventh grade. All of a sudden Mother was making or at least altering a lot of new dresses for me. I think I probably had a new dress to wear to parties at least every other week. It must have been the year Eileen left for college.

Every year as I grew up, it seemed someone else would leave. The house was full of things they left behind. Eileen's and Celia's closets were worth raiding. Someone even left a car be-

hind, which was handy when we were in high school. But the house kept emptying.

Paul and I were very close. When he finally left, the house seemed really lonely. I got close to Charlie that year, but then he left, too.

Mother quit making lunches for us when there were just the three of us in high school and she was teaching. She gave us $2.50 a week to buy our lunches. Paul and I figured out we could sneak into the kitchen in the morning and make peanut butter sandwiches. Then we could get by with spending only 50 cents a week (ten cents per day) for Fritos to go with our sandwiches, and at the end of each week we would have saved $2 each. That was the exact price of a pitcher of beer, and that's exactly where those dollars went every week. Daddy would have wanted us to put those bits and pieces of thousand dollar bills in the bank.

Our friends always wondered how we could all have saved three or four thousand dollars before beginning college. Daddy taught us very early that the only thing you should ever do with money is put it in the bank.

Daddy used to also tell me it was okay to be afraid to spend the night away from home. My phobia about that suited him just fine. The older brothers used to come home and say I would never be able to leave home. Everyone said I would go to college in Chattanooga, and then stay unmarried and live the rest of my life with the parents.

I simply refused to stay away overnight. I literally thought that smoking marijuana would solve that problem. It didn't. What really solved it was drinking. After a few beers I was ready to spend the night at a nearby girlfriend's house. I fell asleep fast, but woke up an hour later in that strange basement. She and our other girlfriend had sneaked out to meet some boys and I was left all alone. Those fears of spending the night away from home were well founded.

One of the brattiest things I ever did was when we went to Baltimore for Harold's wedding and were picnicking in Washington on the filthy Potomac. The idea was to grill hot dogs, but I could eat only one brand — Lay's. Mother looked all over Washington but could not find that Southern regional brand. I threw a fit.

Every morning for ten years my breakfast consisted of a glass of Carnation Instant Breakfast stirred into milk, and a piece of honey toast. Every day. For ten years. I think I'm a creature of habit. If so, I guess I couldn't have chosen a better household to grow up in. Everything we did was just a slow evolution — not even a variation, just an evolution — of the same. The same dinner every night at exactly 5:30. I really wanted to gain weight while in high school because I still weighed much less than 100 pounds, but I just couldn't get hungry by 5:30, which was when we always ate. And people always left, always at the same age, usually leaving for the same place.

But the greatest advantage to being the youngest is that every conceivable sin had already been committed, usually several

times, by the time I was old enough to launch any serious misbehavior.

Even though I did drugs, I was viewed as a pretty good girl
because it was obvious enough to the parents that I did them only
in moderation. And when I moved in with Bill before marrying
him, it was something they had learned to accept from at least
four or five of my elders. Instead of worrying about science club
exhibits, I usually just took one that someone else had already
done.

I'm mostly just a mimic of an Erickson — I just don't know
which one.

— Carol

1 1 0

Baby Beers

Mother and Daddy drank beer every night.

They drank only three beers each, four on a truly exceptional night, and they stretched those out over several hours. It was what they did instead of watching television.

⬤

Daddy drank his beer while reading the evening paper. No one could really spend three or four hours a night reading Chattanooga's thin evening paper, but Daddy always held that paper up

493

like he was reading it. I guess he just wanted to look busy so we would leave him alone.

Mother read *Time Magazine*, or books, or worked on her crocheting while sitting there at the kitchen table drinking her few beers and trying to be left alone.

They talked, sometimes, as they lived out this routine. Especially if Daddy could find something in the paper — maybe a letter to Ann Landers or a quote from Billy Graham's column — that would get a rise out of Mrs. Erickson. Most papers are full of things that can rile intelligent women.

⦿

Daddy liked his beer to be 33 degrees, so, while he was slowly drinking one bottle, the next would be slowly working its way to the freezing point in the freezer section of our refrigerator. Occasionally, a beer's long, brown neck would be clogged with ice after he opened it, and he would have to run warm water over the bottle to bring everything up to 33 degrees. A 34-degree beer, two above freezing, was far too warm.

If Mother and Daddy ever went out at night — which means when they had to go to the annual first and second grade rhythm band recitals or attend the awards ceremony for yet another Eagle Scout — Daddy always placed his beers in the freezer just before leaving so they would be cold enough to drink when he got home.

If Daddy knew their evening entanglement would take longer than his beers could handle in the freezer, he left a note for one of us to take the beers out of the freezer at eight o'clock and place them specifically on the top shelf — the coldest shelf — of the refrigerator. He usually broke away from what he was doing, found a phone, and called us at eight o'clock, under the guise of "checking to see if everything is all right," but determined to make sure we had properly tended his beers.

⦿

I was never cared for by a babysitter. Mr. and Mrs. Erickson manufactured their own sitters.

The biggest disruption to the parents' beer drinking routine was when Mrs. Erickson was in the hospital putting the finishing touches on her newest babysitter. When delivering a baby, Mother was usually kept in the hospital two nights. On each of those nights it was Daddy's job to sneak two beers in for his wife. It was just a little thing that he did after one of the middle babies to show his appreciation for the way she was filling the house with what he always called "the pitter patter of little feet" — which was an expression that, after a few years, never failed to elicit one of Mrs. Erickson favorite retorts: "Poppycock!"

But there was, in fact, an awful lot of pitter patter around our house. As we grew older, we began to suspect there was also a fair amount of hanky panky.

⑩

Smuggling a couple of beers to the new mother, as is true of everything we ever did twice, became an ironclad tradition.

Daddy wrapped them snugly in heavy rolls of newspaper to keep them as cold as possible. He knew a lot about insulation from his years of shipping fragile flowers through the Southern summers.

We were all delivered at Memorial Hospital in Chattanooga. A Catholic hospital. As Mrs. Erickson rolled in for her annual deliveries, of both beer and babies, she became well acquainted with the nuns on the maternity floor. After the third or fourth year, one of the friendly black-habited nuns told her they were wise to the illicit activity, but they didn't mind. Mother and the nuns decided to not tell Daddy so the activity would remain discreet, and he could enjoy this rare opportunity to be clandestine.

People who drink regularly often aren't aware how noticeable beer breath is to a non-drinker. Most of the nuns were non-drinkers.

1 1 1

Daddy's Marijuana Stash

Daddy has some marijuana.

One night he even claimed to have smoked some of it. Mrs. Erickson didn't believe that claim because she has trained herself over the years to not believe anything Daddy ever says. She says, "If he ever does tell the truth it's either something I already know, or something not worth hearing."

Daddy delights in making outlandish statements.

He claimed Franklin Roosevelt committed suicide at the President's retreat in Warm Springs, Georgia. He said the White

House and the press covered it up because of the war. Whenever Daddy made a statement like that, or a statement like anything, Mother, who knew all the answers because she read *Time* magazine, would say, "Show me!" She would say, "I'm from Missouri. So show me!"

Missouri, which is where Mother is from, is called the "Show Me State." I don't know why. I don't know what the motto of Iowa is. Iowa is where Daddy is from. He's from a place in Iowa that doesn't even exist anymore. That place used to be called Badger. It used to be somewhere near Fort Dodge, but no one knows where it is anymore — if you can believe Daddy.

I believe Daddy about Franklin Roosevelt's suicide. About how his mistress caused him too much grief. And about how the world caused him too much grief, too. I've seen first-hand some of the grief that the world, and particularly its mistresses, can cause. Besides, his story is probably more entertaining than the truth. Daddy doesn't believe himself about Roosevelt anymore. I mentioned it to him once, and he forgot he had ever perpetrated such a rumor. I almost talked him into believing it again. But not quite. Just like he has almost started going to church again. But not quite.

⦿

Daddy went to church nearly every day for a hundred years or more.

He used to be a Lutheran and never went to church. Then he became a Catholic so he could marry Mother, and became not just a Catholic but a devout one.

His flower shop was only two short blocks from the downtown church and he started every day of work by opening the store at 6:15, getting his two workers packing some early orders for flowers to meet early bus schedules, then attending 6:30 Mass and praying that nothing happened to all of us kids. I guess that is what he prayed for. He never said. But nothing happened to all of us kids.

Daddy not just started every day of work by going to Mass. He worked every day of his life, Monday through Sunday, until a few years ago when he retired.

As each of us started coming home from college, we were granted the latitude to rebel against having to go to church on Sundays. This prerogative to quit being good Catholics was not as absolute as our right to come home and start drinking beer. It did not automatically begin on our first trip back to Chattanooga. We had to ease into it.

But by the time Carol, the youngest, was old enough to rebel against everything, she was making her own rules. One of her rules said that she could quit going to church when she graduated from high school. She assumed graduating from high school was the equivalent of going to college. In fact, going to college was nothing by the time Carol did it. She was the 14th to get a degree — 15th counting Mother — and the idea of going to and graduating from college had become so routine by the time Carol went through the motions that buying a new toothbrush seemed more novel.

Carol announced the week after her graduation from high school that she was not going to church anymore unless she chose to at some time in the future. This caused a big stir in the mostly empty and unusually quiet house. Especially for Mrs. Erickson, who didn't like seeing the last of her angels falling from the Church.

Daddy, who was going to church only on Sundays by this time because his shop had moved away from town, said to Carol during one of the arguments, "Well, if none of you kids have to go to church anymore, then I guess I don't have to either."

Carol said, "Of course you don't have to go to church."

Daddy said, "Well then, I won't."

Mrs. Erickson didn't believe him. But Daddy was telling the truth this time.

He quit going to church.

499

⫰

About the same time that marijuana became popular in high schools, Ericksons regained their popularity.

For many years, many of us were unpopular. You know you are unpopular when all the popular people pretend you don't exist. But by the time Cecilia, Paul, Charles, and Carol were spread out in the four grades of high school they were loaded with friends.

One of the reasons the Little Kids had so many friends was that they were doing the things they weren't supposed to do. I won't suggest they were playing around with that three-letter word, but I know they were protesting the war and getting involved in the student revolution. And I know they were drinking a lot of beer and smoking a lot of grass with their friends. They also drank a lot of beer and smoked a lot of grass with their older brothers when we came home from college or visited from the real world.

They weren't supposed to drink beer at the kitchen table until they went off to college. We — their elders — knew that we would get in more trouble than them if they were caught. But we usually let it go if we felt sure the parents were finally asleep.

There weren't any rules about when you could smoke marijuana because, as the Big Boys were growing up, the parents didn't have any reason to make such rules. And none of us kids had reason along the way to arbitrate our own rules about marijuana that could be passed down and reasonably enforced. We didn't know at what age someone was too young to be reduced to giggles.

All the kids inventoried their own marijuana. They shared sometimes, but mostly only when some of the older ones were home. It went without saying that everyone had to share an equal amount. Mother probably came across her high schoolers' marijuana papers, pipes, and other paraphernalia several times but never said anything because she didn't have any experience with what to say about such new things and if she could just get by a few more years everyone, including Carol, would be out from under her feet for good. She maybe even came across some of their marijuana a few times, but that commodity was so expensive they kept their baggies carefully hidden just to preclude the possibility of their treasure getting thrown away.

⦿

But one day Daddy found a baggie full of marijuana. He found about an ounce. A valuable amount. He found it lying among some clothes on the floor of the downstairs bathroom.

Carol and some others had been up at the cabin on the lake. We were not prosperous enough to own a cabin on the lake, but over the years we gradually assumed possession of a rustic little cabin that belonged to a man who was a friend of a friend. He hardly ever used it. If he wanted to spend a weekend there, he called the Little Kids to ask if it would be okay with them. The Little Kids were very generous and let the man use his cabin practically every time he asked.

This man we knew mostly through one of John's friends was a successful accountant. Gay. And in the closet. It's likely he bought the cabin tucked into the woods near the lake so he could entertain friends without being seen. We didn't know he was gay, and wouldn't have cared. But we probably ruined his plans for how to use the cabin when we started showing up there without much warning. It was difficult being gay in Chattanooga in the Fifties and Sixties. Unless you were a retail florist. In which case, it was expected.

All the gay florists would say to each new Erickson boy who showed up at age 16 driving the truck and delivering flowers on Saturdays, "Now, which one are *you*?" "Number seven," I would say. Always, "Number seven." Some were particularly flirty. All were nice.

I'm sure it was uncomfortable for Daddy to send all of his sons, one after another, out into this minefield, the hotbed of Chattanooga's homosexual culture. But driving the delivery truck was where the college money was to be earned, and we all survived, passing the word of how to slip in and slip out of those retail shops from teenager to teenager.

The two florists whose shop was next door to and associated with Daddy's wholesale were as openly gay as anyone in Chattanooga. One was among the first men in the city to not wear socks with his Oxford, penny loafers. When that became the overall fashion, and we, like all our classmates, quit wearing socks, Daddy tried, without success, to make us buck that fashion trend. The gay priests and Scoutmaster were not nearly so open and obvious as those florists we delivered flowers to. But we adeptly dodged all of them as well.

When Carol got back from our gay benefactor's cabin that one day she took a shower. But forgot to take her dirty clothes back upstairs. Probably because there is a natural aversion to handling dirty clothes when you are freshly clean. She remembered later that night that her marijuana was in a pocket of her dirty clothes, so Carol hurried back down to the bathroom. The dirty clothes weren't there. She ran back upstairs and found them in her room. The marijuana wasn't with them.

If Mother had found the dirty clothes, she would have laid them at the foot of the stairs and screamed at the top of her lungs, lungs calloused by a million such advisories, "Ca!-rol!! How many times do I have to ask you kids to take your dirty clothes upstairs with you!!? (Loud sigh.)" Only Daddy would have quietly taken her clothes up to her room.

So it was Daddy who had found, and confiscated, her marijuana.

⦿

Daddy was on record as being vehemently opposed to marijuana.

What he was really vehement about was all the things happening to his kids in the Sixties. He was a Republican.

He vented his growing frustrations on marijuana and long hair.

Daddy was so opposed to marijuana that he drove all the way from Chattanooga to the university in Knoxville once just to lecture Eileen and me about our use of it. We hadn't come home during the previous spring break, but our grades had. He thought our grades were too low. He asked over the phone if we smoked marijuana. We said "yes" because it seemed time to break him and Mother into the facts of life.

It wasn't the marijuana that made my grades so low that quarter — it was all the other drugs. I didn't bother to mention that fact.

After talking to Eileen and me on the phone, Daddy stewed about things for several days, then one morning called my apartment to say he and Mother were coming up to talk to us about our drug problems. It was really his drug problem, but he thought it was ours.

I wasn't home so my roommates took the message. My roommates, who are still close friends, had met Daddy and knew he was generally meek, mild, and easy. A very nice man. They also knew he was irrationally concerned about marijuana and long hair and that he spoke harshly on those subjects. They had nick-named him "Thor." Thor Erickson.

I came back from class one spring day and they told me with mock seriousness, "Thor called. Said he's corning up tomor-row to talk with you and Eileen. Didn't say anything else. Just asked us to let you know that Thor is coming."

Daddy hadn't bothered driving to Knoxville for the last two or three graduations, so this was serious. We called in Frank, the second oldest, who was a priest at the time and conveniently sta-tioned at a Knoxville parish. We asked him to moderate. Thor came, said his piece a few times, didn't listen to anything, and left. He never asked us about his drug problem again.

Mother is a Democrat. She wasn't too concerned about marijuana. And wasn't the least concerned about hair.

⟪⟫

Carol was aware of Daddy's emotional instability with regards to marijuana. When she found her baggie missing and determined who must have found it, she knew it could become a serious mess.

Carol solved her problem by making it Douglas's problem.

He, she explained to Douglas, who happened to be home from college that very weekend, would be able to leave again, and would not have to put up with any ongoing difficulties. Whereas she, she explained, was only in the ninth grade, would be carefully watched, and would have to make a lot of unfaithful promises for the next four years. He, she further explained to Douglas, wasn't supposed to smoke marijuana, but was essentially allowed to do whatever he wished because he was in college. She, she explained, was yet a little girl, and should be behaving both herself and her parents.

She, she explained, was already mired in considerable ongoing trouble in the house because the parents were becoming increasingly difficult to deal with, and she really didn't need any more trouble. He, she explained, had just transferred from the school in Knoxville to Duke, which the parents liked; was on full scholarship, which they liked; was in pre-med, which they liked; and was, in general, living one of the most likable lives of anyone in the family at the time. He, she explained to Douglas, should therefore go to Daddy and tell him that the marijuana found in the bathroom belonged to him and that he was only keeping it in Carol's pockets for some reason he could invent on his way downstairs to make this confession.

We always tried to be fair and reasonable. Our firm rules required us to be fair and reasonable. Everything Carol said to Douglas was true — especially the part about the parents being pleased with his life at that time. The parents take turns being especially pleased or upset with our intermittently pleasing and upsetting lives.

So, knowing it would be fairer for him to take a little flack than for Carol to take a lot, Douglas risked a share of the pleasure his life was bringing them by confronting Daddy and claiming ownership of the marijuana. Douglas scoffed at the idea Carol would smoke marijuana — careful not to actually deny that she did — and said he asked her to carry it home from the cabin in case he got stopped by the police because they will often search the driver of a car.

Daddy was very disappointed with him, but believed the story. Douglas promised that he didn't smoke very much, which was true, and said he would probably quit — which he did a few months later.

Daddy said he would keep the marijuana, which he did.

⑩

For the next several years, the issue of where Daddy kept his marijuana stashed inevitably came up as we gathered around the kitchen table late at night.

No one ever looked for it, but we knew that if everyone was ever out it could probably be found.

One weekend when a bunch of us were home we were all out of grass and decided there were enough of us present — a quorum — to make it fair that we raid Daddy's stash. The baggie was found in the big, gray, metal document box he kept in the brown, metal, portable closet in a corner of the ping-pong room upstairs. The only other place it could have been was tucked in the back of the white aluminum linen cabinet. Those were the only two places in the house where Daddy ever kept personal items. The only two places where he would consider hiding anything from Mother.

We only took enough for a couple of joints, leaving the rest for any other family emergencies. Practically everyone quit smoking before there were any other emergencies, so the marijuana is probably still there. Don't tell the police.

①

Daddy drinks beer every night the sun goes down, but has overdone it only twice in the last 20 years.

Once was 15 years ago when he decided for the first and only time to go to Midnight Mass on Christmas Eve. He began drinking beer at his usual hour — eight o'clock — and drank on past his usual bedtime. He had a few more than his daily allotment of three beers. Not too many more. Just enough to make him skip across the floor and pretend to dance with Little Eileen. He quickly recognized the source of this aberrant behavior and sobered up for the rest of the night.

Cecilia's worm, who lives in the kitchen cabinet, survived unharmed.

The other time he got just a little high was one of the nights before Cecilia's wedding. Her wedding had a lot of parties attached to it and, even though it was in Chattanooga, Daddy's routine was thrown off. On one of the nights before the wedding he had gone to a party and not escaped in time to have enough beers at home to relax him before bed without running the risk of drinking more than his limit. He gambled and had a couple of beers more than his limit. We were talking around the table and the conversation turned to marijuana.

Enough of us had quit smoking by this time that we could speak openly about it in front of the parents. We defended its use. Mother was criticizing it, citing recent data from *Time* magazine, her Bible, when one of her disrespectful offspring — it's hard to remember which one — said, "You don't know what you're talking about!"

Daddy perked up and said, "I know what *I'm* talking about. I've smoked marijuana."

This quieted the whole table and drew a ghastly stare from Mrs. Erickson — so Daddy dug a little deeper. "It has a sweet smell to it. Like burning rope. I have some marijuana. Right upstairs I've got my own supply. And I've smoked it."

We knew Daddy had a marijuana stash, but we were not sure whether or not to believe he ever smoked it.

Mother did not say, "Show me!"

She just made him go to bed.

CHAPTER 112

Daddy

Who is Daddy?

I doubt anyone has an answer.

I doubt anyone even knows if Daddy is an intentional mystery — or an accidental one.

⓪

Daddy never had many friends after he became Daddy.

To be more exact, he had one friend, a man he worked with.

And that man died of alcoholism about 30 years ago.

A psychiatrist who was called on one year to bridge a marital gap talked a lot to Daddy. He said Daddy never bothered talking to him. He said Daddy was the only person he had ever met who did not have a single friend.

Daddy got up at six in the morning, seven days a week, and went to work. He came home at 5:15, just in time for dinner. After dinner, he swept the kitchen floor until he was sweeping under Mrs. Erickson's feet, at which point he stopped because she would question his helpfulness.

Next, he would carry out the garbage.

Then he would give baths.

After all the little ones were bathed, Daddy would sit in his chair at the kitchen table and drink his beers and read his newspaper until ten o'clock. Then he would go to bed so he could get up and do all the same things the next day.

Daddy dressed in a suit and tie for work every morning. He took the suit jacket off before dinner, but wore his white dress shirt and tie until he changed at ten into his light blue pajamas, took his thick glasses off, and went to bed.

Since retiring, Daddy still wears his suit pants, dress shirt, and tie most days.

In the winter he wears a checked flannel shirt, and clashing bow ties.

Daddy never went out at night, unless he had to.

The only times he had to were when there were major school functions that he couldn't get out of, or when Mrs. Erickson was at the hospital having babies.

⦿

We had no idea what Daddy would do with himself when he finally had to retire a few years ago. He had worked so long and so steadily that it was bound to be a social shock to him.

He doesn't really do anything now that he's retired — except maybe get in Mother's way more than he used to.

I suggested to him recently that he develop a hobby. He thought about it a minute and decided he didn't need a hobby. He said, "I read in the newspaper that short skirts are coming back into style. I'll keep myself busy by going downtown on windy days. I don't need a hobby."

Mrs. Erickson, of course, didn't like that kind of talk. That's what Daddy's real hobby always has been: coming up with the kind of talk that will get Mrs. Erickson going.

⦿

Daddy is a great talker. He can't hear much because of his bad ears, but everyone who visits the house loves listening to Daddy go on and on about things he knows nothing about.

⦿

Daddy never helped with our homework. If asked to, he would lower his newspaper and say, "Your mother always tells me I don't know 'nuthin'.' So I better not help. She would just have to come back and correct all my mistakes."

Then he would find his place again in his newspaper.

It's hard to say if Daddy did know anything. He should have been illiterate because health problems forced him out of school in the sixth grade. But somewhere he learned something. He wrote a book once. A book I expected to be slow and cumbersome when I finally read it ten years later. A book, a novel, that was actually very impressive.

The book was never published.

Most books are never published.

His was among the best of the books never published. He wrote the book down at his office. As much as anything, it was an excuse to get him out of the house and out from under Mrs. Erickson's feet while she was crashing through menopause.

He would drive back downtown to his store every night after sweeping the floor, carrying the garbage out, and giving baths.

◎

Daddy was an accomplished carpenter and mechanic. And a bit of an entrepreneur. He invented a weight and pulley system for closing large refrigerator doors. There were no orders, but his system worked great for decades on the three doors in his flower shop.

◎

Daddy was a competent, dependable businessman. We thought he never made a lot of money. In fact, he was one of the first of a very small percentage of Americans to, as he phrased it after retiring, "make five figures." He got his annual income to $10,000 when we were kids.

I remember him talking about that well-rounded number several times when his Christmas bonus came in and pushed him over the line. But, given the other numbers he had to contend with at home, $10,000 didn't go very far. Besides, every nickel that didn't have to be spent got saved for the always looming emergencies. Fortunately, we never had any real emergencies. Even if we weren't as poor as we thought, we lived as poor as we could.

Daddy could have done even better, but was never able to fully concentrate on the wholesale flower business. Much of his time, energy, and management skills were devoted to getting kids shuffled around town.

⓪

But, who is Daddy? Here are some of the pieces:

Daddy came from Badger, Iowa. He was raised on a farm by Norwegian immigrant parents. It was a big farm, back before the Depression wiped it out. One of the biggest farms in Iowa, and the only one in the state with white stallions — if you can believe the stories. His family was so wealthy before the Depression that Daddy was driving sleek, shiny cars with names like "Silver Phantom" before he was 16. He drove one of those cars across a very narrow bridge once by simply speeding up to make the car more slender and then closing his eyes to improve his aim — if you can believe the stories.

⓪

Daddy's father died when he was still a child, and his mother re-married. This resulted in a house full of stepchildren. Hampered by Daddy's general reluctance to talk about those days, we grand-stepchildren have never formed a very distinct picture of that past.

⓪

Daddy almost died when he was young. He was lying on the kitchen table after the doctor left, just fading on out, practically in a coma. He remembers one of his stepbrothers saying sort of matter-of-factly, "Harold's gonna die, isn't he."

Daddy lived. But he never walked completely erect after that. He always said, "The doctor left a scalpel in me." Mrs. Erickson always said, "Poppycock!"

He lost some of his hearing during that brush with death, and a lot of his sight. Daddy says he used to be able to shoot flies

off a barn door from a hundred yards away. Says he used to have in-credible hawk-like sight until he lost it while knocking on death's door. No one ever doubted that claim because no one's ever known Daddy to lie about something he would know about.

Daddy had to quit school because of his hearing and vision problems. He has never said much about what he did instead of going to school. He so seldom talks about his past. But Half-Uncle Winston visited once and told us Daddy passed his time by driving sleek, shiny cars over bridges that were far too narrow. Said he made the cars fit by thinning them out with speed.

⦿

In his twenties, Daddy left the farm in Iowa in a Model-T and drove it to California. He was going to become a movie star, or a scriptwriter. This was in the early days of Hollywood. Days so early there were no roads from Iowa to Southern California. Just various widths of dirt paths. He went to California, went un-discovered, returned to Iowa, then drove again to California.

He never did get that casting call, but worked for a while parking cars in a lot frequented by celebrities. Among the people he met in the parking lot were W.C. Fields and Howard Hughes.

⦿

Back in his home territory, he met a pretty girl named Eileen Lorenz. Daddy quit being a Lutheran and became a Catholic. She quit being a Lorenz and became an Erickson.

Harold Alonzo Erickson, born September 4, 1905, Badger, Iowa

Harold Erickson, Age 21, Hollywood casting photo.

CHAPTER 113

Mother

Mother is much easier to figure out than Daddy.

She's a hard woman. She's weathered a lot of ups and downs. Rolled with a lot of life's punches.

She was so busy raising so many kids for so many years that she hardly had time to think. And thinking was always her best suit.

❪❫

Mrs. Erickson was and is a brilliant lady.

She remembers virtually everything she reads, and she reads constantly.

She didn't have much time to use her acute intelligence for many years.

She was too busy being a baby making machine, a diaper changing machine, clothes washing machine, a breakfast-lunch-dinner fixing machine, a dish washing machine, a doctor machine, and a hall monitor machine.

Mother ran the house and raised all the hell — us, and it.

Daddy was so quiet we hardly got to know him until we worked at his store during our high school years.

Mother kept us moving. Her disposition was a balanced blend of love and fear. Neither of the parents ever resorted to physical force, but none of us was willing to risk the wrath Mrs. Erickson could unleash with her machine-like efficiency and overwhelming mental prowess.

Mrs. Erickson with her firstborn. Little did she know what was coming.

Her energy was endless. When she finally got her last baby, Carol, tucked into high school, she relaxed by enrolling in college to complete the education that had been interrupted after one year by the Depression. When she finished her education — graduating *summa cum laude* — she relaxed by going volunteering as a teacher at the small Catholic school Black children had attended before integration, and that many still preferred.

⦾

The former Eileen Marie Lorenz came from a family noted for its intelligence and industry.

Her father got in on the ground floor of popular photography by buying a lot of inexpensive Kodak stock and by opening a photography supply store in St. Joseph, Missouri — the picturesque home of the Pony Express. That's what this town on the Missouri side of the Missouri River — Kansas living on its western shore — was most famous for during our visits in the 1950s. Its second most famous claim to fame was being the town where hero

outlaw Jesse James was shot in the back by a new gang member. That and the Pony Express excited a family of boys a lot more than rarely seen grandparents and distant cousins.

Her father's business suffered during the Depression, but he came out all right once the nation got back to the serious business of taking family photos.

Mother's sister, Gertrude, stayed in the town where Jesse James was shot in the back, and married Uncle Don, a car salesman who had a long career as sales manager of the local Ford dealership. They had a bunch of kids — maybe seven.

Mother's brother, Paul, was the real success story. Though I consider what Mother pulled off equal to his achievements.

Uncle Paul, who had *just* four children, was a corporate go-getter who fought his way up the ranks at Ford Motor Company after graduating from the University of Chicago. His picture was in *Time* magazine a few times over the years as he climbed the ladder. He was close to Robert McNamara and the other renowned "Ford Whiz Kids" who cranked up American industry during and after World War II.

Uncle Paul never made it to the top. Lee Iacocca, a clever charlatan and quintessential back-stabber, kept blocking his progress. Uncle Paul was president of this division and then that division, president of Lincoln-Mercury, and then president of Ford Europe. We were all disappointed when he finally retired from Ford without becoming president of the whole show. Our family's view of "success" is narrow.

Mother had the same wits and tenacity as her brother, Paul. But hers was a much different enterprise.

⚉

Eileen Lorenz was a good Catholic girl who went to good Catholic schools.

Her one year of college before the Depression was at a good Catholic girls' school.

Her Catholic background had a profound effect on our childhoods.

⚉

During the Depression, she worked 38 hours a day folding shirts for a big department store. She was happy to have the opportunity to work so long and hard for about a nickel a week because work was hard to come by. And she was unbeatable at folding shirts back into their original cardboard supports whenever her kids ended up buying a shirt the wrong size that had to be returned.

⚉

Now in her golden years, Mrs. Erickson is finally relaxing.

She teaches only on a substitute basis.

She spends a lot of time turning spools of yarn into elegant afghans, each more intricate than the last. She's probably made 50 by now.

She also reads. Constantly. Best sellers, and obscure books that no one else in the world reads. She still remembers everything. Everything in the books and everything that *Time* magazine and her PBS news programs tell her about what's really going on in the world.

Enjoying one of the many Christmases
she made so memorable for everyone in the family.
(But the crib on the table to the right seems to be
missing a few of the usual starry night visitors.)

One of our favorite pastimes when we gather in Chattanooga is arguing. Mother can't be argued with. She cheats. She uses only raw facts and empirical data to support otherwise untenable positions. She also cheats by not having a sense of humor. It is virtually impossible to argue with someone who doesn't have a sense of humor without getting angry with them.

521

Since we are not allowed to get seriously angry in the house, we don't argue with Mother. Too bad. We never really learned how to talk with each other; just argue. And not many of us talk with Mother as much as we should because we don't like losing the conversations.

Eileen Marie Lorenz, born May 27, 1914, St. Joseph, Missouri

Married Harold Alonzo Erickson, October 26, 1935,
in St. Joseph, Missouri

Became Mostly Pregnant

Wedding photograph. October 26, 1935.

CHAPTER 114

The (Inevitable) End

Dear Nieces and Nephews,

Mr. & Mrs. Erickson, who were born in 1905 and 1914, can't go on forever.

It is inevitable that they will pass on. Grandparents always do.

It will seem natural for Daddy to die because he's been quietly preparing himself for that big outing ever since he almost made it as a kid. We will miss him. We will miss him dearly, and we will make frequent sentimental, heartfelt comments about what a kind and easy person he was.

When Mother dies, we will feel terribly bad about all the nice things we could have done for her, or at least said to her, to show our appreciation for all the nice and selfless things she did for us . . . to show that we understand she devoted her entire wealth of mental and physical energy to one cause: Raising 14 children.

Yes, we will think about that. But more than anything we will find it very hard to believe she is actually gone. Mountains don't just disappear . . . unless, of course, one is pregnant.

Relatively yours,
Uncle Rags

In Memoriam

Eileen Lorenz Erickson
May 27, 1914 — April 1, 1991

Harold Alonzo Erickson
September 4, 1905 October 3, 1994

Allen Edward Erickson
June 1, 1942 July 3, 2004

Table of Contents

Book Three

Book Four

Made in the USA
Las Vegas, NV
21 June 2023